The Literary Criticism of
HENRY JAMES

The Literary Criticism of

HENRY
JAMES

Sarah B. Daugherty

Ohio University Press

Library of Congress Cataloging in Publication Data
Daugherty, Sarah B   1949–
    The literary criticism of Henry James.

    Chapters 1–10 were part of the author's thesis,
University of Pennsylvania, 1973.
    Includes bibliographical references and index.
    1. James, Henry, 1843–1916—Knowledge—
Literature.   2. Fiction—19th century—History and
criticism.   3. Fiction—Technique.   I.   Title.
PS2127.L5D3   813'.4   80-36753
ISBN 0-8214-0440-7
ISBN 0-8214-0697-3 pbk.

Second Printing, 1982
First paperbound edition, 1982

Contents

To my parents and sisters,

and to the memory of my aunt

Acknowledgments

Chapters I through X of this study, in their original version, were part of my doctoral dissertation, written at the University of Pennsylvania in 1973. For their advice and criticism, I am indebted to my director, Professor Daniel G. Hoffman, and to my readers, Professors Robert Regan and Peter Conn.

I am also grateful to Professor Thomas D. Clareson of the College of Wooster, under whose guidance I began my study of James, and to Professor James Walton of Notre Dame, who has read the latter part of this manuscript and has offered valuable comments and suggestions.

As always, my family, and particularly my parents, have been generous in their warmth and encouragement.

An extended version of my discussion of Renan (Chapter X) appeared as "James, Renan, and the Religion of Consciousness," *Comparative Literature Studies*, 16 (December 1979), 318–331. The University of Illinois Press has kindly granted me permission to quote from this article.

Preface

OF ALL MAJOR AUTHORS, Henry James is one of the most
difficult to place within an historical context. To be sure, we
have the invaluable aid of Leon Edel's biography, but the
question of the author's relation to the literary traditions of
his time still remains unsettled. In the light of James's pecu-
liarities, this is hardly surprising. He was, after all, an
expatriate—an American who journeyed to France, where
he met Turgenev, Flaubert, and other members of their
circle, and then settled permanently in Britain, the land of
Eliot, of Trollope, and of Dickens. Moreover, his later
style—the mannerisms by which most readers recognize
him—seems to have been derived from none of his predecessors, French, British or American; his novels, in short,
sound peculiar (or original, if one desires to take a more
favorable view of the matter). Consequently, his critics, both
friendly and hostile, have often regarded him as a curiosity,
a kind of sport in the garden of literature. In 1904, Herbert
Croly, writing of "Henry James and his Countrymen,"
described him as an author whose "method and purpose were
peculiar to himself" and whose primary goal was highly

ix

abstract: "he seeks fullness of insight and perfection of form at any cost."[1] And in subsequent years other writers, often less sympathetic to James than was Croly, still echoed his judgments: Stuart Sherman (1917) stated flatly that the novelist "adored beauty and absolutely nothing else in the world";[2] Granville Hicks (1933) pronounced him an "unrepresentative American" in his "belief in the sanctity and sufficiency of art";[3] Carl Van Doren (1940) called him a writer of "courtly romances in a democratic age";[4] and Albert Baugh (1948), stressing his independence from the Victorian as well as from the American tradition, contended that his books are "documents in the history of a phase of European sensibility as remote from today's actualities as is the *Carte du Tendre.*"[5] Perhaps the most extreme assessment has come from one of James's greatest admirers, Richard P. Blackmur. In his chapter on the novelist in *Literary History of the United States*, he wrote:

> The strangest privation in James . . . was the privation of his relation to the whole body of literature. He was, as Santayana ironically said of himself, "an ignorant man, almost a poet." It was because he knew so little great literature in quantity that to many he seemed excessively literary in manner . . . . He knew well enough the things read around the house as a boy—Dickens and Scott and Hawthorne; he knew even better his chosen masters, Balzac and Turgenev and Flaubert; but . . . he had no organized command of any of the possible general traditions of literature a writer living in his time might have taken up . . . . His critical writing . . . was almost entirely contemporary, of narrow range and narrower sympathies; it is worth reading chiefly as an illumination of his own mind and writing. Only when he tackled the technical problems . . . was he critically at home and master in his house.[6]

Though James was surely a master of technique, this evaluation seems perverse. Granted, as W. C. Brownell first noted, that James's culture was contemporary—that he read Daudet, Trollope, and Gautier rather than Molière, Fielding, or Dante.[7] But is it entirely just to call James "ignorant," when he was in fact thoroughly familiar with the novelists mentioned above and with many other nineteenth-century authors as well? And if James's criticism does illuminate "his own mind and writing," might it not indicate that he was less isolated than Blackmur implies, and that his technical precepts hardly originated in a vacuum?

Other scholars, fortunately, have not allowed James's style or the fact of his expatriation to deter them from exploring his literary background. They, too, however, are faced with a problem, for it is impossible to fit James into a single tradition, great or minor. Indeed, the author read many novels, approving of some, disapproving of others; and undoubtedly his responses affected his creative writing. But more than most novelists, he remained his own master, refusing to join any particular school. To place him in context, therefore, is to deal with a number of traditions, and it is understandable that most studies of his background have been less than comprehensive. Whereas Edwin Cady and Arthur H. Quinn, for example, have dealt with James as an American realist and an ally of William Dean Howells,[8] Clarence Gohdes, in a history edited by Quinn, has treated the author under the heading "Escape from the Commonplace," emphasizing his decision to go to Europe.[9] Although both of these views are defensible, both need modification. Certainly, a number of scholars have made a good case for regarding James primarily as an American author, if not as a realist: Vernon L. Parrington[10] and Harry Hartwick[11] have noted, with some acerbity, his place in the "genteel tradition"; Marius Bewley has related him to Hawthorne, Cooper, and Melville in his preoccupation with his national identity;[12] and Quentin Anderson has read his novels in terms of his father's philosophy.[13] On the other side of the Atlantic, F. R. Leavis has seen James as an exponent of a great British tradition—a tradition that includes George Eliot and Jane Austen, but excludes "the ruck of Gaskells and Trollopes and Merediths" (novelists whom, ironically enough, James also admired).[14] Some writers have even treated the novelist as a member of Flaubert's *çénacle*. Among these critics are Ford Madox Ford, who, eager to prove James's dissociation from the Victorians, stated that he was "in the same boat" as the French authors;[15] Philip Grover, who has discussed his indebtedness to Balzac, Flaubert, and Gautier;[16] and Lyall Powers, who has argued that his work tended "clearly in the direction of the Flaubert circle."[17] There have also been many studies of the novelist's relationship to individual figures, notably Michael Egan's excellent book on James and Ibsen.[18]

Nonetheless, though most of these critics and scholars have had valuable insights to offer, one can hardly help wishing that someone might lay hands on the whole beast in this jungle of criticism, writing not of the American or the British or the French Henry James but of the author whose interests spanned three national literatures and a far greater number of schools within each of these. It is perhaps Oscar Cargill who has best grappled with the complete James, for he has dealt carefully with the sources of his novels, showing his indebtedness to writers so diverse as Holmes, Hawthorne, Daudet, Cherbuliez, and Eliot.[19] Yet one still feels the need for a more comprehensive study—a study treating not only the actual sources of James's works but also the books which shaped his imagination, and not only isolated novels but also the relationship among them.

James's criticism of other authors provides excellent material for such an examination. In addition to the volumes he published during his lifetime—*French Poets and Novelists* (1878), *Hawthorne* (1879), *Partial Portraits* (1888), *Essays in London and Elsewhere* (1893), and *Notes on Novelists* (1914)—he wrote more than 150 essays and reviews, many of them still unanthologized, which have now been identified by Leon Edel and Dan H. Laurence.[20] A number of scholars, recognizing the importance of this material, have dealt with it in some detail; but generally, their studies have been too cursory[21] or have dwelt too much on the limitations of James's taste and theories.[22] Thus, there is still a place for a more complete reading of the essays and reviews which establish his place in literary history. Such a study cannot be totally inclusive: it cannot discuss the books that James read but did not write about, and it cannot deal directly with his Prefaces, which must be treated in conjunction with his own fiction. Nevertheless, it may aid the reader in understanding why the author wrote as he did and how his novels may be related to those of his predecessors.

Among the advantages gained by placing James in an historical context is a better awareness of the conventions he used in his fiction. To cite an obvious example, the women who so often appear as his protagonists have a complex literary ancestry: they are related to the dark heroines of Eliot and Trollope, rebels against a society devoted to narrow moralism and to material prosperity; to the women of Cherbuliez and Droz, rebels against a culture that is aesthetically attractive but morally corrupt; and to the ideal woman sketched by Renan, the embodiment of religious faith in an age of doubt. Even James's late style, which seems peculiar to himself, can be better understood in the light of his preoccupation with the author's unique personality, a concern he derived in large measure from George Sand. Leon Edel's biography shows us the relationship between these aspects of James's writing and his personal experience, but his fiction may become more accessible to us if we realize that he was less idiosyncratic than we might suppose.

A reading of James's criticism may also aid us in avoiding

an error which he himself seldom made—namely, that of regarding his technical pronouncements as absolutes. One thinks, for example, of the work of Ford Madox Ford and Richard P. Blackmur, and most especially of Percy Lubbock, whose influential study, *The Craft of Fiction* (London: Jonathan Cape, 1921), treats the author's method as a standard by which other fiction should be judged. Fortunately, more recent critics have been less dogmatic, perceiving that the works of the Victorians are not mere "fluid puddings," inartistic forerunners of the master's novels. But it is time to reaffirm the insights of Joseph Warren Beach, that James's method grew directly out of his preoccupation with the inner life and that this interest, in turn, stemmed from his cultural concerns as a man of the later nineteenth century.[23] Recognizing this, one can keep James's theories in perspective and thus avoid becoming more of a Jacobite than he was himself.

Finally, his criticism, because it documents his response to his milieu, has a direct bearing upon the controversy surrounding his works. As Philip Rahv has noted, the quarrel between the partisans of James and their enemies is more cultural than critical: it is a battle between "palefaces" and "redskins," between lovers of "art" and lovers of "life," between defenders of tradition and advocates of revolution.[24] James, so the redskins argue, was completely out of touch with the realities of his own age; how, then, can he be of interest to ours? The most famous exponent of this position is Maxwell Geismar, who contends that James "knew nothing at all about the life of his time," that he represents "the most singular curiosity in the whole range of literary history," that he had "no real interest in the social-economic nature of his prosperous, materialistic, post-Civil War American society," and that he suffered from an "ignorance of literature . . . from which he drew only his own peculiar inspiration."[25] Oddly enough, Edward Stone, in taking up the cudgels for the palefaces, does not seriously challenge these arguments. Though he writes of James's artistic strengths, as evidenced especially in his transformation of his source materials, he concedes the author's "aloofness from social history" and his lack of interest in the philosophies of Darwin, Huxley, and Spencer. At one point he even agrees with Stuart P. Sherman, stating that the author claimed for art "an immunity from morality," thus "following in the footsteps of Poe."[26] A reader of James's criticism, however, will feel that Geismar overstates his case and that Stone concedes too much. For one thing, the author, in his distaste for vulgarity, reacted strongly against the Gilded Age; and for another, he hated aestheticism, which posed a direct threat to his own moral idealism. As for Darwinian philosophy, he feared its dehumanizing effects; yet late in his career, he acknowledged the greatness of Gustave Flaubert and Emile Zola despite his fundamental differences from them. He was thus a more broad-minded critic than were many of his detractors.

Even so, the battle of the books will still rage: those who join Geismar in wishing that James had had the virtues of Dreiser will continue to quarrel with those who admire the novelist's "faith in human will and in character."[27] But a study of James's background may at least provide the basis for intelligent discussion. The first step toward an assessment of James in our century is an understanding of his place within his own.

Chapter I

"A Great and Arduous Mission"

The whole scene and the whole time flushed to my actual view
with a felicity and a unity that make them rather a page of
romance than a picture of that degree of the real, that potentially
so terrible truth of the life of man, which has now learnt to
paint itself with so different a brush. They *were*, they flourished,
they temporarily triumphed, that scene, that time, those
conditions. . . . I measure the spread as that of half a century—
only with the air turning more and more to the golden as space
recedes, turning to the clearness of all the sovereign exemptions,
the serenity of all the fond assurances, that were to keep on and
on, seeing themselves not only so little menaced but so admirably
crowned. This we now perceive to have been so much their
mistake that . . . it can only rest with us to write down the fifty
years I speak of, in the very largest letters, as the Age of the
Mistake.[1]

Thus wrote Henry James in 1915. He was referring
specifically to the founding of the *Nation*, the periodical
which had published most of his reviews during the 1860s
and '70s; and more generally, to the aspirations which he and
some of his contemporaries shared with their predecessors,
those whom William Dean Howells called the "Brahmins."
Although it has become unfashionable, since Vernon L.

1

Parrington wrote scathingly of James's "Nostalgia of Culture,"[2] to associate the author with the genteel tradition, his connection with the New England humanists was of cardinal importance in his career. Not only did they edit the journals to which he first contributed, but they also gave him a sense of purpose which he never quite repudiated, his comments on the "Mistake" notwithstanding.

James's first critical essay was published in 1864 by the venerable *North American Review*, which Charles Eliot Norton and James Russell Lowell had begun to edit the previous year. Before then, the *Review* had been declining in quality,[3] because, as Lowell said, "it wasn't lively, and it had no particular opinions on any particular subject."[4] Underlying the editors' hope "to put some life into the dry old bones of the Quarterly" was a serious purpose, most succinctly stated by Norton: "to raise the standards of criticism and scholarship among us."[5] Whatever one may think of these "defenders of ideality,"[6] the young James apparently sympathized with their desire to make the journal a citadel of culture in the Gilded Age. In addition to the evidence of his reviews, we have his revealing commentary in his 1908 essay on Norton. He recalls his impressions on the "autumn day, when, an extremely immature aspirant to the rare laurel of the critic, [he] went out from Boston to Cambridge" in order to offer his first review for publication: "[Norton's] eminent character as a 'representative of culture' announced itself exactly in proportion as one's general sense of the medium in which it was to be exerted was strong; and I seem verily to recall that even in the comparative tenderness of that season I had grasped the idea of the precious, the quite far-reaching part such an exemplar might play." He adds further: "the representative of culture . . . had before him in the United States of those days a great and arduous mission"—a mission that was particularly crucial in "a young roaring and money-getting democracy, inevitably but almost exclusively occupied with 'business success.'"[7]

These statements assume a broader significance because the *Atlantic* and the *Nation*, the two other journals publishing James's first reviews, closely resembled the *North American* in their critical stance. Under the editorship of James T. Fields, the *Atlantic* of the 1860s remained the organ of the Brahmins;[8] according to Howells, who served as Fields' assistant during the latter part of the decade, "The literary theories we [the editors] accepted were New England theories, the criticism we valued was New England criticism, or, more strictly speaking, Boston theories, Boston criticism."[9]

The *Nation*, founded in New York (1865), was broader in scope, but the Bostonians—Norton in particular—were instrumental in its establishment.[10] If anything, the youngest of these Eastern periodicals was even more conscious of its "mission" than were its predecessors. Its prospectus announced: "The criticism of books and works of art will form one of its most prominent features; and pains will be taken to have this task performed in every case by writers having special qualifications for it."[11] This practice of sending out books to qualified critics had seldom been followed by other weekly journals, which had entrusted the task of reviewing to resident "literary gentlemen."[12] But the founders and editors of the *Nation* were eager to break precedent because they believed American letters to be in a state of crisis. C.A. Bristed, for example, wrote in the first issue of the new magazine that American criticism was still in "the childish age, or that of promiscuous and silly admiration";[13] and Norton, in an article denouncing the United States as "The Paradise of Mediocrities," lamented the "lack of men of learning and cultivated critics who would leaven the whole mass of popular ignorance."[14] It is therefore highly significant that Edwin L. Godkin, the editor of the *Nation* and himself an influential social critic,[15] personally sought out James at his Boston residence and asked him to contribute to the new journal.[16]

The seriousness with which James took his duties is apparent in his 1865 review of Matthew Arnold's *Essays in Criticism*. Quoting Arnold's statement that the object of criticism is "to know the best that is known and thought in the world" without regard to "practical consequences or applications," James stressed the pertinence of this standard to American letters. Criticism, he continued, should

> exalt, if possible, the importance of the ideal. We should perhaps have said the intellectual; that is, of the principle of understanding things. Its business is to urge the claims of all things to be understood. If this is its function in England, as Mr. Arnold represents, it seems to us that it is doubly its function in this country. Here is no lack of votaries of the practical, of experimentalists, of empirics. The tendencies of our civilization are certainly not such as foster a preponderance of morbid speculation. . . . American society is so shrewd, that we may safely allow it to make application of the truths of the study. . . . Let criticism take the stream of truth at its source, and then practice can take it half-way down.[17]

There are two points to be noted here. The first is James's acceptance of the Arnoldian definition of criticism; for him, the literary critic was not the narrow formalist, but rather the cultural, social, and moral critic. Though James sometimes played down his "missionary" role (in this essay, he neatly avoids calling his countrymen "Philistines" by suggesting that they might take a more enlightened view of Arnold than had the British),[18] the implication of many of his reviews is clear enough. Moreover, he seldom criticized literature without considering the author's purpose and the effect of his work on the readers. In this respect his views were strikingly similar to those held by other Eastern critics, who agreed with his high estimate of Arnold.[19] Also important is James's desire to emulate Arnold's posture: to remain aloof from the vulgar herd, to observe the world from an intellectual height, to see life steadily and see it whole. Indeed, when he invoked such undefined terms as "the truth" and "philosophy," he was referring less to any system than to the philosophic mind—the mind that could understand the world without being overwhelmed by it, that could observe life and then pass judgment on it. Later, when he became acquainted with the naturalists, he attacked them chiefly because they denied the power of mind—of consciousness—as a unifying force.

James's approval of Arnold's stance is also apparent in his essay on Edmond Schérer, whom he called "a solid embodiment of Arnold's ideal critic" and whose *Etudes* he praised for their combination of "intellectual eclecticism" and "moral consistency." Such a critic, added James, was "a compromise between the philosopher and the historian"— between one who dealt exclusively with ideas and one who was solely preoccupied with "facts." Sainte-Beuve fell short of the ideal because he was too much of an historian, observing phenomena without judging them; so also did Taine, because he was "too passionate, too partial" to mediate between his roles as observer and thinker. Schérer, in contrast, struck exactly the right balance; he made "the journey round the whole sphere of knowledge," then returned "at last with a melancholy joy to morality."[20]

Although James did not cite specific examples to prove his case, a reading of "Madame Roland," an *étude* he particularly recommended, will help to clarify his meaning. This is ostensibly a review of her memoirs, yet Schérer concentrates primarily on her role as an historical figure. Sometimes he criticizes her, balancing her virtues against her defects: "Une femme modeste qui lâche des mots grossiers, une femme pure qui appelle *Faublas* 'un joli roman,' une femme sensible qui demande des têtes, voilà de ces disparates, en présence desquelles on se trouve quand on étudie Madame Roland." Sometimes he adds a generalizing comment, as when he writes of (supposedly) platonic love: "Nous avons tant mis de physiologie dans notre psychologie, que nous sommes en danger de confondre l'amour avec les appétits ou les plaisirs." Finally, he assesses her ultimate value: "On éprouve le besoin de s'assurer qu'au milieu même de ces saturnales [e.g. the French Revolution], la vertu humaine ne s'est pas laissée sans quelque témoinage; et alors, chose étrange, ce sont les femmes qui attirent et consolent le regard; . . . c'est Madame Roland, enfin, avec son grand coeur et ses illusions sublimes."[21] As we shall see, many of Schérer's attitudes—his distaste for vulgarity and violence, his distrust of "les appétits," and his faith in the virtuous woman as a civilizing force—were almost identical with James's own. What is most important here, however, is Schérer's use of the "higher criticism"—the term James later used to designate the criticism of history and culture from a moral point of view.[22]

James's negative reviews of many works, especially those written by Americans, may best be understood in relation to this ideal. Consider, for example, his notorious assessment of Walt Whitman's *Drum Taps*. Like many of his contemporaries, he took Whitman to task for his "adoption of an anomalous style"; yet he was most severe not in his comments on poetic form, but in his chastisement of the poet for failing to do his cultural duty. The true poet, according to James, viewed facts "from a height":

> Every tragic event collects about it a number of persons who delight to dwell upon its superficial points—of minds which are bullied by the *accidents* of the affair. The temper of such minds seems to us to be the reverse of the poetic temper; for the poet, although he incidentally masters, grasps, and uses the superficial traits of his theme, is really a poet only in so far as he extracts its latent meaning and holds it up to common eyes. And yet from such minds most of our war-verses have come, and Mr Whitman's utterances . . . are in this respect no exception to general fashion.

In this passage James anticipated Santayana; he accused Whitman of losing himself in the phenomenal world to such a degree that he could not interpret it for the general public, who, one infers, were badly in need of teaching. True, James complimented the people as he lectured the poet: "You must respect the public which you address; for it has taste, if you have not. . . . This democratic, liberty-loving, American populace, this stern and war-tried people, is a great civilizer.

It is devoted to refinement."[23] But the critic's fear that Whitman might be only an extreme example of American barbarism seems stronger than his faith in the nation as a whole.

These same concerns were often evident in James's reviews of fiction, in which he deplored the representation of vulgarity even if the author's intentions were obviously satirical or didactic. One novel he attacked was Henry Sedley's *Marian Rooke*, a study of the greed and materialism typical of the United States and especially of New England. The hero, Hugh Gifford, loses his first love, Virginia Chester, to a prosperous merchant, because her father has convinced her that Hugh will not be able to get enough California gold to suit her needs. According to the narrator, Hugh's disappointment is symptomatic of a larger problem: Americans "are taught from their youth up that gold is the only good, and find that democracy has done too much to establish that maxim."[24] Moreover, the book seems to be a partial apology for the American South; standing in sharp contrast to the greedy Virginia is the girl whom Hugh finally chooses, Marian Rooke, daughter of a Louisiana planter and his slave. Though James himself objected to American materialism, he castigated the author for his "magnificent loathing" of New England and for his portrayal of the Yankees as being sycophantic, snobbish, and puritanical. The James of the 1860s apparently revered New England more than would the author of *The Bostonians;* and his ambivalence toward the United States as a whole—his distaste for its vulgarity and his hope for its refinement—probably made his attack on Sedley's patriotism the more vigorous. He pronounced the novel to be a "very bad book" serving no purpose except to entertain "those jolly barbarians who read novels only for what they call the 'story.'"[25]

At times James was even harder on errant writers than were his elders. J. R. Lowell wrote Godkin in 1868: "The criticisms in the *Nation* often strike me as admirable. I sometimes dissent, but I am getting old and good-natured, and know, moreover, how hard it is to write well, to come even anywhere near one's own standard of good writing."[26] And on at least two occasions, Norton rejected James's criticism of authors generally admired by the Brahmins.[27] The first of these unpublished reviews deals with *John Godfrey's Fortunes* by Bayard Taylor. The hero of this novel is a young writer who almost loses his love when she sees him with his arm around "an unfortunate young girl" (James's words) whom he has just saved from a burning brothel. Like *Marian Rooke*, the novel also includes some satirical portraits of the New York "fashionables" whom the aspiring author tries to impress. James lamented the "general tone of vulgarity which made us regret that the author had seen fit . . . to emphasize the American character of his work"; Taylor, he said, lacked "that union of good sense and good taste which forms the touchstone of the artist's conceptions."[28] The second review is of Elizabeth Stoddard's *Two Men*, a novel of sexual passion concerning a father and son's rivalry for the love of a young girl. This book, James said, is full of "a savage violence" which is a poor substitute for "the quiet seriousness of genius."[29]

There is thus ample evidence of James's zeal in upholding the standards of the New England humanists—standards that some critics have called "neo-classical" because they emphasized tradition, taste, and reason as opposed to Transcendental enthusiasm.[30] This Brahmin strain, moreover, would reappear in James's later criticism; his moral seriousness, his dislike of vulgarity, and his concern for the relationship between literature and culture persisted throughout his career. But as Henry Seidel Canby has pointed out, the young James, whose roots were in the Middle States rather than in New England, eventually found Boston "too professionally intellectual for his artist's mind."[31] His early reviews also show a second, conflicting tendency, a tendency to celebrate emotion as opposed to reason and to return to the past instead of criticizing the present.

This appears quite dramatically in the review of Arnold cited above. In a digression, James mused: "It is hard to say whether the literary critic is more called upon to understand or to feel. It is certain that he will accomplish little unless he can feel acutely; although it is perhaps equally certain that he will become weak the moment that he begins to 'work,' as we may say, his natural sensibilities. The best critic is probably he who leaves his feelings out of account, and relies upon reason for success." The conflict here is obvious. As a "higher critic" living in a post-Romantic age, James distrusted pure feeling, which he associated with nostalgia and hence with an impulse toward escapism. Therefore, like Arnold, he decided to play the rationalist—or so it would seem. But a few sentences later, he praised Arnold for "boldly saluting [Oxford University] as the Queen of Romance: romance being the deadly enemy of the commonplace; the commonplace being the fast ally of Philistinism, and Philistinism the heaviest drag upon the march of civilization." Perhaps feeling might be better than reason as a weapon against vulgarity. Even more significant is a passage near the end of the review in which James remarked on "a peculiar character of melancholy" in Arnold's essay: "that melancholy which arises from the spectacle of the old-fashioned instinct of enthusiasm in conflict (or at all events in contact) with the modern desire to be fair,—the melancholy of an age which not only has lost its *naiveté*, but which knows it has lost it."[32] One easily infers that James shared this melancholy, not only from this review but also from his circumstances at the time he wrote it. In the foreground were Lowell, Norton, Fields, and Godkin, who encouraged him to be a critic of the age; but in the background were the Romantics—particularly his Swedenborgian father, Henry James, Sr., who regarded self-consciousness as original sin and spontaneity as a cardinal virtue.[33] Little wonder, then, that James had doubts concerning his critical role.

The same conflict occurs on a more basic level in his analysis of Nassau W. Senior's *Essays on Fiction*, his first published review and the one he timidly presented to Norton. He began by criticizing Senior for his old-fashioned impressionism and for his failure to write a "critical treatise on fiction" surveying "the nature and principles of the subject." Paying a snide compliment to the tired businessman and the harried housewife, James conceded that the judgments of such "intelligent half-critics" might be "very pleasant in conversation; but," he added, "they are hardly worth the trouble of reading." The implication is that Senior and those for whom he wrote used literature as a means of escape. But in the remainder of his essay, a panegyric on Sir Walter Scott, James became the kind of critic whom he belittled. Scott's romances, he said, "are emphatically works of entertainment" and should be cherished and preserved as such. Their value lay in the pleasure they gave the reader: "In retracing one by one these long-forgotten plots and counter-plots, we yield once more to something of the great master's charm."[34] Despite his demand for reason, culture, and high seriousness, James was obviously fascinated by works to which such standards could not be applied.

But because he thought the nostalgic impulse to be regressive, he seldom followed it without apologizing for his weakness. The only reviews of the sixties in which he gave full vent to his feelings are those of William Morris's poetry. Of *The Life and Death of Jason*, he wrote: "To the jaded intellects of the present moment, distracted with the strife of creeds and the conflict of theories, it opens a glimpse into a world where they will be called upon neither to choose, to criticise, nor to believe, but simply to feel, to look, and to listen."[35] And he praised *The Earthly Paradise*, a series of mythological tales, for its gratification of man's "latent tenderness for the past" and for its depiction of "men and women . . . simpler and stronger and happier than we."[36] Rarely was James so explicit as this; but in him as in many of his contemporaries, the sense of the past, and the feeling associated with it, remained strong.[37] This emotion would come to the surface many times in his career, notably in his criticism of romance and poetry and in the fiction of his "major phase."

Chapter II

Criticism of Fiction, 1864–1868

DURING THE 1860s, James's ideal of the novelist was closely related to his conception of the critic. In a review of *Our Mutual Friend*, he wrote that a "truly great novelist" (as opposed to a mere "observer" or "humorist" like Dickens) is not simply an "artist," but a "moralist" and a "philosopher" as well; that is, he knows "*man* as well as *men*" and can therefore make "those generalizations in which alone consists the real greatness of a work of art." Such a figure is closely reminiscent of Arnold and Schérer as James perceived them. James even went so far as to suggest that the writer assume the Arnoldian posture—that he understand mankind's "elementary passions" while telling his story "in a spirit of intellectual superiority to those passions." At the same time, and in partial contradiction to this statement, the critic suggested that the novelist should write "out of the fulness of his sympathy" with human emotion.[1] Thus, James thought that the good writer, like the good critic, possessed both intellectual and intuitive insight, the former predominating over the latter.

But how was the novelist to translate such insights into fictional form? This was obviously the problem which James had to solve. During the decade, the novel had become the most popular literary genre (especially among magazine readers),[2] while the Eastern critical tradition still retained its vitality. Few critics, however, had seriously attempted to relate theory and practice, as James himself had indicated when he wrote of the need for a "critical treatise" on fiction.[3] Since writers like Nassau Senior failed to supply this desideratum, James had to work out his own formulations.

Perhaps his most important step toward the achievement of this goal was his recognition of the difference between "philosophy" and the novel, a distinction he clearly made in his 1865 review of Goethe's *Wilhelm Meister*. He praised the book highly as a "treatise on moral economy,—a work intended to show how the experience of life may least be wasted, and best be turned to account."[4] Undoubtedly, James was impressed by the hero's desire to *live* and by his progression from illusion to clarity of perspective—two themes which the critic was to develop in his own *bildungsromanen*, notably *The American* and *The Ambassadors*. But it would be a mistake to assume, as does Cornelia P. Kelley, that Goethe "more than anyone else was responsible for James's introspective, psychological fiction."[5] In fact, James found so little psychology in *Wilhelm Meister* that he refused to classify it as fiction:

> Although incidentally dramatic, . . . *Wilhelm Meister* is anything but a novel, as we have grown to understand the word. As a whole, it has, in fact, no very definite character; and, were we not vaguely convinced that its greatness as a work of art resides in this very absence of form, we should say that, as a work of art, it is lamentably defective. A modern novelist, taking the same subject in hand, would restrict himself to showing the sensations of his hero during the process of education; that is, his hero would be the broad end, and the aggregate of circumstances the narrow end, of the glass through which we were invited to look; and we should so have a comedy or a tragedy, as the case might be. But Goethe, taking a single individual as a pretext for looking into the world, becomes so absorbed in the spectacle before him, that, while still clinging to his hero as a pretext, he quite forgets him as a subject.

Here, in embryonic form, are a number of the technical principles that James was to develop in the course of his career, including those of "drama," point of view, and structural coherence. But behind all these was his concern with character, the connecting link between "philosophy" and the novel. Despite his admiration for Goethe's "pages of disquisition," he found them only a partial compensation for the author's failure to dramatize his ideas, to express them through his hero's personality. As a treatise, then, *Wilhelm Meister* succeeded; as a novel, it did not. And so far as "fulness of sympathy" was concerned, James strongly implied that Goethe had none; though the critic was moved by the episode of Mignon, the pathetic child who dies of a broken heart, he thought the rest of the book appealed "exclusively" to the reader's understanding.[6] Once again, it was the absence of sympathetic figures that led James to this judgment.

The young critic was thus less interested in a novelist's abstract "philosophy" than in its expression through the figures he created. His chief preoccupation in his early reviews of fiction was with different types of characters, whom he divided into two broad categories: those who were "natural" or "true to nature," and those who were not.[7] Truth to nature, of course, is an ancient literary criterion;[8] but to understand James's specific uses of the term, one must consider the individual characters whom he accepted or rejected.

Though as a child James had enjoyed reading Dickens and watching dramatized productions of his works,[9] that author's grotesques were among his chief critical dislikes. Reviewing *Our Mutual Friend*, he complained: "every character here put before us is a mere bundle of eccentricities, animated by no principle of nature whatsoever." Obviously, James was unable to accept Dickens's technique of using his characters as symbols representing their socioeconomic circumstances. He called Jenny Wren, the dwarf victimized by her deformity and her poverty, "a little monster . . . unhealthy, unnatural." And with the two rival suitors, Eugene Wrayburn and Bradley Headstone, he was equally dissatisfied; he conceded that a conflict between a gentleman and a man of the people might be interesting, but regretted that Dickens had "made them simply figures" rather than characters. (The point of the novel, of course, is that the men's personalities have been stunted by their social positions: Wrayburn is one of Dickens's cynical lawyers, finally redeemed from his indifference by a woman's love; Headstone is a "mechanical," Utilitarian schoolmaster, driven to insanity when his passion is first aroused and then thwarted.) James was also displeased with Dickens's villains: not with Rogue Riderhood, whose malice he found "sufficiently natural," but with the more subtle Lammles (the bourgeois couple who swindle their peers) and Mr. Fledgeby (the Gentile usurer). Such characters he labeled "aggressively inhuman."[10]

Why was James so harsh in his criticism? Despite his wish that Dickens's figures were three-dimensional, he was not primarily concerned with psychological realism as such; in fact, he stated that the reader could easily accept "a certain number of figures or creatures of pure fancy" if he were "repaid for his concession by a peculiar beauty or power in these exceptional characters." But James could not abide those figures in whom want or greed had overcome *"humanity,"* "intelligence," "natural sense and natural feeling," and "those elementary passions in which alone we seek the true and final manifestation of character." Using James's terminology in the Whitman review, one may say that he disliked characters who were too much affected by the "accidents" of life. This explains why the critic, who in his early years considered characters as expressions of their creator's mind, called Dickens "nothing of a philosopher."[11] James's own "philosophy," then, in its emphasis on those traits of character which could not be altered by social or economic conditions, was profoundly anti-deterministic—a fact which explains his later hostility toward Flaubert and his followers. Indeed, as we shall see, his distaste for their extreme cynicism was to make him relatively more tolerant of authors such as Dickens who simply lacked his own idealism.

The critic's attitude toward character, like his related concern for his "mission," was shaped in large measure by his elder compatriots. There is, for example, a striking parallel between the young critic's review and an address given four years previously by his father, Henry James, Sr. In his speech delivered on the Fourth of July, 1861, the elder James castigated Dickens for failing to appreciate the United States. This, he said, was the result of the author's typically European interest in "persons" rather than in "man"; preoccupied with social distinctions, he could not understand America, "the country of all mankind."[12] Although the young James's review is overtly neither anti-British nor pro-American, one can easily see the relationship between son and father in their common concern for universal man.[13] More generally, it seems clear that James's belief in "man" or in "character" was derived from his American predecessors: the Transcendentalists, who stressed the passions shared by everyone, and the Brahmins, who emphasized the "natural sense and natural feeling" by which "[s]ociety is maintained."[14]

If James was opposed to characters like those of Dickens—grotesques misshapen by social pressures—he was even less sympathetic with those distorted by internal forces such as sexual passion. The clearest evidence of his aversion was his attack on the sensation novel, a sub-genre he mentioned by name in his review of M. E. Braddon's *Aurora Floyd*.[15] The strong-willed heroine of this novel, while still a school-girl, defies convention and secretly marries a horse-trainer. Believing him dead, she weds a simple but respectable Yorkshireman, with whom, after many tribulations—including persecution and blackmail by the jockey and false accusation of his murder—she lives happily ever after. Since Aurora is not introduced until after she has had her youthful fling, there is nothing particularly shocking about the book. Nor does the narrator hold her up as a paragon of virtue, though he does suggest that she is lovable, sympathetic, and above all, fascinating.[16] Not to James, however. He belittled the author's attempts to "save the proprieties" by making the jockey Aurora's first husband and accused her of exploiting the "romance" of "vice." He added that her work appealed to a public "which reads nothing but novels, and yet which reads neither George Eliot, George Sand, Thackeray, nor Hawthorne"—a public avid for novelties like bigamy and murder but indifferent to "human nature," which "is very nearly as old as the hills."[17]

On similar grounds James objected to Elizabeth Stoddard's *Two Men*, an American novel of sensation. Referring to Jason Auster, the unfortunate hero who loves the same young girl as does his son, James asked, "Is he a man? Is he a character, a mind, a heart, a soul? . . . What is his formula? Is it that like Carlyle's Mirabeau he has swallowed all formulas?"[18] A reading of the novel shows that Jason does indeed fit a formula, though not exactly the one James had in mind. Consider, for example, Jason's reaction to the heroine, Philippa: "his heart stopped beating, then bounded forward, and dragged him into the terrible development which made him a *man*. One by one his savage instincts were revealed to him."[19] Of course, it is easy to see how James could and did dislike such books on literary grounds; most were marred by melodramatic plots, stereotyped characters, and, as he said, "a violent style."[20] His comments, however, reveal not only his impatience with the authors' deficiencies but his reluctance to consider lust and violence as fundamental human motives.

The most dramatic and amusing example of James's bias in this respect is his review of Mrs. Seemüller's *Emily Chester*. The theme of the novel, though obscured by the author's prudishness and bad prose, may be simply stated:

it concerns a woman who loves and remains faithful to her husband despite her sexual aversion to him and her attraction to another man. James, however, refused to accept the obvious; he doubted that a heroine "so admirably self-poised as Mrs. Crampton" could suffer from "a vagrant passion which has neither a name nor a habitation." Concerning human nature in general, he stated: "Beasts and idiots act from their instincts; educated men and women, even when they most violate principle, act from their reason, however perverted, and their affections, however misplaced." Thus, he defined "psychology" as "the observation of the moral and intellectual character"—that which is distinctively human—and chastised the novelists who dealt instead with their characters' "temperament, nature, constitution, instincts . . . their physical rather than . . . their moral sense."[21] Once again, James anticipated his later reaction to the naturalists in his defense of an ideal view of human character.

Yet it is possible to exaggerate this aspect of his criticism, for he was almost equally adamant in rejecting the figures who appeared in the religious, didactic, and sentimental novels of the day. One must say "almost," because when he felt constrained to choose between the author of *Aurora Floyd* and the creator of an impossibly virtuous cripple, he opted for the latter: "as matters stand at present," he concluded, "to say that we prefer. the sentimental school to the other, is simply to say that we prefer virtue to vice."[22] But as a rule his treatment of "the sentimental school" and its creations was satirical or at best condescending. One of his pet peeves was the "orthodox little girl"[23] serving as the author's mouthpiece—a figure like Mrs. Charles's Grace Leigh, who uttered such profundities as "All sermons are nice" and "Everything is pleasant."[24] And when this sort of child became the victim of puppy love, as did Mrs. Train's young heroine in *The Gayworthys*, James exploded: "Heaven defend us from the puerile!" Such a theme, he added, was as "fatal to the dignity of strong passion as the most flagrant immoralities of French fiction."[25] Still another object of his disdain was the ridiculously "moral" hero, a stock figure in the American sentimental novel. There was Mrs. Davis's Dr. Broderip, the Northern doctor who felt duty-bound to tell his haughty Southern fiancée that he had a trace of Negro blood;[26] her Dallas Galbraith ("worse than a woman's man— a woman's boy"), who voluntarily spent five years in prison for the crimes of another and behaved "like a hysterical schoolgirl" thereafter;[27] and Louisa May Alcott's Adam Warwick, a manly idealist (or so the reader was supposed to think) who carried on a high-minded, strictly Platonic affair with his friend's wife. "Women," wrote James, "appear to delight in the conception of men who shall be insupportable to men."[28]

Naturally James laughed at the absurdity of such creatures, but he was serious in his plea that novelists create characters rather than puppets. Reviewing Mrs. Davis's *Waiting for the Verdict*, he described her figures as "a crowd of ghastly, frowning, grinning automatons,"[29] clearly implying that like Dickens's grotesques, they were "lifeless, forced, mechanical."[30] Thus, sensation novelists were not the only ones who could stray from truth to nature; so, too, could genteel authors, particularly when they suffered from "moralism on a narrow basis," a "hankering after a ghastly moral contortion in every natural impulse."[31] In these phrases one again detects the influence of the elder James, who used the term "moralism" to designate the puritanical self-righteousness which he thought his country's worst failing.[32] Perhaps it was inevitable, then, that his son should condemn moralists as well as sensation-mongers, neither of whom could create "natural" characters. This idea, which he gradually developed in his reviews of the sixties, was to be a major theme of his 1884 essay "The Art of Fiction."

In all of these reviews James dealt with characters whom he considered grotesque or distorted. Hence, when he stated that they were not "true to nature," he meant that they were not "realistic" in the sense that Howells was later to use that adjective; they were not, in other words, true to common experience. But as various critics have noted, James neither shared Howells's love for the commonplace nor adhered to strict realism in his own fiction, especially when presenting his ideal of human character.[33] Not surprisingly, then, there are a number of reviews in which he invoked "truth to nature" against flat realism and demanded that characters be superior to humanity at large.

The cultural significance of James's distaste for "vulgarity" has been discussed in Chapter I. Sometimes, as in his review of Sedley's *Marian Rooke*, James treated vulgar figures as mere caricatures of living persons. But his objections extended to figures whose only fault was to be ordinary. A case in point was his criticism of John Godfrey, Bayard Taylor's aspiring journalist: "We are struck . . . by the incongruity between the character which Godfrey affirms of himself and that which he actually exhibits. . . . [H]e falls below his presumptive Self. He impresses us as a thoughtful, gentle, affectionate and charitable youth with a very matter-of-fact and prosaic view of the world and a good newspaper style."[34] Obviously James was commenting on the disparity between the protagonist's words and his deeds; but since Godfrey is in fact rather self-deprecating (for example, he quotes Browning: "What I seem [sic] to myself, do you ask of me? / No hero, I confess"),[35] one infers that James was troubled less by the inconsistency in characterization than by Godfrey's blatantly unheroic nature. Perhaps only half-consciously James was looking for a fictional hero, one who could appeal to the imagination and intelligence of the reading public.

Because he failed to discover this hero in the works of the Victorians, he often judged them severely, his former veneration of them notwithstanding.[36] Thackeray escaped his censure, probably because his characters, despite their lack of heroism, seemed larger than life; James referred to the protagonist of *Vanity Fair*, for example, as "Becky Sharp the Great."[37] But Anthony Trollope and George Eliot, both believers in the commonplace as fictional material, became the object of James's criticism and occasionally, of his irony.

One of his more interesting reviews is that of Trollope's *Miss Mackenzie*, the "history of the pecuniary embarrassments of a middle-aged spinster" who inherits and loses a fortune, then marries the cousin to whom she has relinquished it. After confessing a "partiality for Trollope of which [he was] yet . . . somewhat ashamed," James proceeded to discuss the inadequacies of the author's novel and its characters: "Literally . . . Mr. Trollope accomplishes his purpose of being true to common life. But in reading his pages, we were constantly induced to ask ourselves whether he is equally true to nature; that is, whether in the midst of this multitude of real things, of uncompromisingly real circumstances, the persons put before us are equally real." James mentioned two respects in which Trollope's characters were deficient. In the first place, he said, Trollope "diminished the real elements of passion" in his heroine for fear of making her ridiculous, and consequently failed to excite the reader's imagination. Then, too, he said that Miss Mackenzie and her friends took life *"stupidly,"* and that therefore, even the best part of the book—"the development of Miss Mackenzie's affections"—was "a phenomenon unworthy of an intelligent spectator." Clearly, Trollope's figures appealed neither to James's sensibility nor to his "philosophic" mind. The underlying reason for this was their status as social creatures: "Detach them from their circumstances, reduce them to their essences, and what do they amount to? They are but the halves of men and women."[38] In a way this is comparable to James's criticism of Dickens; both novelists, he thought, damaged their characters by subordinating them to their environment. But whereas Dickens's figures were "unnatural" because they were abnormal, Trollope's were all too normal: "true to common life," but not "true to nature."

James went even further in his review of the author's *Can You Forgive Her?*, the story of a young woman (Alice Vavasor) who deserts her true lover (John Grey) for a scoundrel (George Vavasor), but soon realizes her mistake and returns to the hero. Finding all this a bit too tame, James suggested that Trollope should have made Alice more passionate: "For ourselves, we were very much disappointed . . . that on eventually restoring herself to Grey she should have so little to expiate or to forget, that she should leave herself, in short, so easy an issue by her refusal to admit Vavasar [sic] to a lover's privilege. Our desire for a different course of action is simply founded on the fact that it would have been so much more interesting." James also complained because the hapless George departs for America instead of committing suicide, the latter outcome being the one for which the reader's "excited imagination hankers."[39] If juxtaposed with James's criticism of the sensation novel, this review appears strangely contradictory. But it illustrates the extent to which he could rebel against excessive dullness in fiction. And he did find most of Trollope's novels dull, because his characters lacked either passion, as in *Can You Forgive Her?*, or intellect, as in *The Belton Estate*, which James pronounced "a *stupid* book." A "good observer," but "literally nothing else,"[40] Trollope could seldom create the superior figures that James desired.

To George Eliot, a more serious novelist, the young critic showed greater respect. His 1866 review of her *Felix Holt* praised her "extensive human sympathy, that easy understanding of character at large, that familiarity with man, from which a novelist draws his real inspiration." He stated, moreover, that few English novelists possessed these attributes, which in his view were the hallmark of the "philosophic" writer. Thus, he never accused Eliot of writing "stupid" books or creating "stupid" characters. He implied, nonetheless, that she was comparable to Trollope in her preoccupation with ordinary figures and her disregard of passion: "As a novel with a hero," he said of *Felix Holt*, "there is no doubt that it *is* a failure." And he went on to characterize Felix as a "thorough young Englishman" who, "in spite of his sincerity, his integrity, his intelligence, and his broad shoulders," had "nothing in his figure to *thrill* the reader." One infers that Felix's priggishness and asceticism, as evidenced by his reluctance to pursue Esther Lyon, were difficult for the critic to accept. So far as Esther herself was concerned, he allowed that she had "great merits of intention" (and indeed, the novel does present her as a woman of fine sensibilities), but he said she had no "chance" because of her subordination to the dispassionate Felix. James concluded, therefore, that despite her breadth of mind—her "masculine comprehensiveness"—Eliot was a "feminine" writer: "She has the microscopic observation, not a myriad of whose keen notations are worth a single one of those great synthetic guesses with which a real master attacks the truth." And her books, according to James, were not novels of character; rather, they belonged "to a kind of writing in which the English tongue has the good fortune to abound— that clever, bright-colored novel of manners which began with the present century under the auspices of Miss Edgeworth and Miss Austen."[41] Thus, her "familiarity with man" notwithstanding, he believed Eliot to be somewhat similar to Trollope.

A second, more general essay, "The Novels of George Eliot," makes it clear that James criticized her works not because he misunderstood her aesthetic but because he disagreed with it. Citing the passage from *Adam Bede* in which Eliot defends her treatment of her "everyday fellowmen," James said of her characters: "The word which sums up the common traits of our author's various groups is the word *respectable*.... They all share this fundamental trait,— that in each of them passion proves itself feebler than conscience." This, from James's point of view, was detrimental to Eliot's fiction: "I profoundly doubt whether the central object of a novel may successfully be a passionless creature." And he applied this principle to Adam Bede as he had earlier done to Felix Holt: Adam, the virtuous hero, he found "too good" and "too stiff-backed," lacking in "spontaneity and sensibility"; Dinah Morris he judged too "cool-headed" and "temperate" for one "exalted by religious fervor"; and as for Arthur Donnithorne, who at least had the merit of being a seducer, James wished he were "either better or worse," a hero or else a real villain unredeemed by suffering. Also significant were James's objections to *Romola*. Though he considered the faithless Tito to be among Eliot's more interesting figures, he had reservations about the "moral lesson" of the book, the idea that "Our deeds determine us as much as we our deeds." He acknowledged that this lesson was "salutary," but objected that like the characters who conveyed it, it was "essentially prosaic," making "no demand upon the imagination of the reader."[42] Once again, James revealed his anti-determinism, his belief that denying a character's free will led either to distortion or—as in this case—to dullness.

These reviews anticipate James's later objections to bourgeois realism, particularly in the works of the "Anglo-Saxons." If moralism could cause a writer to produce monsters like Mrs. Davis's, it could also make his creations lifeless—not false, but simply uninspiring. And once again, James's views were shared by many of his countrymen. Throughout the sixties and seventies, Trollope was commonly treated as a novelist whose insight was "anything but profound";[43] and whereas Eliot, at the time James wrote his first reviews, was more highly regarded, eventually critics began to complain about her anti-heroic philosophy and her characters' lack of spontaneity.[44] James was thus one of a number of reviewers whose idealism prevented their wholehearted acceptance of the commonplace, especially with regard to characterization.

This outlook, moreover, was to have a profound effect on James's own theory and practice of fiction. To appreciate his abiding concern for the extraordinary in character and his distaste for the merely banal, one has only to read any of his major novels or to recall his succinct statement in the Preface to *The Princess Casamassima:* "I confess I never see the *leading* interest of any human hazard but in a consciousness (on the part of the moved and moving creature) subject to fine intensification and wide enlargement."[45] And as John O'Neill has demonstrated in his excellent study, *Workable Design,* James as author was less interested in simple realism than in the depiction of a certain ideal of human character, one which stressed the values of freedom and consciousness.[46] This ideal, of course, was evolved by James during his years as a practicing novelist; but two statements in his early reviews anticipate the evolution of his own heroes and heroines.

The first of these occurs in his 1865 essay on Henry Kingsley's *The Hillyars and the Burtons.* Noting the inadequacy of "the muscular system of morals"—an ethic emphasizing honesty, energy, and duty—James said: "there is in the human heart a sentiment higher than that of duty—

the sentiment of freedom; and in the human imagination a force which respects nothing but what is divine."[47] A year later, he developed this idea in the conclusion of his essay on George Eliot: "In morals [Eliot's] problems are still the old, passive problems. . . . What moves her most is the idea of a conscience harassed by the memory of slighted obligations. Unless in the case of Savonarola, she has made no attempt to depict a conscience taking upon itself great and novel responsibilities. . . . Both as an artist and a thinker, in other words, our author is an optimist; and although a conservative is not necessarily an optimist, I think an optimist is pretty likely to be a conservative."[48] Extrapolating from these statements, one may construct the ideal Jamesian hero. In the first place he has "the sentiment of freedom"; far from being satisfied with his environment, and further still from being utterly a creature of it, he rebels against the status quo to seek new experiences. He is not, however, a libertine, for his conscience makes him aware of his "novel responsibilities." But high-mindedness does not guarantee success; his new situation may in turn prove too much for him, and having relinquished his security, he may come to a tragic end.

Obviously James was to be the most eminent creator of Jamesian heroes. One has only to think of Isabel Archer, Lambert Strether, Milly Theale, and Maggie Verver, or— on a lower level—Roderick Hudson, Christopher Newman, and Daisy Miller; each breaks the bonds of tradition, and each deals with his new obligations more or less successfully. It may fairly be said, then, that as an author James was to meet the specifications which he first laid down as a critic. To a considerable degree these standards resulted from his dissatisfaction with the fictional heroes of his day; yet in the character of the rebellious or suffering heroine—a stock figure in the mid-nineteenth-century novel—he found the prototype for his own creations.

Even in his reviews of novels he disliked, James invariably singled out this figure for praise. Discussing Eliot's *Adam Bede*, for example, he commented admiringly on Hetty Sorrel, the young girl who has an affair with Donnithorne and murders their illegitimate child. According to James it is she, not the pious Adam, who is the "central figure of the book, by virtue of her great misfortune." Though he admitted that she is "vain" and "superficial," he sympathized with her far more than does the narrator of Eliot's novel: "there is something infinitely tragic in the reader's sense of the contrast between the sternly prosaic life of the good people about her, their wholesome decency and their noonday probity, and the dusky sylvan path along which Hetty is tripping, light-footed, to her ruin." Clearly, James preferred Hetty, who had a sense of freedom if not a conscience, to the light heroine, the conventional Dinah; in fact, he liked her better than any of Eliot's other women. His second favorite, quite naturally, was Maggie Tulliver of *The Mill on the Floss*, another figure whose passions place her in opposition to her peers. James only wished that she were a little less conventional—that Eliot, instead of killing her off in the flood, had allowed her to return to Stephen Guest.[49]

One finds the same pattern in James's criticism of Trollope; when he discovered a spirited heroine in the author's works, his attitude changed from condescension to respect. Reviewing *Can You Forgive Her?*, he had kind words for Lady Glencora, "the only really poetic figure in the novel." A woman caught between the dull, insensitive politician she has married and the passionate lover she has rejected, she obviously moved James: "Lady Glencora, young and fascinating, torn from the man of her heart and married to a stranger, and pursued after marriage by her old lover, handsome, dissolute, desperate, touches at a hundred points almost upon the tragical." Nonetheless, James implied that like Eliot, Trollope lacked the imagination to handle such a fascinating character; he complained that Lady Glencora is subordinated to her less interesting cousin, Alice Vavasor, and that the conclusion of her tragedy (in which she is reconciled with her husband and bears his child) is out of keeping with her character.[50]

For Trollope's *Linda Tressel*, however, James expressed unqualified admiration. Compelled by her aunt to become engaged to a grimly puritanical gentleman thirty years her senior, the young German heroine of this novel elopes with a man whom she knows to be a rogue; but before they can be married, he is captured by the police, and she, unwilling to regain her social status by marrying the first suitor, dies of a broken heart. This, said James, is a story in which "human nature recognizes herself"; though Linda is "essentially a *common* girl," she represents "the sublime of prose." It is easy to understand his preference for Linda; more virtuous than Hetty Sorrel, she is the author's sole heroine, and more spirited than Maggie Tulliver or Lady Glencora, she refuses to yield to convention but struggles— as James triumphantly noted—"to the death."[51] Perhaps it is not too far-fetched to see her as a figure behind his own Daisy Miller. A second novel which he considered prosaic but sublime was Mrs. Gaskell's *Wives and Daughters*, in which the dark heroine, Cynthia, possesses "an unconscious power of fascination" over men and is tormented by uncontrollable passions. (She apologizes to the light heroine, Molly, as she prepares to woo the latter's beloved: "[S]teady everyday goodness is beyond me. I must be a moral kangaroo!")[52] It hardly need be said which girl James preferred; he thought Molly appealing, but Cynthia delightfully mysterious and suggestive of "infinite revelations of human nature."[53]

So far as character delineation was concerned, however, James gave the highest honors to Charles Reade, who by virtue of his "great synthetic guesses" was in the critic's opinion "the most readable of living English novelists" and "a distant kinsman of Shakespeare."[54] He mentioned in particular "the much-abused 'Griffith Gaunt,'"which had created quite a scandal when, after its serial publication in the *Atlantic*, it was criticized as immoral by other more conservative magazines.[55] Kate Gaunt, Reade's high-spirited heroine, excites the jealousy of her narrow-minded husband by her strictly virtuous (though obviously unwise) attachment to an "ethereal" Catholic priest. Thereafter, Griffith commits bigamy, and when he flees to escape her righteous anger, she is accused of his murder and is forced to stand trial and to endure public humiliation. The novel, then, follows the conventional melodramatic pattern. And significantly, it was a favorite not only of James but of his colleague William Dean Howells, who praised it as a "study of passions and principles that do not change with civilizations," claimed that the "reader himself falls in love" with its heroine, and lamented only its anti-climactic denouement, in which she takes back her unworthy husband.[56] Howells's critique thus echoes many of James's reviews.

This resemblance indicates that James's preferences were again not idiosyncratic; rather, they exemplified the literary trend discussed at length by William Wasserstrom in his *Heiress of All the Ages: Sex and Sentiment in the Genteel Tradition*. This study shows that many American writers conceived of the heroine as a woman of destiny who, through a combination of high-mindedness and passion, could liberate a puritanical, materialistic society.[57] And though Wasserstrom deals only with American fiction, it is obvious that authors like James and Howells found their prototypes in the works of foreign authors, including the Victorian novelists and (at a slightly later date) Cherbuliez, Droz, and Turgenev. To be sure, James's reviews of British novels had a peculiarly American quality, as witness his eagerness to invest figures like Hetty Sorrel with a greater value than they possessed in the original works and his reluctance to accept their return to conventional domestic life. But at a time when he found few characters to his taste, he took consolation in the passionate heroine—a figure who satisfied both his desire to criticize society and his impulse to celebrate feeling.

As James's attitudes toward character and "truth to nature" were the product of his milieu, so his conception of the novel as a literary form derived largely from his ideas on character. His criticism of Goethe's *Wilhelm Meister* shows that even in 1865, he thought of the protagonist as a compositional "center"; without a true hero, he said, the novel lacked form, and its author had "no principle of selection" to follow.[58] In his early reviews, then, James began to criticize the novels that he was later to call "large loose baggy monsters"[59]—that is, fiction in which a central figure or small group of figures does not determine structure.

One of his chief complaints against the British novelists was that they sacrificed the portrayal of the hero to the depiction of society at large. He suspected, in fact, that they did so because of their superficiality of mind. If a novelist collects "a large number of persons," he said in his review of T. A. Trollope's *Lindisfarn Chase,* he has "no space to refine upon individuals."[60] James elaborated this point in his criticism of Henry Kingsley: "His main dependence is his command of that expedient which is known in street parlance as 'collecting a crowd.' He overawes the reader by the force of numbers; and in this way he is never caught *solus* upon the stage; for to be left alone with his audience, or even to be forced into a prolonged tête-à-tête with one of his characters, is the giant terror of the second-rate novelist."[61] Anthony Trollope, too, was an habitual offender in this respect: James lamented that he should have deserted Alice Vavasor for her "vulgar" aunt and equally "vulgar" suitors[62] and that he should have seen fit to devote an entire chapter of *Miss Mackenzie* to the description of a shabby dinner party—"an anomaly in a work of imagination."[63] And of Eliot's novels, James said that they had "much drawing" but "little composition"[64]—again, a criticism stemming directly from his concern for the protagonist. This interest, of course, served him well when he came to write his own fiction, but it limited him as a critic of novels dealing primarily with society rather than with individual characters.

American novelists also incurred James's censure, though in these cases his criticism was more justified. Typically,

his countrymen—or women, one should say, because the
offenders were invariably female—allowed their fondness
for description to distract them from their task of characterization. James thus inveighed against the "picturesque school
of writing,"[65] including such "painters" as Mrs. Stoddard,
Mrs. Charles, and Miss Prescott.[66] Miss Prescott was clearly
the worst culprit; her *Azarian*, though ostensibly the story
of a young girl driven to despair by her cruel lover, seems
written primarily for the sake of description. ("There [the
leaves] lay, . . . here as if wine had been poured upon them,
blazing there in vermeil ardency, one opaque with a late
greenness full of succulence and studded with starry sprinkle
and spatter of splendor, another dancing on its airy stem.")[67]
James made the obvious objection to this "ideal descriptive
style," but his chief criticism was that such passages diverted
the reader's attention from "the history of two persons' moral
intercourse."[68] And as a contrast, he cited the example of
Honoré de Balzac, whose *Eugénie Grandet* (which was to be
the source of his own *Washington Square*)[69] illustrated the
proper use of descriptive detail: "The scene and persons of
[Balzac's] drama are minutely described. Grandet's house,
his sitting-room, his habits, his appearance, his dress, are
all reproduced with the fidelity of a photograph. The same
with Madame Grandet and Eugénie. . . . And yet our sense of
the human interest of the story is never lost. Why is this? It
is because these things are all described *only in so far as
they bear upon the action*, and not in the least for themselves."[70]

By "action," James also implied "character," or as he
said, "human interest"; for in his view, character was the
center not only of structure but of plot as well. This point,
implicit in his 1865 review, becomes more explicit in his
subsequent criticism of Trollope and Eliot; when he commented on the former's uninteresting plots and subplots[71]
and on the latter's "*langeurs* of exposition,"[72] he made it
clear that these failings resulted from the authors' inability
to create strong central figures.

His most interesting statement concerning plot occurs
in his 1866 essay on George Eliot. Noting the anti-climactic
ending of *Adam Bede* (in which the protagonist marries
Dinah, the virtuous heroine), James suggested that Eliot
might have followed Balzac's example and written a second
novel continuing Adam's adventures. Or, he said, she had a
second alternative:

I. . . hold that it would be possible tacitly to foreshadow [Adam's marriage] at the close of the tale. . .—to make it the logical consequence of Adam's final state of mind. Of course circumstances would have much to do with bringing it to pass. . . ; but apart from the action of circumstances would stand the fact that, to begin with, the event was *possible*. The assurance of this possibility is what I should have desired the author to place the sympathetic reader at a stand-point to deduce for himself. In every novel the work is divided between the writer and the reader; but the writer makes the reader very much as he makes his characters. . . . In making such a deduction as I have just indicated, the reader would be doing but his share of the task; the grand point is to get him to make it. I hold that there is a way. It is perhaps a secret; but until it is found out, I think that the art of story-telling cannot be said to have approached perfection.[73]

The advantages which James saw in making plot the outgrowth of character were twofold. First, such a method insured dramatic consistency, providing a safeguard against the arbitrariness that he found at the end of *The Mill on the Floss;* to have done Maggie justice, he said, Eliot should have left her "to her own devices."[74] Second, it might prevent the author from "telling all" and thus leaving nothing to the reader's imagination—an idea also related to James's emphasis on character, for the sake of which this faculty had to be brought into play. James's belief in the value of suggestiveness was to remain an important part of his theory[75] and practice; his contemporaries' reviews of his fiction (especially of *The American* and *The Portrait of a Lady*, which baffled critics because of their inconclusive endings) testify to his efforts at making the readers work, and often, to their dislike of being "made."[76]

So far as narrative technique was concerned, James's criticism reveals his early attempts to assess the value of "dramatic" and "pictorial" methods. Here, too, characterization was the end and technique the means; nearly all of his comments on this subject have to do with the ways an author can lend stature and dignity to his central figure, thus making him more heroic.

In his review of Bayard Taylor's *John Godfrey's Fortunes*, James noted the disadvantages of first-person narrative, which he called "the most dramatic form possible." "To project yourself into the consciousness of a person essentially your opposite," he said, "requires the audacity of great genius"—and evidently Taylor was no genius. Though he could conceive of a character "with various nerves and magnetic sensibilities," he could not make him relate his autobiography in such a way that the reader would believe him to be a hero.[77] The implication is clear, and highly unflattering to the author: ordinary writers had best not attempt the dramatic representation of characters "different from" (especially, superior to) themselves; otherwise, they merely displayed their own limitations. Nonetheless, James did not criticize the first-person technique as such, but simply stated that it was difficult for an author to make his "second story" (the manner in which a character tells of his life) consistent with his "first story" (that of the character himself.)[78]

James was more strongly opposed to the overuse of dialogue as a means of characterization, primarily because of his interest in the protagonist's inner being. In contrast to the first-person narrator, the character who dramatized himself only in his speeches to others was unlikely to project his personality to the reader and thus needed the author's aid in doing so. James made this point as he reviewed *Two Men*, criticizing Mrs. Stoddard for shifting "all her responsibilities as a story-teller upon the reader's shoulders" and for "manufacturing incoherent dialogue" and "uttering grim impertinences about her characters. . . . Take her treatment of her hero. What useful or profitable fact has she told us about him?"[79] Clearly, James thought that not all of Jason's complexities could be revealed through dialogue and that the author should have made greater use of a third-person narrator. At the same time, however, he usually objected to narrators whose preaching supposedly edified the readers but added nothing to characterization; for example, he wrote disparagingly of "Thackeray's trivial and shallow system of moralizing."[80] A good artist, in James's view, conveyed his "philosophy" indirectly through his creations, not directly through a persona.

Moreover, James believed that an excessively analytical technique might rob characters of their human interest, reducing them to mere illustrations. Hence, reviewing *Wives and Daughters*, he praised Mrs. Gaskell for making her commentary unobtrusive, at least with respect to the dark heroine: "She contents herself with a simple record of the innumerable small facts of the young girl's daily life, and leaves the reader to draw his conclusions. He draws them as he proceeds, and yet leaves them always subject to revision; and he derives from the author's own marked abdication of the authoritative generalizing tone which, when the other characters are concerned, she has used as a right, a very delightful sense of the mystery of Cynthia's nature and of those large proportions which mystery always suggests."[81] James thus approved of the absence of narratorial analysis for the same reason that he advocated an open-ended plot: such methods stimulated the reader's imagination, making him sense the complexities of human nature.[82] More generally, James implied that too much analysis interfered with the dramatic illusion. Acknowledging the merits of *Adam Bede* "as a picture, or rather as a series of pictures," he stated: "The author succeeds better in drawing attitudes of feeling than in drawing movements of feeling."[83] Elsewhere he called Eliot "a critic rather than a creator of characters" who "thinks for them more than they think for themselves."[84] Brief as these statements are, they foreshadow James's later use of "internal drama" and his attempt to surround his figures with an aura of mystery.

In James's early criticism there are also two allusions to the "reflector" as a rhetorical device. These occur not in his commentaries on fiction, but rather in his reviews of Swinburne's poetic drama, *Chastelard*, and of Eliot's half-dramatic, half-narrative poem, *The Spanish Gypsy*. Though *Chastelard* is ostensibly the tragedy of Queen Mary's lover, James considered the heroine to be the central figure. He therefore wished that her suitor had dwelt less on her sensuous beauty and more on his own emotions regarding her, the better to convey an idea of her charms: "The only way, in our judgment, to force home upon the reader the requisite sense of Mary's magical personal influence was to initiate him thoroughly into its effects upon Chastelard's feelings."[85] But James's praise of Eliot's Don Juan, the minstrel who observes the heroine as she is torn between love and duty, suggests quite a different role for the reflector: "In every human imbroglio, be it of a comic or a tragic nature, it is good to think of an observer standing aloof, the critic, the idle commentator of it all, taking notes, as we may say, in the interest of truth. The exercise of this function is the chief ground of our interest in Juan."[86] Between these two statements there is obviously a dichotomy—one which reflects the conflict of James's impulse to celebrate passion with his desire to be judicious.[87] Both his reviews imply that dialogue can be supplemented by a reflector; but in the first case, this is a means of involving the reader with the characters, while in the second, it is a device for increasing his distance from them. The later James was to recognize this discrepancy and to exploit it as a source of ambiguity in his own fiction.[88] The early James, however, did not fully explore this problem. Although he noted correctly that Juan is "a man of action, too" and a would-be suitor of Fedalma, he said nothing further on this point.

Despite the tentativeness of James's statements, it is obvious that in the sixties he was beginning to formulate his own ideas of structure, plot, and narration. He could do this because his cultural background had given him a clear idea of "truth to nature" from which, in turn, he could derive his technical concepts. There was one problem, however, that could not easily be subsumed under "character," and that was the matter of genre. Throughout his career James labored to distinguish between the romance and the novel, though at times he confessed his inability to do so. His first such attempt was in an 1868 review of George Sand's *Mademoiselle Merquem*, one which included a brief contrast between her and Balzac:

> An intelligent reader of both authors will, at times, be harassed with the feeling that it behooves him to choose between them and take up his stand with the one against the other. But, in fact, they are not mutually inimical, and the wise reader, we think, will take refuge in the reflection that choosing is an idle business, inasmuch as we possess them both. Balzac, we may say, if the distinction is not too technical, is a novelist, and George Sand a romancer. There is no reason why they should not subsist in harmony.[89]

A few months later the critic made a somewhat more explicit discrimination when he stated that Eliot's *Spanish Gypsy* was "emphatically a *romance*. . . . Whether the term may be absolutely defined I know not; but we may say of it, comparing it with the novel, that it carries much farther that compromise with reality which is the basis of all imaginative writing."[90] This latter definition, of course, is still tentative; yet it anticipates the one in James's preface to *The American*, written some forty years later: "Romance deals with experience liberated . . . ; experience disengaged, disembroiled, disencumbered, exempt from the conditions that we usually know to attach to it and . . . drag upon it."

These formulations, both early and late, are extremely broad; conceivably, they could apply to any literature "uncontrolled by our general sense of 'the way things happen.'"[91] And since the dramatic illusion is a matter of degree, James never made a clear distinction between the romance and the novel. His initial comments on romance dealt primarily with plot; a "strong story," in his view, showed a character's power to perform great deeds in the grand manner and hence his freedom from the circumstances governing—and limiting—ordinary mortals. Obviously, then, James's fondness for romantic story was the most extreme result of his anti-determinism. But despite his faith in the superiority of "character," he also believed that modern man, almost by definition, was a creature of "experience" with a limited capacity for heroic action. This point is at least implicit in his reviews of the poetry of William Morris, particularly of *The Life and Death of Jason* and *The Earthly Paradise*. On the one hand, he revealed his love for romantic myth (for example, the quest myth of warriors "embarking upon dreadful seas" in search of "a jealously watched, magically guarded relic.");[92] yet on the other hand, he wrote, Morris was retelling the stories of "men and women . . . simpler and stronger and happier than we."[93] Here and elsewhere, James associated his liking for romance with the nostalgic, uncritical impulse discussed in Chapter I. Readers of Hawthorne and Melville, of course, are accustomed to conceiving of romance as a genre presenting serious ideas. But Melville was probably unknown to James, and Hawthorne was in his view a special and complex case; and thus, writing of pure romance, he referred instead to Sir Walter Scott and George Sand, whose chief gift was that of "improvisation"—in simplest terms, the ability to tell an entertaining but improbable story, often based on a character's acting against overwhelming odds.

This conception of romance led to a characteristic tension in James's criticism. As a man of sensibility, he was fond of the "strong story"; but as a "higher critic," he wanted to avoid the charge of escapism. Therefore, when he himself ventured to write romance, he felt guilty of neglecting his cultural mission;[94] and when he reviewed works of this genre, he sometimes assumed an air of condescension, perhaps in self-defense. For example, he ridiculed the complex plot of Victor Hugo's *Les Travailleurs de la mer*[95] and stated that Charles Kingsley's *Hereward*, the story of the first of the knights-errant, was "picturesque" but devoid of intellectual interest.[96] More often, however, he self-consciously revealed his affection for the genre, as when, in the middle of his serious review of Senior's *Essays on Fiction*, he commended Sir Walter Scott for his "dazzling array of female forms," for his "poetic plots," and for his "stream of wondrous improvisation." The adjective he applied to Scott's works—"irresponsible"—conveys the ambivalence with which he regarded them. On the simplest level, "irresponsible" could mean "amusing"—a desirable quality in the eyes of the man of sensibility, but an equivocal one from the point of view of the cultural missionary. It could also mean "non-didactic," as James clearly indicated when he opposed Scott to his predecessors, the "preachers and moralists."[97] Regarded in this light, the romance or "irresponsible" novel could be a valuable weapon; James was to use it first against the Mrs. Grundys and later against the naturalists, both of whom, in his opinion, sacrificed imagination to dogma. Finally, "irresponsible" could imply the modern catchword "irrelevant"; that is, lacking in contemporary significance.

James's mixed feelings about romance are even more apparent in his review of George Sand's *Mademoiselle Merquem*. This heroine, as seen through the eyes of the man she eventually marries, is definitely a liberated woman, capable of almost anything: she drives her first suitor nearly insane, turning him away because his ideas on women are too conservative; she cares for a young child, exciting suspicion that it may be hers; she tests the loyalty of a second suitor by making him think that she has had an affair with a disreputable marquis; and she plays "godmother" to an entire fishing village as an expression of her democratic sympathies. All this apparently made James uneasy, for after dismissing the book as "decidedly not one of the best of [Sand's] works," he devoted his commentary to Sand in general, saying little about the romance in particular. Obviously he had a certain taste for Sand; he praised her in much the same way that he had Scott, dwelling on her "extraordinary facility in composition," her ability to tell stories that "beguil[ed]" the reader far better than did Balzac's novels. Moreover, he gave her credit for using romance as a means of combating moralism; though unlike Scott, she had her own axes to grind, James noted that her ideas were iconoclastic and that during the Transcendental era her works were regarded as "scandalous, dangerous, and seditious." Yet far from dealing seriously with her conceptions of democracy and women's rights, he wrote instead of the vagaries of her imagination: "It is indefatigable, inexhaustible; but it is restless, nervous, and capricious; it is, in short, the imagination of a woman."[98] He did not go into further detail, but the meaning of this remark is illuminated by a later essay which cites Mademoiselle Merquem's adoption of the child as a "striking instance" of Sand's "want of moral taste."[99] Irresponsibility, if carried to extremes, could come perilously close to libertinism.

We shall see that in subsequent years, James was to return many times to the romancers—particularly to Sand, whose works provided an antithesis to those of the naturalists. Generally, however, his early reviews set the pattern of his later criticism; almost invariably, he believed romances to be lacking in seriousness, though he regarded them as evidence of their authors' imaginative power. He thus considered himself to be a novelist, not a romancer, and turned to other novelists as his primary models. But his reviews also show his dissatisfaction with the conventions of realism, which, as he knew, made it difficult for writers to depict the extraordinary characters whom he himself preferred:

> Sir Charles Grandison . . . was possible to the author, and is tolerable to the reader, only as the product of an age in which nature was represented by majestic generalizations. But to create a model gentleman in an age when, to be satisfactory to the general public, art has to specify every individual fact of nature; when, in order to believe what we are desired to believe of such a person, we need to see him photographed at each successive stage of his proceedings, argues either great courage or great temerity on the part of a writer, and certainly involves a system of bold cooperation on the reader's side.[100]

Conversely, James thought that the figures of "empirical"[101] novelists like Trollope were generally undistinguished. And because he had read the works of Flaubert and his school, he associated "realism" not only with the non-hero but with the anti-hero as well. In 1865 he noted: "It is just now very much the fashion to discuss the so-called principle of realism, and we all know that there exists in France a school of art in which it is associated with great brilliance and great immorality." Mentioning Flaubert and Gérôme in particular, he proceeded to give thanks that American realists, at least, concentrated only on "objects and sensations of the most unquestioned propriety."[102]

Morover, while James was reluctant to accept characters totally "liberated" from the ordinary conditions of life, he also thought that mere puppets were untrue to nature. In his earliest reviews (especially those of 1865), this anti-determinism led him to assume a dichotomy between character (or motive) and circumstance—a gap that obviously had to be bridged before he could accept the novel as a literary form. One observes this tendency in his review of *Miss Mackenzie*, when he suggested that it is possible to "[d]etach [characters] from their circumstances";[103] in his comments on T. A. Trollope's *Lindisfarn Chase*, which he disliked because the author had "forge[d] his interest out of the exhibition of circumstance rather than out of the analysis of motive";[104] and in a digression on Wilkie Collins, whom he first praised highly for "having introduced into fiction those most mysterious of mysteries, the mysteries which are at our own doors," but then criticized because he dealt with "circumstances" rather than with the criminal himself.[105]

James, then, could not fully accept either the romance or the realistic novel and thus had to find a means of combining the two genres. The solution of this problem was to be one of his main concerns throughout his career; as we shall see, it was the focal point of his *Hawthorne* (1879) and of most of the essays he wrote after 1884. Even in the sixties, however, he began to examine the various means of incorporating the elements of romance into the novel form. One such means was provided by the heroine of sensibility, whom he was to use as a source of "poetry" in his own fiction.[106] This point is implicit in his 1866 review of *Wives and Daughters*, a novel, he said, which might easily have been "dull" except for its interesting young girls. He added: "If an author can be powerful, delicate, humorous, pathetic, dramatic, within the strict limits of homely prose, we see no need of his 'dropping into poetry,' as Mr. Dickens says."[107] His 1868 commentary on *Linda Tressel* is more explicit:

> The atmosphere of the tale . . . becomes positively heavy with despair and madness and coming death, and it is not too much to say that it recalls forcibly that brooding thunderous stillness which . . . our imagination associates with the last pages of "The Bride of Lammermoor." . . . There are a great many different ways by which an effect may be reached. Scott travelled through romantic gorges and enchanted forests, and scaled the summits of mountains crowned with feudal towers. Mr. Trollope trudges through crowded city streets and dusty highways and level garden paths. But the two roads converge and meet at the spot where a sweet young girl lies dying of a broken heart.[108]

Thus, the character whom James found truest to nature was also a means of reconciling the novel with the romance. She could easily be related to her circumstances, which were the cause of her suffering, though not the only forces shaping her personality. Moreover, she was sufficiently attractive in herself to bear realistic portrayal. As James noted in reviewing a translation of Sainte-Beuve's *Portraits de femmes*, a writer who could depict women as they were, "neither ideally beautiful nor ideally gifted," was in fact "deeper and more disinterested" in his passion for the sex than were "the great poets and romancers."[109]

Then, too, the heroine, if she were not treated too analytically, was a subject whose "mystery" transcended the banalities of surface realism. As Peter Brooks has observed,

James's ultimate quarrel with the realists was epistemological; whereas the latter focussed on empirical data—"the things we cannot possibly *not* know, sooner or later, in one way or another"—James assumed the existence of occult, ineffable truths—"the things that, with all the facilities in the world, . . . we never *can* directly know; the things that can reach us only through the beautiful . . . subterfuge of our thought and our desire."[110] And clearly the figure of the young girl, with her sensitive consciousness and her impulse toward freedom, belonged in this realm beyond the limits of scientific psychology. We must remember, of course, that it took James several decades to formulate a definition of romance that did not depend on traditional ideas of plot and accessories; yet his comments on Trollope and Mrs. Gaskell foreshadow his later, more sophisticated criticism.

A second strategy for incorporating romance into the novel was to make the social milieu itself a source of picturesque interest. In this respect James found George Eliot to be a good model. Though he regarded most of her heroes as prosaic, he greatly admired her descriptions of setting and especially, her depiction of English "low-life." He filled several pages of his essay on her works with the humorous dialogue of the rustics in *Silas Marner*, the speeches of the practical Mrs. Poyser in *Adam Bede*, and those of the hard-headed Mrs. Denner in *Felix Holt*. These, he said, are "the author's *touches*. She excels in the portrayal of homely stationary figures for which her well-stocked memory furnishes her with types." That he thought it easier to discover these types in England than in America is suggested by his statement that "the figure of a New England rural housewife" would lack Mrs. Poyser's "picturesque richness of color," there being no "superincumbent layer of 'gentlefolks'"to enhance her characterization.[111] This comment, of course, anticipates James's thesis in his *Hawthorne*. From the beginning of his career, the writer was fascinated by the density of English and European society—by the color which contrasted sharply with the drabness of American life, and which lent charm to the works of Eliot and Balzac no less than to those of Scott and Sand. One might even say that for James, Europe possessed a fascination comparable to that of the mythic world described by Morris. The European milieu could thus serve to unite the novel and the romance, since the author who dealt with it, however realistic his techniques, might still treat colorful and typical figures against a picturesque background.

The heroine of sensibility and the European setting—
these, then, were the elements of fiction which could satisfy
James's demand for "philosophy" and his yearning for
"poetry." And as he himself traveled to the old world near
the close of the decade, his tastes were satisfied by the
French social romancers, especially Victor Cherbuliez
and Gustave Droz, who combined these elements in a
manner that was to have a lasting effect on his own fiction.

Chapter III

Travel Literature
and the Society Novel

To UNDERSTAND James's reviews of fiction during the late sixties and early seventies, one should also examine his comments on travel essays and other sketches of European life. His own attitude toward Europe, which has long been recognized as an important influence on his fiction, had an equally significant effect on his criticism. Writing to Thomas S. Perry in 1867, he expressed "a vague desire to do for our dear old English letters and writers *something* of what Ste.-Beuve and the best French critics have done for theirs." But, he added, an American should emulate the Frenchman only in his "intelligence and his patience and vigour," not in his general posture:

> One feels—I feel at least, that [Sainte-Beuve] is a man of the past, of a dead generation; and that we young Americans are (without cant) men of the future. I feel that my only chance for success as a critic is to let all the breezes of the west blow through me at their will. We are Americans born—*il faut en prendre son parti*. I look upon it as a great blessing; and I think that to be an American is an excellent preparation for culture. We have exquisite qualities as a race, and it seems to me that we are ahead of the European races in the fact that more than either of them we can deal freely with forms of

36

civilization not our own, can pick and choose and assimilate and in short (aesthetically &c) claim our property wherever we find it. To have no national stamp has hitherto been a regret and a drawback, but I think it not unlikely that American writers may yet indicate that a vast intellectual fusion and synthesis of the various National tendencies of the world is the condition of more important achievements than any we have seen.[1]

Prompted by his sense of cultural mission and, as suggested in the previous chapter, by his passion for the picturesque, James did indeed journey to Europe in 1869, 1871, and 1875, becoming a permanent resident of London in 1876.[2] Not surprisingly his "empiricism"—his interest in details of social milieu that he had once considered superficial—increased markedly during this phase of his career. If in 1864 his critical model was the Arnoldian man of culture looking down on the world from his mountain-top, by 1867 or '68 it was the observer moving, notebook in hand, within the populous town. And though he continued to stress the importance of the "moral consciousness," the "spiritual lightness and vigour" which he thought especially characteristic of his countrymen,[3] he gave added emphasis to the values of civilization and the picturesque which for him were invariably linked with Europe. One observes these tendencies not only in James's travel sketches but in his observations on the works of other passionate pilgrims.

Chief among these was William Dean Howells, whose *Italian Journeys* James reviewed in 1868. Part of his enthusiasm for this book derived from his interest in its subject; Italy, he said, possessed "a sort of half-sacred character" because of its monuments of art and culture. But he also gave due credit to Howells as an observer, praising the "vitality" of the author's "sympathies," his abilities as a "poet," and his "imagination." The only danger, said James, was that Howells's sensibilities might warp his judgment:

It is doubtless unfortunate for the Italians, and unfavorable to an exact appreciation of their intrinsic merits, that you cannot think of them or write of them in the same judicial manner as you do of other people, . . . but that the imagination insists on having a voice in the matter, and making you generous rather than just. Mr. Howells has perhaps not wholly resisted this temptation; and his tendency, like that of most sensitive spirits brought to know Italy, is to feel . . . that much is to be forgiven the people, because they are *so* picturesque.

On the whole, however, James seems to have been satisfied that Howells used his head as well as his heart, for he also praised his friend's "keenness of . . . observation," his intelligence, his powers as a "moralist," and his "healthy conscience."[4] Apparently James was here referring to the brief commentaries Howells interspersed among his descriptions, such as those on the Italians' vices (duplicity and vanity) and their poverty, concealed though these were by their picturesque charm.[5] Howells was thus an observer and a man of feeling who yet retained his ideals and his moral sense. As such, he won James's approval.

In opposition to Howells, the critic placed his predecessor, Hawthorne. According to James, the latter author's works, unlike *Italian Journeys*, were "only half descriptive. [Hawthorne] kept an eye on an unseen world, and his points of contact with this actual sphere were few and slight. One feels through all his descriptions,—we speak especially of his book on England,—that he was not a man of the world,—of this world which we after all love so much better than any other."[6] "This world," of course, was the only one left in the post-Romantic era; and James, while admiring Hawthorne's idealism, criticized his failure to observe and to appreciate the life around him during his European travels. The critic developed this theme in his 1872 review of the author's posthumously-published *French and Italian Journals*. There, James referred to "the fascination of seeing so potent a sovereign in his own fair kingdom of fantasy so busily writing himself simple, during such a succession of months, as to the dense realities of the world." Hawthorne's deficiency, he continued, was most evident in his views on art and aesthetics, notably in his objections to nude sculpture and his deafness to "the Parisian harmonies." Hawthorne was therefore "the last pure American—attesting by his shy responses to dark canvas and cold marble his loyalty to a simpler and less encumbered civilization."[7] The implication is clear: modern Americans must come of age. This explains why the critic, throughout the seventies, wrote favorable reviews of sketches marked by their American authors' fervent (and often naive) admiration for Europe—books such as John Burroughs's *Winter Sunshine*, E. S. Nadal's *Impressions of England*, and Augustus J. C. Hare's *Days Near Rome*.[8] (It also explains why he never alluded to the most famous of the travel books, Mark Twain's *Innocents Abroad*.) Despite his reference, in his review of Howells, to the dangers of the picturesque, he seems to have believed that his countrymen could profit from the European experience. Their moral judgment was strong, but their aesthetic sense needed to be developed.

In his criticism of Théophile Gautier, however, James

discussed the limitations of one who was overly fond of the "surface" of things. Gautier, of course, was no American but a Frenchman who had long been a proponent of "art for art's sake." This doctrine, according to James, was at once his strength and his weakness. Writing of the author's *Tableaux de siège*, his sketches of "the picturesque aspect of his country's troubles" during the Franco-Prussian War, James commented: "We have in English no literary analogue of Théophile Gautier. No English writer has as yet taken stock of the capacity of our language for light descriptive prose; and indeed, for that matter, the turn for light analytical description is decidedly less common in the English than in the French mind. M. Gautier is the apostle of visual observation—the poet of the look of things." As an example of Gautier's skill, James cited his description of an emaciated dog, "raw-boned, dissected by leanness, his spinal column like a rosary of beads, the tuberosities of his joints nearly piercing his skin, his sides like a series of hoops, his hide as rugged and rough as dry turf."[9] Clearly, the reviewer was impressed by the vividness of such imagery. But he strenuously objected to the author's final chapter on Paris, which, he said, revealed "a moral levity so transcendent and immeasurable as to amount really to a psychological curiosity." Reading the chapter, one may find the source of James's disgust: Gautier celebrated Paris as a city "trop raffiné, trop élégant . . . pour s'abaisser à des plaisirs grossiers"; he defended the practice of prostitution there on the grounds that it testified to the number of women whose virtue could not be attacked; and with a flourish, he dismissed those whose moral seriousness was offended by Parisian *légèreté:* "Le sérieux! cette belle invention du *cant* moderne pour déprécier les talents aimables, . . . ce morne refuge où les sots silencieusement ruminent leur absence d'idées!"[10] Whether James felt personally affronted by this, one can only speculate. In any case his response was highly indignant: "The ineffable frivolity of [Gautier's] peroration recalls irresistibly that sternly unsavory Scriptural image of the dog and his vomit."[11]

This notice, written in 1872, sets the pattern for James's subsequent reviews of the author's works. Sometimes he was condescending, as when he called Gautier "the prince of travellers" but credited him with "powers of reflection . . . about equivalent to those of an intelligent poodle."[12] Sometimes he was pitying: "Poor Gautier seems to stand forever in the chill external air which blows over the surface of things; above his brilliant horizon there peeped no friendly refuge of truth purely intellectual."[13] And sometimes he was complimentary, praising the author's "perception of material beauty" and his ability "to make an image."[14] Always, however, James's theme was the same: Gautier was a superb painter, but he never found the substance of life beneath its surface. And what, in the critic's view, was substance? In the first place, it was "moral consciousness"; one has only to contrast Howells's comments on Italian shortcomings with Gautier's unconcern for French vice to understand James's position. In a fictional context, substance was "character" or as James was later to say, "the deeper psychology." This point is explicit in his 1873 memorial essay on Gautier, which deals with his poetry and fiction as well as his sketches. "Gautier's figures," said James, "are altogether pictorial; he cared for nothing, and knew nothing in men and women but the epidermis." Thus, though he acknowledged his enjoyment of the author's "chiselled and polished verses" and of his picaresque novel, *Capitaine Fracasse*, he judged him as one whose development was "inexorably circumscribed."[15] We shall see that this was also James's attitude toward some of the fashionable novelists of his own generation.

If a writer's love of "facts"—especially picturesque facts—could make him superficial, it could also render him materialistic, inclined not only to disregard substance but to equate it with surface. The latter failing James perceived in Hippolyte Taine, whose work he first admired but then rejected because of the author's "philosophy." Taine, a member of the circle that included the Goncourts and Flaubert,[16] was one of the first proponents of rigid scientific determinism. James summarized the author's methods in an 1868 review of his *Italy: Rome and Naples*: "M. Taine, in effect, studies man as a plant or as a machine. You obtain an intimate knowledge of the plant by a study of the soil and climate in which it grows, and of the machine by taking it apart and inspecting its component pieces." No reader of James's criticism or fiction could suppose that he shared the French writer's view of humanity. Yet at this date, the critic's remarks were conciliatory:

> The question remains . . . with each reader as to whether . . . [Taine's] famous theory of *la race, le milieu, le moment* is an adequate explanation of the various complications of any human organism—his own (the reader's) in particular. But he will be willing, at least, to admit that the theory makes incomparable observers, and that in choosing a travelling companion he cannot do better than take him from the school

of M. Taine. For, in fact, you can do you own moralizing and sentimentalizing; you can draw your own inferences and arrange your own creed; what you wish in a companion, a guide, is to help you accumulate *data*, to call your attention to facts.

Despite his reservations, James clearly appreciated Taine's talent for "broadly picturesque" description (an ability he shared with Gautier) and his power of minute observation (an "intellectual" skill in which he had no peer). As an example, James cited his passage on Ribera's painting "A Descent from the Cross": "The sun struck upon the head of Christ through the half-drawn curtain of red silk. The darksome background seemed the more mournful beside this sudden radiance of luminous flash, and the dolorous Spanish coloring; the expression, here mystical, there violent, of the passionate figures in the shadow gave to the scene the aspect of a vision." Such lines, added James, "are assuredly picturesque writing; but it seems to us that they serve to illustrate the difference between the picturesque as practised by a writer with his facts in hand, and one who has nothing but fancies."[17] In making this remark, he might have been contrasting Taine with Harriet Prescott and the other women "painters."

One finds similar comments in James's 1872 review of *Notes on England;* he praised the author for his careful observation of English manners and "his admirable faculty for presenting his impressions as pictures." But this time, James made his objections to materialism more explicit, noting, "The French possess that lively aesthetic conscience which, on the whole, is such a simplifier." And though he agreed with Taine's claim that the English had little artistic sense (or for that matter, "intellectual agility"), he defended their "exposition of the facts of human character, the mysteries and secrets of conscience and the innumerable incidents of life. The English genius for psychological observation has no correlative in France."[18] A few months later he repeated these themes in his review of another product of Taine's British journeys, his *History of English Literature*. In this essay James contended that the author lacked "spiritual initiation" into his subject and that unlike Sainte-Beuve, a true empiricist, he oversimplified the mysteries of the human mind and its creations. Far from suggesting that Taine was a good historian because of his theories, James said that he was most perceptive when he ignored them: "his best strokes are prompted by the independent personal impression."[19]

James's strongest reaction against Taine, however,

occurred in 1875, when he reviewed an English translation of his *Notes sur Paris: La Vie et opinions de M. Frédéric-Thomas Graindorge*. In this book, perhaps the most cyncial of his works, Taine uses a persona to observe Paris from a materialistic point of view. (A typical comment is Graindorge's advice to his nephew on the need of dressing fashionably for the ladies: "you are a commodity, and commodities are not disposed of unless properly exhibited.")[20] After the first appearance of this book in 1867, James seemed almost willing to overlook its "philosophy" for the sake of its descriptions of the theater, embassy balls, dinner parties, and so forth. Referring to it in his review of *Italy*, he wrote: "Of feeling in the work there is none; of ideas there are very few; but of images, pictures, description, style, a most overwhelming super-abundance."[21] Yet by the mid-seventies, James was less than overwhelmed. He accused Taine of hiding behind his persona, and added:

> M. Graindorge is the most brutal of materialists, and the more he watches the great Parisian spectacle, the greater folly it seems to him to be otherwise. He finds it all excessively ugly, except in so far as it is redeemed by a certain number of pretty women in beautiful dresses, cut very low. But though it is ugly, it is not depressing; exaltation and depression have nothing to do with it; the thing is to see—to see minutely, closely, with your own eyes, not to be a dupe, to find it very convenient that others are, to treat life and your fellow-mortals as a spectacle, to relish a good dinner, and keep yourself in as luxurious a physical good-humour as possible until the "machine" stops working.[22]

The irony is self-explanatory.

These reviews are particularly interesting because they parallel James's essays on fiction during the same period. In the latter, too, one discerns the tension between his fondness for the European scene—especially when it included high society—and his suspicion that it distracted the author from his proper concern for truth to nature. This conflict underlies all of James's comments on the fashionable novel or social romance.

An English example of the genre is *Lothair* (1870), Disraeli's immensely popular *roman à clef*[23] about a young Scottish nobleman who, after flirting with Catholicism on the one hand, and fighting for the Italian patriots on the other, is finally reconciled to traditional Anglicanism. James, however, expressed no interest in the characters' resemblance to actual persons or in the author's religious views, but commented instead on the dukes and duchesses, the "jewels, castles, horses," and "riches of every kind" that had been "poured into the story": "We are forever complaining, most of us, of the dreary realism, the hard, sordid, pretentious accuracy, of the typical novel of the period, of the manner of Trollope, of that of Wilkie Collins, of that, in our own country, of such writers as the author of 'Hedged In,' and the author of 'Margaret Howth'. We cry out for a little romance, a particle of poetry, a ray of the ideal." *Lothair*, he added, "puts in a claim for the romantic, for the idea of elegance and opulence and splendor." In other words, it represented the picturesque, the meeting-ground of romance and reality. Yet James was not wholly satisfied with the book, for he thought that its author, out of his "joy in being one of the initiated among the dukes," had turned the sublime into the ridiculous: "Here we have a novel abounding in the romantic element, and yet for the most part we do little but laugh at it."[24] (Actually, as the British reviews suggested, Disraeli's exaggerations were in part a burlesque of high life.)[25] Moreover, James complained of the passive hero's "provoking immateriality," especially since the presence of three heroines (a Catholic, an Italian patriot, and an Anglican) offered him a number of dramatic opportunities. Despite these reservations, however, the critic stated that *Lothair* "left us much more good-humored than it found us."[26] This reaction is similar to his attitude toward Gautier; he appreciated picturesque works, yet found them inferior to more serious ones.

Most society novels, of course, were written by the French—not by the naturalists, who detested the genre, but by the conservative school which published in one of James's favorite journals, the *Revue des Deux Mondes*.[27] The fashionable novelist *par excellence* was Octave Feuillet, whose *Monsieur de Camors* James reviewed in 1868. Like most French novels of this kind, *Camors* deals with adultery; the protagonist, a politician and social-climber whose outlook resembles that of Taine's Graindorge, marries an innocent young girl (the daughter of a widow whom he had courted unsuccessfully) while carrying on an affair with the wife of his benefactor, a kindly old general. As might be expected, James's attitude toward the novel was highly ambivalent. On the positive side, he admired its elegant setting and especially, its social drama. For example, he praised one exciting scene in which the adulteress, knowing that her husband is spying on her and Camors, manages to alert her lover and to remove the eavesdropper's suspicions through an ingenious ploy: she tells Camors that he *must* marry the girl who does, indeed, become his wife.[28] Noting that Feuillet was also a playwright, James pronounced him "a master of dramatic form," implying that the novel had not only the picturesqueness of romance but something of its thrilling action as well. Then, too, he liked the suffering heroines, Mme. Camors and her mother: "the virtue . . . of these two ladies is above all things elegant, but it has a touch of the breadth and depth of nature." Nonetheless, he could accept neither Camors, "a most unreal and unsubstantial character," nor the adulteress (Mme. de Campvallon), whom he found "cold, artificial, and mechanical." And he added that Feuillet's works, like "those of most of the best French romancers, . . . wear, morally, to American eyes, a decidedly thin and superficial look. Men and women, in our conception, are deeper, more substantial, more self-directing; they have, if not more virtue, at least more conscience; and when conscience comes into the game human history ceases to be a perfectly simple tale."[29] Again, one notes James's idealistic view of man and his insistence that morality be conveyed through character. (He was unimpressed by the narrator's comments on the necessity of religion.) Moreover, one sees the dichotomy he so often made between the "deeper psychology," which he usually associated with American and English works, and the depiction of the "surface," which he increasingly regarded as the French *métier*.

In several French novels, however—those by Dumas *fils*, Gustave Droz, and Victor Cherbuliez—he found these opposites reconciled. Such works resembled other social romances in that their settings were picturesque and their plots involved sexual adventure, even adultery. But their heroes, unlike Feuillet's protagonists, invariably had a conscience—a moral sense placing them in opposition to society at large, to its cynicism, its heartlessness, and its inflexible conventions. If James admired English heroines for the "sentiment of freedom" that prompted their revolt against bourgeois moralism, he admired their French counterparts for the feeling of responsibility that made them stand out in a superficial world. The latter characters, one may speculate, appealed to his own ambivalent feelings about Europe and its significance to Americans.

The first novel dealing with such a figure was Dumas' *Affaire Clémençeau*, which James reviewed in 1866. This first-person narrative is ostensibly a legal memorial written by a man justly accused of his wife's murder. Ordinarily one would not expect James to have approved of this theme, especially since the protagonist takes pains to stress the "fatalité héréditaire" and the "instinct" which determined his actions. Nonetheless, while somewhat concerned about the depressing nature of the book, James sympathized with its hero, who, as the novel clearly implies, is more sinned against than sinning. The illegitimate son of a laundress, Clémençeau must suffer the taunts of his friends at school. Then, just as he begins to establish himself as a sculptor, he meets a *femme fatale* at a fancy-dress party and marries her as soon as she comes of age in the faith that she is the ideal woman. ("Pour moi," he says at one point, "ce n'était pas une jeune fille, ce n'était pas une enfant, ce n'était pas une femme, c'était la Femme: Symbole, Poëme, Abstraction, Énigme éternelle."[30] One perceives why James thought him "a man of the deepest feeling and the richest understanding"!) But alas, Iza commits adultery with a number of men, and Clémençeau, when he finally discovers the truth, is driven to murder, hence ruining his artistic career. As James suggested, then, the book treats the *belle dame* theme in a social context: "It traces the process of the fatal domination acquired by a base and ignoble soul over a lofty and generous one."[31] It also deals with the conflict between the innocent soul and society, for presumably, if Clémençeau had been a man of the world, he would have discovered the truth far sooner and experienced less shock when he did. Dumas' novel thus develops the same themes that James was to treat in *Roderick Hudson* and *The Princess Casamassima;* indeed, Viola Dunbar has correctly cited it as the principal source of the former novel, the study of a young American artist literally destroyed by his passion for a woman and more generally, by his experience in Europe.[32]

One also finds approving criticism in James's 1871 essay on Gustave Droz, which deals with his *Cahier bleu de Mademoiselle Cibot* (1867) and an English translation of his *Autour d'une source* (first published in the *Revue des Deux Mondes,* 1868). Droz, as James noted, was best known as a fashionable novelist and light satirist "at home in that cool *demi-jour* of well-appointed drawing-rooms, in which the accustomed eye finds it of profit to detect and compare the subtler gradations of social fact." In this review, however, he praised the author for having turned his attention to serious subjects and for having used his gifts to delineate character, adding that his *Mademoiselle Cibot* deserved "to stand among the very best fictions of recent years." The heroine of this novel, like Dumas' Clémençeau, is guilty of wrongdoing (in this case, adultery); but also like him, she is the victim of a society too cynical for her. Forced into a marriage of convenience by her ambitious and greedy mother, she is rendered miserable both by her husband's insensitivity and by her own sexual fears, acquired in the course of her education at a grim convent school. For consolation she turns to a neighbor, the Count de Marsil, who resembles James's Osmond in his passionless aestheticism. Ultimately he casts her off, and in despair she drowns herself. Said James: "There is an admirably sagacious irony in the contrast between the clear, deep-welling passion of Adèle and the shallow, cynical self-possession of the lover on whose condescension she lives and from whose indifference she dies."[33]

The same kind of contrast exists in *Autour d'une source*, a novel James applauded for its "unfolding of those personal passions and motive accidents which lurk beneath the surface of broad public facts, like the little worms and insects we find swarming on the earthward face of a stone." In this book there are two victims: a countess, herself sophisticated in the Parisian way, who nonetheless suffers because of her husband's infidelity; and the simple priest of the mountain village where the story takes place, who in turn is captivated by the lady's wiles. Although he retains his sexual honor, he is forced by the countess's father—"a Frenchman of the Yankee type"—to assent to a fake "miracle," which leads to the commercialization of the town and its spring. Thus, as James said, the "supreme interest of the story" lies in the conflict between "the large and dusky soul of the stalwart Abbé, lighted only by the votive taper of his simple primitive faith," and the "fierce irruption of modern life into the little mountain parish."[34] In this context, it should be noted, "modern life" means not only the corruption that James and Droz linked with Paris but the materialism that the critic associated with his own country as well. The sensitive soul had to struggle against the worst of both worlds.

James also admired these books on technical grounds, which, as always, were closely related to his thematic preferences. In the first place, he commented on the "unity of effect" in *Mademoiselle Cibot* and the "moulded plot" of *Autour d'une source*, contrasting the latter with "those mere measured chains of consecutive incident which suggest a yard-stick as their formative implement." Here again one may note James's taste for the simple plot involving a central figure as opposed to the complex plots of Dickens, Eliot, and other social novelists. Secondly, he praised the texture of Droz's works, calling him "a master of . . . sensuous detail" who understood "the relation between the cultivated fancy and the visible, palpable facts of the world." This, of course, was a tribute not only to the author's skill as a realistic "painter" but to his gift in selecting the details which illuminated his characters. James added that Droz's work "suggests the interesting reflection that intelligent realism, in art, is sure to carry with it its own morality." Apparently this is a reference to the author's narrative technique; instead of relating Mademoiselle Cibot's story "in the vulgarly sentimental manner," he told it "in its hard material integrity,"[35] letting the characters, and the facts about them, speak for themselves. (Part of *Mademoiselle Cibot* is a first-person narrative in the form of a diary.) Once again it can be seen that *intelligent* realism—as opposed to the realism of the commonplace or that of the "surface"—was in James's view dependent on the intelligent character.

Another writer who published in the *Revue des Deux Mondes* was Victor Cherbuliez, a native of Geneva. Reviewing his *Meta Holdenis* in 1873, James referred to him as "an old friend" and proceeded to discuss his earlier works, nearly all of which dealt with a sensitive protagonist at odds with a decadent society. In *Comte Kostia* (1862), the hero is an idealistic young tutor who saves a lonely girl from the clutches of her father, a Byronic figure tortured by the thought of his late wife's infidelity and his child's possible illegitimacy; in *Ladislas Bolski* (1870), the central character is (as James stated) an "unbalanced but heroic young Pole, the dupe of his generosity and the victim of his passionate illusions"; and in *La Revanche de Joseph Noirel* (1871), which James pronounced the most "brilliant" of the author's works, there are two poetic figures—an "enchanting and appealing woman" married to an evil count, and a frustrated artisan who tries to become her lover and ultimately kills both her and himself. *Paule Méré* (1864), which was the source of James's *Daisy Miller*,[36] has the same basic configuration as these other novels; its heroine suffers a broken heart because her suitor, at the urging of his friends, misjudges her spontaneity as impropriety. For this kind of fiction the critic professed an obvious enthusiasm, expressing his admiration for Cherbuliez's "vastly thrilling" plots and for the characters which set his works apart from those of Octave Feuillet.[37]

But though James stated that Cherbuliez was at his best when his fiction included a "poetic element," he disliked the writer's tendency toward satire and irony. Even Paule, a more sophisticated figure than James's own Daisy, impressed the critic as being less than "natural"; and Meta Holdenis, a "German Becky Sharpe" who plays fast and loose with two men, was in his view a completely distasteful character, one who failed to provide a contrast to the society around her. Discerning Cherbuliez's intention to ridicule

German idealism, he lamented that the writer had subordinated his characters to his "obtrusive *parti pris*" and that he had become "fatally clever," like the novelists who dealt with life's surface. "The hard metallic glitter of his style," James concluded, "is a disagreeable substitute for the charming atmosphere of his early works."[38]

These essays on Dumas, Droz, and Cherbuliez are of special interest because of their direct relationship to James's fiction. In them one finds not only his comments on some specific sources of his novels[39] but also indications of the literary tradition behind most of his work. Since the minor French novelists have passed into oblivion, scholars have underestimated their influence on James, seeing this only in his early writings.[40] Yet especially in his novels of the "major phase"—*The Ambassadors*, *The Wings of the Dove*, and *The Golden Bowl*—one discovers a pattern similar to that of the better social romances: an innocent character is placed in opposition to an aesthetically attractive but morally bankrupt society. True, James's heroes and heroines are American, and his treatment of this theme is so original that one cannot criticize his fiction as being derivative. Nonetheless, his reading of *La Revue des Deux Mondes* was probably of cardinal importance to his own career. This hypothesis seems all the more likely because, as we shall see, James at first found little to admire in the naturalistic novels of the mid-seventies and eighties, and because, as Matthiessen has noted,[41] his disillusionment during the nineties caused him to look backward toward a more idealistic age.

Furthermore, this criticism reveals that James, despite his idiosyncrasies, shared the taste of his era. Both Cherbuliez and Droz were extremely popular among the readers of the Eastern periodicals,[42] and both found favor with other critics, whose comments were strikingly similar to James's. Like him, they praised the authors' depiction of sensitive characters against colorful backgrounds, at the same time expressing doubts concerning their French "cleverness."[43]

But the fiction of Droz and Cherbuliez, despite its popularity, marked the end rather than the beginning of an era. In spirit, at least, these novelists were citizens of the Empire, a social order destroyed by the Franco-Prussian War (1870-71). James himself acknowledged this when he wrote that *Autour d'une source* "already" had "something of the value of an historical document" and that Droz told "the latest social news of the France of the past."[44] Then, too, the "cleverness" James discerned in *Meta Holdenis*,

Cherbuliez's attempt to capture the spirit of the new age, reappeared in subsequent novels by this writer and his contemporaries. In 1875 Droz published *Une Femme gênante*, the story of a Breton apothecary who exhumes his late wife's body, embalms it, provides it a suite of rooms, and ministers to it (until he falls in love with his neighbor's daughter). Referring to this novel in a brief note, James used one adjective: "inconceivable."[45] And the same year, Cherbuliez wrote *Miss Rovel*, a book relating the adventures of a spoiled, insolent English flirt. The critic reviewed this novel with great sorrow; it represented, he said, "the most striking example of the eclipse of a great talent that we have ever encountered." He added that Cherbuliez had gone "to Paris... at any rate intellectually," and that this was the more disappointing because he had seemed the only French novelist capable of that most "difficult feat": the characterization of "a young girl brought up in the Anglo-Saxon fashion."[46] As for Dumas and Feuillet, the former deserted the novel in favor of didactic plays and prefaces (a fact which James regretted);[47] the latter continued to write fiction which the critic found clever and dramatic, but superficial. (In 1876, he noted: "There are writers who began with doing better things— Flaubert, Gustave Droz, and Victor Cherbuliez—but they have lately done worse, whereas M. Feuillet never falls below himself.")[48]

Thus, as the decade progressed, James became dissatisfied with the authors whom he had once admired. Furthermore, he himself probably realized that his taste for novels of a simpler age—the kind that depicted a pure hero (or heroine) suffering in an impure world—was somewhat outmoded. A certain ambivalence is apparent in his 1874 review of "Jean de Thommeray," a story by another writer in the *Revue des Deux Mondes*, Jules Sandeau.[49] By and large, James found him preferable to his contemporaries:

> Now that ... the sun of Madame Sand's genius has dipped pretty well into the horizon, and M. Gustave Flaubert seems to have told the one good story he had to tell, and M. Octave Feuillet breaks his long silences to no great purpose, and M. Dumas *fils* . . . has taken to writing prefaces to his own and other people's masterpieces—in this not very brilliant state of affairs we know no French novelist whom we prefer on the whole to M. Jules Sandeau. His novels, some time ago, brought him into the Academy, which was natural enough, as they rigorously respect all the proprieties, moral and literary.

But James commented with a certain embarrassment on the author's story, a tale about a young man, almost "fatally corrupted" by Parisian life, who redeems himself when the War arouses his patriotic feelings. Noting the lack of verisimilitude in the protagonist's eleventh-hour conversion, James commented: "If we were a German professor of chemistry, in spectacles, who had lived through the siege of Paris, we are afraid we should laugh at [the story]. But in that case, twenty to one we should be utterly insensitive to its charm of style."[50] Obviously, there was a conflict between the critic's sensibility and his literary judgment.

It was James himself who revitalized the themes of the French social romances, dealing with them in a more complex and less sentimental fashion. First, however, he had to come to terms with the contraries that made progression possible: the works of the naturalists.

Chapter IV
The Naturalists

GUSTAVE FLAUBERT and his followers—Edmond and Jules de Goncourt, Emile Zola, and Alphonse Daudet—were among the novelists whom James knew personally, having attended their weekly meetings during his visit to Paris in 1875-76. Leon Edel's biography and various collections of James's letters show that he was at once fascinated and horrified by the conversations he heard at Flaubert's gatherings; that he admired the naturalists' artistic interests—especially their search for the "mot juste"—while deploring their subject-matter; that he was unpleasantly surprised by their unfamiliarity with English writers and by their disrespect for Cherbuliez, Droz, and Feuillet;[1] and that finally, after declaring he was "turning English all over,"[2] he left Paris to take up permanent residence in London.

Less well-known, but equally important, is the history of James's critical reaction to these novelists as found in his reviews of their works. Some of this criticism—his notice of Edmond de Goncourt's *La Fille Elisa* (1877) and his essays on Zola's *Une Page d'amour* (1878) and *Nana* (1880)—was written after his Parisian sojourn and may have been affected by his personal impressions. Other essays, however, including his "Minor French Novelists,"[3] were written before his meeting with the naturalists. Possibly, then, his prior knowledge of the authors' writings affected his judgments of the persons themselves. In any case his initial attitude toward their novels was largely negative. Only in later years, after he had become far more flexible in his judgments, was he able to regard them in a more favorable light.

To understand why this was so, one must read James's reviews in the context of his earlier criticism. In the late sixties his acceptance of the novel as a genre depended primarily on two assumptions: first, that the novelist might create characters who were "true to nature," possessing both a conscience and a sense of freedom; and second, that he might emulate the romancer, placing these figures in picturesque circumstances to which they would be partially yet not completely subordinated. Moreover, we have seen that James found these requirements met by the novels of Dumas, Cherbuliez, and Droz, fiction that expressed his own ambivalence toward the European "surface." The naturalists, in contrast, deliberately violated the conventions which James valued. They created figures governed by their heredity and environment, not by their spiritual nature; and they placed them in surroundings which were either dull, sordid, or "picturesque" in a sense that James thought perverted.

If the heroines of the French romancers were tiresomely virtuous, those of the naturalists were invariably corrupted. This, of course, was no accident, for the writers of the new school reacted against their predecessors, attempting to show that the separation of character from circumstances was utterly factitious.[4] First among the anti-heroines was Flaubert's Madame Bovary, who dreams of a romantic escape from her dull, provincial life but poisons herself after being deserted by the two lovers whom she once idealized. James's comments on Flaubert in his "Minor French Novelists" reveal his ambivalence toward this figure. Initially, he observed, "The reader may protest against a heroine who is naturally depraved. You are welcome, he may say, to make of a heroine what you please, to carry her where you please; but in mercy don't set us down to a young lady of whom, on the first page, there is nothing better to be said than that." One receives the impression that the hypothetical speaker is James himself, or at least one of his personae. On the other hand, he argued, "Mme. Bovary is typical, like all powerfully conceived figures in fiction. There are a great many potential Mme. Bovarys, a great many young women, vain, ignorant, leading dreary, vulgar, intolerable lives, and possessed of irritable nerves and of a high natural appreciation of luxury, of admiration, of agreeable sensations, of what they consider the natural rights of pretty women, who are more or less launched upon the rapid slope which she descended to the bottom."[5] James's attitude toward Madame Bovary seems comparable to his view of Hetty Sorrel; he found both characters sympathetic, at least to some extent, because of their craving for "elegance and opulence and splendor." For their sake, then, he set aside his scruples against "depraved" women.

But he also stated: "Realism seems to me with 'Madame Bovary' to have said its last word. I doubt whether the same process will ever produce anything better."[6] And indeed, he was adamant in rejecting the literary descendants of Flaubert's protagonist. For example, he clearly disapproved of Daudet's Sidonie Chèbe (*Fromont jeune et Risler aîné*), a vulgar woman who seduces her husband's business partner and his brother, forcing her hapless spouse to bankruptcy and ultimately to suicide. Such a character, in James's view, was "cold, false, vicious, luxurious, essentially corrupt"—an imitation of Madame Bovary with no redeeming qualities. "If we are to write the natural history of the prostitute on this extended scale," he queried, "on what scale shall we handle that of her betters?" In fact, Sidonie does not become a prostitute until the end of the novel; but, said James, "At night all cats are grey . . . , and past a certain level all women of the habits of Mesdames Bovary and Risler may be lumped together."[7] Similarly, he had little patience with the heroine of Zola's *Une Page d'amour*, whom he described sarcastically as "this singular figure of the exceptionally virtuous widow, who throws herself into the arms of her daughter's physician, and then gets so bravely over it." In thus characterizing Hélène Grandjean, he ignored both the extenuating circumstances of her lapse from virtue—her loneliness as a widow in Paris—and the subtle irony of her regarding herself as "honnête" when, after her daughter's death (the result of the girl's distress at her affair), she makes a "respectable" marriage.[8] James's idealism, then, often caused him to overlook the complexities in the naturalists' works.

It was their depiction of real prostitutes, however, which truly disgusted him. Goncourt's treatment of his protagonist in *La Fille Elisa* is a case in point: a pathetic figure, more a victim than a victimizer, she wastes away in an inhumane prison after murdering the man whom she really loves. (Ironically, his attempt to rape her causes her to commit the crime.) Referring to the author's didactic intentions, James wrote: "M. de Goncourt's theory is perfectly respectable; novelists are welcome to become as serious as they please; but are the mysteries of such a career as Elisa's the most serious thing in the list? M. de Goncourt's fault is not that he is serious or historical or scientific or instructive, but that he is intolerably unclean."[9] Here one finds a theme that James stressed repeatedly, not only in his criticism of the naturalists but in his other reviews as well—the idea that an author's selection of his subject-matter (in a novelistic context, his protagonist) is at least as important as his treatment of it. He was later to modify this judgment, arguing that a writer must be allowed his *donnée;* but even in subsequent years, he strongly preferred the heroine to the prostitute.

His most violent objections were directed against the anti-heroine of Zola's *Nana,* a thoroughly vicious woman who preys on a succession of wealthy lovers. The narrator, it should be noted, stresses her corruption without attempting to excuse it, though he does attribute this to her heredity and upbringing. At one point, for example, he says of her: "la mouche envolée de l'ordure des faubourgs, apportant le ferment des pourritures sociales, avait empoisonné ces hommes, rien qu'à se poser sur eux."[10] But James, the seeker of characters who were true to nature, was hardly appeased by such moralizing. In his 1880 review he invoked the same standard that he had used fifteen years earlier: "Does [Zola] call that vision of things of which *Nana* is a representation, *nature?* The mighty mother, in her blooming richness, seems to blush from brow to chin at the insult! On what authority does M. Zola represent nature to us as a combination of the cesspool and the house of prostitution?" Apparently the critic found Nana false to nature in a double sense. On the one hand, she was too commonplace: "The figure of the brutal *fille,* without a conscience or a soul, with nothing but devouring appetites and impudences, has become the stalest of the stock properties of French fiction." On the other, she and her victims were caricatures, at least from James's point of view:

> The human note is completely absent, the perception of charac-
> ter, of the way that people feel and think and act, is helplessly,
> hopelessly at fault; so that it becomes almost grotesque at last
> to see the writer trying to drive before him a herd of figures that
> never for an instant stand on their legs. This is what saves us in
> England, in spite of our artistic levity and the presence of the
> young ladies—this fact that we are by disposition better psy-
> chologists, that we have, as a general thing, a deeper, more
> delicate perception of the play of character and the state of the
> soul.

To some extent, as Lyall Powers has noted, James's objections to the novel were based on aesthetic grounds: "It is not [Zola's] choice of subject that has shocked us," he concluded, "it is the melancholy dryness of his execution, which gives us all the bad taste of a disagreeable dish with none of the nourishment."[11] One feels, nonetheless, that the critic protests too much; his metaphors strongly convey his antipathy toward Zola's protagonist.

So far as the picturesque was concerned, James found the new novels devoid of even superficial charm. Significantly, he devoted the first part of his "Minor French Novelists" not to Flaubert's *cénacle* but to Charles de Bernard, a writer "more enjoyable than many of his highly perfected modern successors." Though he conceded that Bernard, who wrote in the late 1830s and '40s, had "no moral imagination," he nonetheless praised him for being "gentlemanly," "extremely amusing," and "picturesquely humorous." In short, he represented "the old French cleverness as distinguished from the new." The critic dwelt particularly on *Gerfaut*, a novel about a young man of letters who seduces an unhappily married countess. Like most works of its kind, the book is highly melodramatic: ultimately Gerfaut kills the count in a duel and his remorseful wife commits suicide. James ignored the main characters in the novel but wrote favorably of its colorful minor figures and its romantic plot and setting: "There is an old castle, and a good deal of killing, a secret closet in the wall, and a very good portrait of a feudal nobleman born too late." Bernard, then, like Cherbuliez, Droz, and Feuillet, was yet another social romancer. In an interesting digression James stated why such writers appealed to him:

> [The critic] remembers often turning over, as a child, an old back-parlor volume of the "keepsake" genus, bound in tarnished watered silk, as such volumes were apt to be. It was called, if memory serves him, the "Idler in France."... There was the good old crooked, dirty, picturesque Paris of Charles X and Louis Philippe.... There were pictures of the old Boulevards and the Palais Royal, the staircase at the Opera, the table d'hôte at the Hôtel des Princes, a *salon* in the Chaussée d'Antin.... The Paris of these antediluvian Parisians seemed to my fancy a paradise; and I suppose that a part of my lurking tenderness for Charles de Bernard rests upon the fact that it appears to live again in his pages.[12]

Again, one notes that Europe—especially France—had acquired an almost mythic value in James's eyes.

It was this image of Europe, together with the old ideals of human nature, which the new novelists set out to destroy. In the portion of his essay dealing with Flaubert, James commented on *Madame Bovary* as "an elaborate picture of small rural *bourgeois* life," adding: "Into all that makes life ignoble, and vulgar, and sterile M. Flaubert has entered with an extraordinary penetration. The dulness and flatness of it all suffocate us; the pettiness and ugliness sicken us." This passage calls to mind James's early reviews of Trollope, though in the French author's works, he found repulsiveness added to vulgarity. Nonetheless, he bravely acknowledged the merit of the most unpleasant incident in the novel, Charles Bovary's unsuccessful operation on the clubfoot of the ostler. At first, said James, the reader wonders whether Flaubert was not guilty of "a sort of artistic bravado . . . a desire to complete his theory of realism by applying his resources to the simply disgusting." Yet the critic noted the "metaphysical value" of the episode in its characterization of Bovary, the community at large, and indirectly, the protagonist.[13]

But as James argued for the uniqueness of Madame Bovary, so he felt that Flaubert's "picture" was also a special case. He clearly disliked the author's *Education sentimentale,* the account of another dreamer, Frédéric Moreau, who wastes his life in pursuing an unattainable woman. Because the novel contrasts Moreau's ideals with the realities of his existence, its action is unexciting and its descriptions emphasize the tawdry aspects of high society. To James this ironic technique was intolerable. He pronounced the book "elaborately and massively dreary," adding: "That a novel should have a charm seems to me the most rudimentary of principles, and there is no more charm in this laborious monument to a treacherous ideal than there is perfume in a gravel-heap."[14] On similar grounds, he condemned the works of Zola, citing the "atmosphere of low-class Parisian cockneyism" in *Une Page d'amour*[15] and the "dryness," "solemnity," and "air of tension and effort" in *Nana.*[16] These qualities may all be contrasted with the urbane, "gentlemanly tone" which he found in Bernard's treatment of "the *monde élégant.*"[17]

The Goncourt brothers, whom he discussed in the third part of his "Minor French Novelists," presented a special problem. Noting their background as art students, he admitted that their imagination was, indeed, *"raffiné":* "realism for them has been altogether a question of taste—a studio question, as it were." In other words they did have a strong sense of the picturesque. James thought this was a virtue, so long as they dealt with subjects like the heroine of *Renée Mauperin,* a young girl who prevents her ambitious brother from stealing the title of a noble family. But he strenuously objected to the aestheticism he perceived in *Soeur Philomène*, a novel about a sister of charity in a hospital and the surgeon whom she admires from afar, an alcoholic who finally commits suicide by injecting himself with some poisonous material obtained from a cadaver. Acknowledging that the novel was "a masterpiece" of "writing and of visual observation," James said: "there is something ineffably odd in seeing these elegant erudites bring their highly complex and artificial method—the fruit of culture, and leisure, and luxury—to bear upon the crudities and maladies of life, and pick out choice morsels of available misery upon their golden pen-points."[18]

Though he cited no examples, the following passage—a description of the surgeon as he drinks absinthe—will serve to clarify his meaning: "Il versait au fond du verre l'absinthe d'où montait aussi-tôt l'arome des herbes enivrantes. De haut, et goutte à goutte, il laissait tomber dessus l'eau, qui la troublait et remuait dans de petits nuages les blancheurs nacrées d'une opale. . . . La morte se transfigurait en une image pâlissante. Le souvenir ne faisait plus que flotter en lui sous un linceul rose."[19] Such writing, which James called "the analysis of sensation raised to its highest power," was in his view a perversion of the quality he had found in the Goncourts' predecessors: "The sense of the picturesque has somehow killed the spiritual sense; the moral side of the work is dry and thin."[20] And for the same reasons, he also attacked Flaubert's *Tentation de Saint Antoine* (a prose poem "abounding in the grotesque and the repulsive, the abnormal and the barely conceivable")[21] and the poetry of Poe and Baudelaire.[22] He thus condemned aestheticism as well as naturalism, rejecting the union of picturesqueness and morbidity.

To a twentieth-century reader James's tastes may appear to have been hopelessly conservative, yet they seem less so if judged not by present-day standards but by those of his own era. Other Eastern critics joined him in condemning the "black picture of corruption" in *L'Education sentimentale*[23] and the aestheticism of Flaubert (in *Saint Antoine*), the Goncourt brothers, and Baudelaire.[24] Above all, they hated the figure of the vicious heroine and thought *Nana* represented a literary nadir. Thomas S. Perry stated that the novel "reek[ed] with every kind of beastly sin," adding, "Zola lacks, more than anything else, gentlemanliness";[25] and A. K. Fiske, in an article entitled "Profligacy in Fiction," accused the author of "opening . . . the sewers of human society into the gardens of literature."[26] Parallels to James's criticism may also be found in various essays appearing in the *Revue des Deux Mondes*. Ferdinand Brunetière, for one, thought *Madame Bovary* the best of Flaubert's novels because of its exploration of "un psychologie raffinée," condemned Zola for his grossness and the Goncourts for "Le Faux Naturalisme," and called for more inspiring heroines, such as those of George Sand.[27] Another critic, Charles Bigot, argued against the naturalists' exclusive preoccupation with the lower classes in terms that James himself might have used: "Si les drames humains se passent surtout dans la conscience, si c'est là qu'est la véritable intérêt littéraire, ces drames sont particulièrement attachans . . . où la conscience est la plus complexe et la plus développée."[28] And Charles de Mazade, a critic whom it is certain that James read, attributed the decline of French literature to the doctrine of art for art's sake, naming Sand, Feuillet, Cherbuliez, Sandeau, and Droz as the authors who could counteract this tendency.[29]

James was thus hardly alone in his distrust of the new school. It is all the more remarkable, then, that to some degree he was able to overcome his cultural bias. Even as he inveighed against the French writers' "uncleanness," he warned the "Anglo-Saxons" against their opposing tendency to be puritanical and too unconcerned about literary merit. As he stated in his review of Zola's *Nana:* "Half of life is a sealed book to young unmarried ladies, and how can a novel be worth anything that deals only with half of life? . . . [I]t may be said that our English system is a good thing for virgins and boys, and a bad thing for the novel itself, when the novel is regarded as something more than a simple *jeu d'esprit*, and considered as a composition that treats of life at large and helps us to *know.*"[30] This same idea, it should be noted, reappears in "The Art of Fiction," James's attempt to weigh the claims of the French writers against those of the Mrs. Grundys.

Furthermore, he praised the naturalists' artistry, especially their rendering of the "pictorial side of life" and their attempts to find the expression corresponding to the object (the "mot juste"). These, of course, were the qualities he had previously admired in the works of Balzac, whom he identified as the naturalists' predecessor, and in those of Gautier, Taine, and Gustave Droz. Even when he wrote of loathsome descriptions—that of Charles Bovary's operation on the ostler, for example, or that of Jeanne Grandjean's death in *Une Page d'amour*—he treated these as *tours de force*, commenting on the authors' artistic powers.

Then, too, James thought that the writers' practice could at times transcend their theories. We have seen, for instance, that he exempted *Madame Bovary* from his general condemnation of the naturalists' works, although his praise of the novel was rather backhanded: "In spite of the elaborate system of portraiture to which [Madame Bovary] is subjected, in spite of being minutely described in all her attitudes and all her moods, from the hem of her garment to the texture of her finger-nails, she remains a living creature, and as a living creature she interests us."[31] One notes that James said "in spite of," not "because of"; as he had earlier objected to Eliot's overuse of description, so he implied that Flaubert might be depriving his characters of life if he delineated them too minutely. And consequently, one sees the force of Peter Brooks's contrast between Flaubert, with his "attitude of deconstructive and stoic materialism," and James, with his desire to fathom the "abyss" underlying surface appearances.[32] Yet one also notes James's admiration of Flaubert's "living," "typical," and "powerfully conceived" protagonist, and of "the intensity of illusion" created by the novel. Intuitively, then, James recognized that Flaubert could be a symbolist as well as a realist, an author who could suggest the truths "beneath and behind" the surface in spite of his devotion to "the pictorial side of life."[33]

This perception may account for a subtle revision upward in James's estimate of Flaubert. In the original version of his major essay, published in the February 1876 issue of *Galaxy*, he classified the author as one of the "Minor French Novelists," thus placing him in the same category as Bernard and the Goncourt brothers. Moreover, James used his last paragraph to contrast these authors with his old favorites: "the brilliant talents—Octave Feuillet, Edmond About, Victor Cherbuliez"; Gustave Droz, whose *Mademoiselle Cibot* he called "a masterpiece, and a capital example of the charm that intense reality may have when it is reached by divination, by the winged fancy, rather than by a system more or less ingenious"; Emile Erckmann and Alexandre Chatrian, co-authors of a series of local color novels characterized, James said, by their presentation of "the decent, wholesome, human side of reality"; and George Sand, whom he thought superior to all her successors: "She has the true, the great imagination—the metaphysical imagination. She conceives more largely and executes more nobly; she is easy and universal and—above all—agreeable."[34] But in the version of the essay published in *French Poets and Novelists* (1878), this peroration was dropped, as was the final, negative section on the Goncourts; and the title was changed to "Charles de Bernard and Gustave Flaubert." Flaubert, then, was no longer a "minor" novelist; and the structure of the essay now heightened the contrast between him and Bernard, which (in both versions) was not entirely in the latter's favor. True, James displayed an instinctive preference for "the old French cleverness as distinguished from the new"; yet, as Lyall Powers has noted, he was forced to admit that Bernard was "persistently second-rate ... because he had no morality," whereas Flaubert, despite his theories, was a "potent moralist" and hence a major author: "Every out-and-out realist who provokes curious meditation may claim that he is a moralist, for that, after all, is the most that the moralists can do for us."[35]

Similarly James showed his respect for Zola, even in his negative reviews. Though he wished that the author had "more horizon," he called his work on the *Rougon-Macquart* "one of the most remarkable literary tasks of our day"; and though he disliked both *Une Page d'amour* and *Nana*, he praised *L'Assommoir* (the history of Nana's parents and their progressive alcoholism) for its "power," its "brilliancy," and its "extraordinary technical qualities."[36] True, he said, the book was "pervaded by [a] ferociously bad smell," making its perusal "very much such an ordeal as a crossing of the Channel in a November gale," but still it "constantly rewarded" its readers' "patience" and "perserverance."[37] Perhaps James was impressed by its sympathetic characters; Coupeau is an honest workman until an accident encourages him to start drinking, and Gervaise, sober and chaste until after her husband's downfall, retains her sense of shame even in the end. More generally, James seems to have admired Zola's ability to make his characters "magnificent"—larger than life—and to plan his novels on an epic scale.

We shall see that in later years, James increased his admiration for Flaubert and Zola, accepting the "uncleanness" of their works and applauding their transcendence of surface realism. But in the 1870s, he could not fully accept the naturalists, and he was therefore left with a dearth of literary models. Droz and Cherbuliez had disappointed him, while the majority of American novelists had in his opinion failed to distinguish themselves as artists. Hence, James turned backward, writing lengthy essays on authors whom he had previously read and whom he considered as foils to Flaubert and his *cénacle*. These may be divided into three groups: the social novelists, especially Balzac and Daudet, whom he associated with the naturalists but set apart because of the picturesque nature of their fiction; the psychological novelists, Eliot, Trollope, and Turgenev, who were notable for their understanding of character; and the romancers—Sand, the "irresponsible" authoress, and Hawthorne, the only writer to combine romance with the "deeper psychology." James's criticism of these writers will be examined in the following chapters.

Chapter V

The Social Novelists:
Balzac, Daudet, and Dickens

IN HIS "Minor French Novelists," James wrote that it was
Balzac who had established the "realistic, descriptive novel"
as the "most characteristic" genre in France: "Gustave
Flaubert is of the school of Balzac; the brothers de Goncourt
and Emile Zola are of the school of Flaubert."[1] As we have
seen, James respected Balzac's descendants yet had comparatively little taste for their theories or their art. His treatment
of their literary ancestor, however, was largely favorable.
Both his "Honoré de Balzac" (first published in 1875, two
months before his essay on the naturalists) and his review
of Balzac's letters (1877) deal sympathetically with the
author—a fact that is the more significant because James
reprinted these essays, together with his criticism of Flaubert, in his *French Poets and Novelists* (1878). One may ask,
then, why he chose to single out Balzac for praise.

To some extent, of course, Balzac's works foreshadowed
those of the naturalists, both in their strengths and in their
weaknesses. As in his essays on Flaubert and Zola, James
commented favorably on the author's ability to weave a dense
"web," giving his novels an "extraordinarily firm" texture:
"Balzac is always definite; you can say yes or no to him as you

61

go on; the story bristles with references that must be verified."
Conversely, James's distrust of Balzac's schematization of
experience recalls his reservations concerning the naturalists'
scientific bias:

> Balzac's "Comédie Humaine" is on the imaginative line very
> much what Comte's "Positive Philosophy" is on the scientific.
> These great enterprises are equally characteristic of the French
> passion for completeness, for symmetry . . . of its intolerance
> of the indefinite, the unformulated. The French mind likes
> better to squeeze things into a formula that mutilates them,
> if need be, than to leave them in the frigid vague. The further
> limit of its power of arrangement (so beautiful as it generally
> is) is the limit of the knowable. Consequently we often see in the
> visions and systems of Frenchmen what may be called a
> miniature infinite. The civilization of the nineteenth century
> is of course not infinite, but to us of English speech, as we survey
> it, it appears so multitudinous, so complex, so far-spreading,
> so suggestive, so portentous—it has such misty edges and far
> reverberations—that the imagination, oppressed and over-
> whelmed, shrinks from any attempt to grasp it as a whole.

And yet, he added, Balzac's *Comédie Humaine*, though
"a very reduced copy of its original," was nonetheless cast
in a "mould . . . of enormous dimensions"; further, he argued,
"it was in the convenient faculty of persuading himself that
he could do anything that Balzac found the inspiration to do
so much."[2] Here and elsewhere, James described Balzac as a
writer of epic proportions, a colossus who towered over
his successors.

This preference was based in part on the picturesque
element in Balzac's fiction. Unlike the naturalists, whose
theories caused them to dwell on banal and sordid subjects,
Balzac believed "that human life was infinitely dramatic and
picturesque, and that he possessed an incomparable analytic
perception of the fact." Moreover, James continued, the
author's other convictions were subordinate to his aesthetic
faith: he was "a Tory of the deepest dye" because a "monar-
chical society is unquestionably more picturesque, more
available for the novelist than any other," and a Catholic
because a "hierarchy is as much more picturesque than a
'congregational society' as a mountain is than a plain."[3]
Hence, in this respect, Balzac was less the forerunner of the
naturalists than of Charles de Bernard, whose "old French
cleverness" had so appealed to James.

But Balzac's taste for the "ideally real" was more than
superficial. Thanks to Hippolyte Taine, whose essay on the
author was in James's view the only one "essentially worthy

of its subject,"[4] the American critic had learned to see Balzac as a symbolist. Referring to Balzac's depiction of "les grands personnages" and his use of "le grand style," Taine had written: "[La force] nous tire hors de nous-mêmes; nous sortons de la vulgarité où nous traînent la petitesse de nos facultés et la timidité de nos instincts."[5] Similarly James, following Taine's lead, described Balzac as a writer of "realistic romance" whose greatest gift was "the incomparable vividness of his imagination." This meant that he was able to transcend the normal confines of realism, creating "portentous" settings and characters emblematic of essential human passions.[6]

Consider, for example, *Le Père Goriot*, which James believed to be the greatest of Balzac's works. Writing of the novel, the critic quoted at length from the famous passage describing Madame Vauquer's "greasy, dusky dining-room," an obvious instance of Balzac's "overmastering sense of the present world." Yet James perceived that the setting was not only realistic but also symbolic: "the shabby Maison Vauquer, becoming the stage of vast dramas, is a sort of concentrated focus of human life, with sensitive nerves radiating out into the infinite." Likewise, he commented on the symbolic nature of the novel's protagonist, Eugène de Rastignac: "the situation of the young man, well born, clever, and proud, who comes up to Paris, equipped by his family's savings, to seek his fortune and find it at any cost, and who moves from the edge of one social abyss to the edge of another . . . until at last his nerves are steeled, his head steadied, his conscience cased in cynicism, and his pockets filled—all this bears a deep imaginative stamp. The *donnée* of 'Le Père Goriot' is typical." And once more following Taine, James likened Goriot to King Lear: "Nowhere else is there such a picture of distracted paternal love, and of the battle between the voice of nature and the constant threat of society that you shall be left to rot by the roadside if you drop out of the ranks."[7]

For several reasons these comments mark an important development in James's critical outlook. First, we see his new interest in symbolic figures, including those whose psychology was simple rather than complex. Writing of Dickens, he had protested against the author's grotesques in the name of "truth to nature"; but writing of Balzac, he waived the question of psychological realism: "behind Balzac's figures we feel a certain heroic pressure which drives them home to our credence—a contagious force of illusion on the author's own part. The imagination that produced them is working at a greater heat; they seem to proceed from a sort of creative infinite, and they help each other to be believed in."[8] Moreover, we see James's new acceptance of the social novel—a genre he had failed to appreciate in the 1860s, when he had stressed the opposition between "character" and "circumstances." Most importantly, we note James's realization that Balzac had incorporated romance into his novels, not through the depiction of exotic settings or spirited young girls, but through his use of a technique suggesting the mysterious, emblematic nature of all his characters and symbols. This technique is the subject of Peter Brooks's recent study, *The Melodramatic Imagination*. Both James and Balzac, Brooks argues, were melodramatists; both created figures larger than life in order "to perceive and image the spiritual in a world voided of its traditional sacred."[9]

An excellent example of Balzac's method occurs in the opening of "L' Interdiction," which describes the features of Popinot, "the type of the upright judge." Clearly impressed by the "energy and vividness" of this portrait, James translated the passage at length:

> If nature, therefore, had endowed M. Popinot with an exterior but scantily agreeable, the magistracy had not embellished him. His frame was full of angular lines. His big knees, his large feet, his broad hands, contrasted with a sacerdotal face, which resembled vaguely the head of a calf, soft to insipidity, feebly lighted by two lateral eyes, altogether bloodless, divided by a straight flat nose, surmounted by a forehead without protuberance, decorated by two huge ears, which bent awkwardly forward. His hair, thin in quantity and quality, exposed his skull in several irregular furrows. A single feature recommended this countenance to the student of physiognomy. The man had a mouth on whose lips a divine goodness hovered. These were good big red lips, sinuous, moving, with a thousand folds, through which nature had never expressed any but high feelings—lips which spoke to the heart.[10]

In descriptions such as this, Balzac not only rendered physical detail but also showed how the essence of his character was (to quote Brooks) "both indicated within and masked by the surface of reality."[11] Here, then, was the fundamental difference between Balzac and his "grandsons"; whereas the naturalists had embraced materialism, Balzac had an intuitive sense of "the infinite," and conversely, of the "abysses" underlying everyday life. This was true, James implied, despite his commitment to "the knowable."

In this early essay, however, James's acknowledgment of Balzac's profundity was almost overshadowed by his sense of the author's superficiality. Indeed, he was obviously bemused by Balzac's "extraordinary union of vigor and shallowness," his "incomparable power" yet lack of "that slight but needful thing—charm."[12] Having read Taine, James was keenly aware of the novelist's preoccupation with that most vulgar of realities, money. And while Taine believed that Balzac's financial hardships added to his social insight (il comprit que l'argent est le grand ressort de la vie moderne"),[13] James contended that the unevenness of his works betrayed his "want of leisure" and that his emphasis on money was reductive: "Each particular episode of the 'Comédie Humaine' has its own hero and heroine, but the great general protagonist is the twenty-franc piece."[14] Then, too, James commented on Balzac's "fathomless Parisian cockneyism," as seen especially in his portrayal of aristocratic figures: "They are so conscious, so fatuous . . . that they really seem at times as if they might be the creatures of the dreams of an ambitious hairdresser who should have been plying his curling-irons all day, and reading fashionable novels all evening."[15]

But James's most serious charge was that Balzac, unlike Eliot, Sand, and Turgenev, was "morally and intellectually so superficial." True, he argued, Balzac had made "this palpable world" seem "ideally real," yet he "had no natural sense of morality." By this he meant that Balzac judged conduct primarily from an aesthetic viewpoint, praising duplicity because it was "more picturesque than honesty." Further, James charged, Balzac could portray magnificent vice but was unable to depict "superior virtue." As proof, he noted the equivocal nature of the novelist's "good" women— for example, Madame de Mortsauf (*Le Lys de la vallée*), who refuses to yield to her lover's entreaties yet sighs on her deathbed for the fleshly joys she has rejected. Such a character, said James, was "a kind of fantastic monster." Similarly, he disliked Madame Hulot (*La Cousine Bette*), who offers herself to a man she despises in order to pay the debts of her unfaithful husband. "[P]urity in Balzac's hands," the critic noted, "is apt to play us the strangest tricks." And predictably, he objected to Balzac's courtesans, for whom society was "a deadly battle for lovers, disguised in a tissue of caresses. To my sense this whole series of figures is fit only to have a line drawn through it as a laborious and extravagant failure."[16]

Even so, one detects a curious ambivalence in James's account of Balzac's greatest courtesan, Madame Marneffe (*La Cousin Bette*). "Balzac aime sa Valerié," Taine had observed; and despite his moral strictures, James could only agree:

> It is not, however, certainly, that here [Balzac's] energy, his force of color, his unapproached power of what the French call in analytic portrayal "rummaging"—to *fouiller*—are not at their highest. Never is he more himself than among his duchesses and courtesans . . . . [Mme. Marneffe] is, according to Balzac's theory of the matter, a consummate Parisienne, and the depravity of a Parisienne is to his sense a more remunerative spectacle than the virtue of any *provinciale*. . . . Never does he so let himself go as in these cases—never does his imagination work so at a heat. Feminine nerves, feminine furbelows, feminine luxury and subtlety, intoxicate and inspire him; he revels among his innumerable heroines like Mahomet in his paradise of houris.[17]

Notwithstanding his reservations, there is no mistaking the enthusiasm in James's description. This passage, then, suggests the Balzacian inspiration behind such figures as Madame de Bellegarde,[18] the Princess Casamassima, and Kate Croy; and equally, it foreshadows James's later essays on Balzac, which celebrate the "intensity" of the author's portrayals despite their lack of moral profundity.

A lesser novelist, but one who also transcended the confines of naturalism, was Alphonse Daudet. In 1875 James had regarded him as a "disciple of M. Flaubert" whose *Fromont jeune* was yet another "natural history of [a] prostitute";[19] but in 1882 and 1883, he wrote two appreciative essays on the author, giving *Fromont* and his subsequent works—*Jack* (1876), *Le Nabab* (1878), *Les Rois en exil* (1879), and *Numa Roumestan* (1880)—his qualified approval.[20] Perhaps the most interesting aspect of this criticism is his contrast of Daudet with his French contemporaries. Whereas the naturalists simply took notes, he said, Daudet had "the faculty of feeling as well as seeing"; he was "a passionate observer, . . . not perhaps of the deepest things of life, but of the whole realm of the immediate, the expressive, the actual." In Flaubert's followers the sense of beauty was absent or (in the Goncourts' case) perverted; but in Daudet, it coexisted with analytical power: "The Parisian has been added to the Provençal, fortunately without crowding him out." And in contrast to the other naturalists, who in James's view were serious, "uncompromising," and too keenly aware of their "terrible responsibilities," their Southern colleague projected the "irresponsible, illuminating day upon material supplied out of hand." Finally, Daudet was aware that fiction should be pleasing—a literary principle that the naturalists had neglected to follow.[21] For many of these observations, ironically enough, James was indebted to Emile Zola, who had written a highly sympathetic essay on his countryman in *Une Campagne* (1880–1881). Though James went further than did Zola in approving of the idealism which colored Daudet's pictures of his native Provençe, he quoted the French critic directly when he said that nature had placed the author "at that exquisite point where poetry ends and reality begins," and when he commented on the "irony" and "geniality" of *Numa Roumestan*.[22] Zola, then, led James to appreciate a writer on the periphery of Flaubert's circle, not in its center.

Like Balzac, Daudet appealed to James's sense of the picturesque, but unlike the older novelist, he wrote fiction characterized by its "charm" and "poetry." The meaning James attached to these terms may be inferred from this description of a Provençal festival in an ancient theater, taken from one of his favorite novels by Daudet, *Numa Roumestan:*

> Ce ciel si pur, ce soleil d'argent vaporisé, ces intonations latines conservées dans l'idiome provençal, ça et là . . . des poses immobiles que la vibration de l'air faisait antiques, presque sculpturales, le type de l'endroit, ces têtes frappées comme des médailles avec le nez court et busqué . . . .tout complétait l'illusion d'un spéctacle romain, jusqu'au beuglement des vaches landaises en écho dans les sousterrains d'où sortaient jadis les lions et les éléphants de combat.[23]

Consider, too, this passage on the Latin quarter in *Les Rois en exil*, a novel in which James found "the *article de Paris* in supreme perfection":[24]

> Au milieu des transformations du quartier Latin, de ces larges trouées par lesquelles s'en vont en poudre de démolitions l'originalité, les souvenirs du vieux Paris, la rue Monsieur-le-Prince garde sa physionomie de rue écolière. Les étalages de libraires, les crémeries, les rôtisseries, les marchands fripiers, "achat et vente d'or et d'argent," y alternent jusqu'à la colline Sainte-Geneviève, et les étudiants l'arpentent à toute heure du jour, non plus les étudiants de Gavarni aux longs cheveux s'échappant d'un béret de laine, mais de futurs avocats, . . . avec d'énormes serviettes en maroquin sous le bras, et déjà des airs futés et froids d'agents d'affaires; ou bien les médecins de l'avenir, un peu plus libres d'allures.[25]

These pictures show not only the correspondence between character and setting, but that between past and present; they are evocative as well as descriptive. Hence, whereas Balzac created powerful symbols of the nineteenth century, Daudet often suggested its relationship to a more poetic age. It was probably this suggestiveness that appealed to James, making him appreciate Daudet's social panoramas at least as much as his major figures.

The characters themselves, however, were also a source of poetic charm. Those whom James particularly admired fell into two categories. First were the suffering heroines: women like Hortense Quesnoy (*Numa Roumestan*), who dies of a broken heart after she is cruelly used by a Provençal tambourine-player and his scheming sister, and Frédérique (*Les Rois en exil*), the long-suffering queen who endures a double tragedy—her husband's infidelity and her son's being accidentally blinded by his tutor, a man for whom she feels a chaste passion. As usual James approved of such figures; he defended Hortense against the irony of Zola (who had found her romance factitious) and called Frédérique "a pure and noble heroine," an embodiment of the essential difference between "royal personages" and "common mortals."[26] This, of course, is the same kind of criticism one finds in James's essays on Cherbuliez, Droz, and their peers.

More significant was his liking for a second group of characters—the vain, selfish, yet charming men who make the heroines suffer. These were a particular specialty of Daudet's and appear in most of his novels. One such figure is Delobelle (*Fromont jeune et Risler aîné*), a former actor who allows his wife and daughter to support him while he dreams of establishing his own theater and discourses on "l'art sacré." In his 1875 review James wrote that the actor and his family partially redeemed *Fromont*[27]—a point he developed further in his later criticism: "the blooming and sonorous Delobelle, ferociously selfish and fantastically vain, under the genial forms of melodrama, is a beautiful representation of a vulgarly factitious nature." James showed equal enthusiasm for other characters of this type, including Valmajour, the "picturesque" tambourine-player of *Numa Roumestan;* Numa himself, a boastful Provençal whose extra-marital affairs drive his wife nearly to distraction; D'Argenton (*Jack*), a literary deadbeat who abuses his stepson while working on his magnum opus; and Christian (*Les Rois en exil*), an exiled king turned playboy who leaves his spouse to bear the royal responsibilities. Obviously James delighted in the sheer bravado of such figures, the representation of "egotism pushed to the grotesque." Furthermore, he appreciated the humor with which they were portrayed: "Daudet's gayety is a part of his poetry, and his poetry is a part of everything he touches."[28] This humor, of course, contrasted sharply with the seriousness that marked Balzac's treatment of his dandies. And it also made Daudet comparatively vulnerable, both to criticism and to self-deception: whereas Balzac, a great novelist, had a sense of the "abysses" underlying Parisian life, Daudet, "a great little novelist," was beguiled by the charm of his native Provence.[29] But like his predecessor, Daudet led James to accept figures whom he might earlier have rejected—characters who were interesting as picturesque types, not as fine consciences.

Once again, however, the critic's demand for psychological depth limited his appreciation of such figures. Sometimes, he complained, Daudet fell "into the trap laid for him by his taste for superficial effects" and produced caricatures with no redeeming qualities—"mechanical doll[s]" such as Sidonie Chèbe, his adulterous woman, and the protagonist of *Jack*, his sentimental portrait of a youth "broken down by his tribulations and miseries." Similarly, James disliked the main figures in *L'Evangéliste* (1883)—Eline Ebsen, who deserts her widowed mother and her fiancé in the name of religion, and Madame Autheman, a fanatic who persuades the young girl to make these sacrifices. Daudet, he said, had missed "a great opportunity for spiritual portraiture," as he had shown the reader "nothing about Madame Autheman's soul" and very little about Eline's. The critic then repeated his old demand for truth to nature: "there is a general human verity which regulates even the most stubborn wills, the most perverted lives; and of this saving principle the author, in the quest of striking pictures, has rather lost his grasp." Still, he praised the humor and "vivacity" of the novel,[30] later using it as the source of *The Bostonians*, his treatment of his own society from a half-satirical, half-comic point of view. Quite obviously, then, he appreciated Daudet's ability to render the picturesque appearance of his figures and their surroundings, although he himself dealt with the psychological aspects of his subject in a way that the French author did not.[31]

As the result of his reading of Balzac and Daudet, he also acquired a taste for a third novelist whom he had previously denigrated—Charles Dickens. A digression in his essay on the letters of Balzac shows that he believed the authors to be comparable and that he regarded both in a sympathetic manner:

Each was a man of affairs, . . . with a temperament of almost . . . phenomenal vigor and a prodigious quantity of life to expend. . . . In intensity of imaginative power, the power of evoking visible objects and figures, seeing them themselves with the force of hallucination, and making others see them all but just as

> vividly, they were almost equal. Here there is little to choose between them; they have no rivals but each other and Shakespeare. But they most of all resemble each other in the fact that they treated their extraordinary imaginative force as a matter of business; that they worked it as a gold mine, violently and brutally; overworked and ravaged it.[32]

Obviously James was aware of the limitations imposed on the authors by their financial needs; but he was equally impressed by their temperaments, and more importantly, by their art, their capacity to make their figures "ideally real." In this respect, of course, they far surpassed the naturalists, whom he regarded as being literal-minded and unimaginative. And in his 1882 essay on Daudet, he argued that Dickens was actually superior to his French successor, and that whereas "Dickens's absent qualities were as striking as those he had[,] . . . on his own ground he was immeasurable."[33] He thus became far friendlier to Dickens than he had been in the sixties, when he had focused exclusively on the author's lack of "philosophy" and on the superficiality of his characters.

The three social novelists—Balzac, Daudet, and Dickens—were to become more important to James in subsequent years. Not only did they inspire *The Bostonians* and *The Princess Casamassima* (1885), but they also broadened his critical outlook, enabling him to see the picturesque and symbolic value of figures and settings which he had previously ignored. And in the later eighties and nineties, when he had lost some of his youthful idealism, he was to return to these authors who, whatever their failings as moralists and psychologists, had the gift of seeing "visible objects and figures . . . with the force of hallucination." But despite his later concern for "intensity," he continued to oppose character to social texture, "depth" to "breadth," and "quality" to "quantity." We must therefore turn to the novelists whose heroes and heroines satisfied his ideal of human character: Eliot, Trollope, and Turgenev.

Chapter VI

The Psychological Novelists:
Eliot, Trollope, and Turgenev

> The French possess that lively aesthetic conscience which, on the whole, is such a simplifier. . . . [I]n English imaginations it is the moral leaven that works most strongly; their home is the realm of psychology, and their fondest exercise not the elaboration of theories, but the exposition of the facts of human character, the mysteries and secrets of conscience and the innumerable incidents of life. The English genius for psychological observation has no correlative in France.[1]

This passage in James's review of Taine's *Notes on England* (1872) describes the polarity he perceived between the French concern for form and the English concern for character. During the early seventies his reading of Taine, Feuillet, and Flaubert led him to make this distinction; and later in the decade, when he became acquainted with the younger naturalists, he was all the more adamant in stressing it. As we have seen, he hoped to reconcile form and substance but opted for the latter if forced to choose between them. Consequently, he came to appreciate two novelists whom his early reviews had rather belittled—Eliot and Trollope.

Writing on *Middlemarch* in 1873, James showed a new respect for Eliot: "The author has commissioned herself to be real, her native tendency being that of an idealist, and the intellectual result is a very fertilizing mixture. . . . [I]n that broad reach of vision which would make the worthy historian of solemn fact as well as wanton fiction . . . George Eliot seems to us among English romancers to stand alone." Undoubtedly James's attitude toward the writer was influenced by the superior nature of her heroine, whom he described as "that perfect flower of conception of which her predecessors were the less unfolded blossoms." An "ardent young girl" who, hoping to marry a great man, becomes the victim of a pedant, Dorothea was the ideal example of a character who always fascinated him—a figure "framed for a larger moral life than circumstance often affords, yearning for a motive for sustained spiritual effort and only wasting her ardor and soiling her wings against the meanness of opportunity."[2] As such, she became the model for his own Isabel Archer.[3]

Yet the difference between this heroine and her less refined prototypes (especially Maggie Tulliver) was only one reason for his change in judgment. Another factor was his growing opposition to materialism, which strengthened his belief in the quasi-religious nature of such figures. During his 1873 visit to Rome, he wrote an interesting letter to his old friend Charles Eliot Norton, who at this point was espousing agnosticism:[4] "As to Christianity in its old implications being exhausted, civilization, good and bad, seems to be certainly pretty well leaving it out of account. But the religious passion has always struck me as the strongest of man's heart, and . . . it is hard not to believe that some application of the supernatural idea, should not be an essential part of our life." He then added, rather self-consciously, that he had sent him his essay on *Middlemarch:* "If you positively don't at all like *M.* you will probably say that such criticism as that ought to be silenced."[5] Turning to the review itself, one may see the connection between the two comments. Dorothea, wrote James, "exhales a sort of aroma of spiritual sweetness, and we believe in her as in a woman we might providentially meet some fine day when we should find ourselves doubting of the immortality of the soul."[6] Thus, he invested the heroine with an even greater value than he had assigned to her predecessors. And it seems quite probable that he wrote this essay and others like it in response to the new skepticism, offering the "deeper psychology" as a substitute for traditional faith.

One observes this same tendency in James's comments on Lydgate, the doctor whose dreams are thwarted by his materialistic wife, Rosamond. The conflict between the two, said the critic, was "that typical human drama, the struggles of an ambitious soul with sordid disappointments and vulgar embarrassments." In other words, it was a version of the *belle dame* theme which he had previously admired in Dumas' *Affaire Clémençeau*. But there was a crucial difference between Eliot's art and that of the Frenchman: "Lydgate is a really complete portrait of a man, which seems to us high praise. It is striking evidence of the altogether superior quality of George Eliot's imagination that, though elaborately represented, Lydgate should be treated so little from what we may roughly (and we trust without offence) call the sexual point of view." Obviously James minimized the sexual side of Lydgate's downfall, arguing, in fact, that Rosamond's "instincts of coquetry" were "a discordant note." Such remarks may be opposed to his early comments on the passionlessness of Eliot's figures. Sexual rebellion had become commonplace; purity, in James's view, was now a welcome novelty. Hence, he remarked that the author was superior to Fielding, Thackeray, and Charles Reade, who had "won great praise for their figures of women" but owed their fame, "in reversed conditions, to a meaner sort of art, . . . to an indefinable appeal to masculine prejudice—to a sort of titillation of the masculine sense of difference."[7]

Another change in James's attitude was his increased tolerance for less heroic figures. Though in the sixties he had chastized Eliot for her love of the commonplace, he now commended her for her sympathetic treatment of human frailty. Of Rosamond, he stated: "The author's rare psychological penetration is lavished upon this veritably mulish domestic flower"; and regarding Casaubon, he wrote: "To depict hollow pretentiousness and mouldy egotism with so little of narrow sarcasm and so much philosophic sympathy, is to be a rare moralist as well as a rare story-teller." Moreover, he admired even the minor figures in the novel (Brooke, the worldly politician, Farebrother, the temporizing minister, and Celia, "as pretty a fool as any of Miss Austen's"),[8] contrasting them with those of "coarser artists" working in "vulgar black" rather than in fine shades. He did not identify these lesser novelists, but one thinks of the cynical and ironic Feuillet and the serious, equally ironic Flaubert.

Despite his new taste for Eliot, however, James conceded that *Middlemarch* had some weaknesses. In the first place, he wrote, the novel seemed "a mere chain of episodes, broken into accidental lengths and unconscious of the influence of a plan"—a "treasure-house of details, but . . . an indifferent whole." And he added that because of its diffuseness, it set "a limit . . . to the development of the old-fashioned English novel. . . . If we write novels so, how shall we write History?" This criticism is in keeping with James's earlier regrets that the author failed to place her heroines at the "center" of her novels. Indeed, notwithstanding his admiration for the lesser figures in *Middlemarch*, he still lamented the author's "tendency to make light of the serious elements in the story" —Dorothea's problems in particular—"and to sacrifice them to the more trivial ones."[9] James's taste for compact structure had also been developed through his reading of French fiction; one recalls his praise of Gustave Droz, who achieved "unity of effect" by focusing on his heroine (Mademoiselle Cibot), and of Flaubert, who attained similar results in the portrayal of his anti-heroine (Madame Bovary). During the seventies, then, his protests against the English "padded" novel became all the stronger. The difference between British and French fiction, he wrote in 1876, was that "between a copious Irish stew, . . . with its savory and nourishing chunks and lumps, and a scientific little *entrée*, compactly defined by the margin of its platter."[10]

Yet in another respect James believed that Eliot had weakened her novel by emulating the French too closely, for his second criticism was that *Middlemarch* lacked "the great dramatic chiaroscuro." Dorothea, he argued, was "altogether too superb a heroine to be wasted; yet she plays a narrower part than the imagination of the reader demands." As he well knew, he was objecting to the design of the book itself, since Eliot's narrator repeatedly states that all human beings— including potential Saint Theresas—are caught in a web of circumstances. But James took exception to such philoso- phizing, complaining that *Middlemarch* was "too often an echo of Messrs. Darwin and Huxley."[11] Obviously, he disliked Eliot's deterministic view of the universe—an attitude which interfered with her plotting, if not with her characterization. In making this objection, James was not alone; several American critics, including those writing in the *Atlantic*, the *Nation*, and the *North American Review*, commented on the undramatic nature of the novel and expressed dismay at its "ironic gloom."[12]

The longer James stayed in Europe, however, the more he was inclined to excuse Eliot's failings as an artist and to distinguish her from her "scientific" contemporaries. In February, 1876—the date of his meeting with Flaubert and his circle—he wrote his sister that he had been enjoying Eliot's new novel, *Daniel Deronda*, "partly for the pleasure of reading it in this beastly Paris, and realizing the superiority of English culture and the English mind to the French."[13] Yet several months later, in a letter to his brother William, he admitted that its idealized hero was "indeed a dead, though amiable failure," adding: "the book is a large affair; I shall write an article of some sort about it."[14] This review, which appeared the following December in the *Atlantic Monthly*, reflects the conflict expressed in these letters. On the one hand, James was eager to defend Eliot's idealism against French cynicism, but on the other, he was aware of the imperfections of her art and the naiveté of her perspective. Thus, not surprisingly, he cast most of his essay in the form of a dialogue, the participants in which express his own various points of view.

The first speaker and strongest defender of the novel is Theodora. As she argues, she works on a piece of embroidery, inventing the design as she proceeds but "being careful," says the narrator, "to have a Japanese screen before her, to keep her inspiration at the proper altitude." From these details one may infer her romantic idealism and anti-aestheticism, which are also evidenced by her disdain for French novels. Though conceding the imperfections of Eliot's art, she says, "There is something higher than form—there is spirit," the latter being embodied in the novelist's characters: in "poor, grand Mordecai," the Jewish patriarch who struggles to preserve the culture of his people; in Daniel ("the most irresistible man in the literature of fiction"), who nobly accepts his Jewish heritage; and in Gwendolen ("a perfect picture of youthfulness"), who suffers both from her husband's brutal selfishness and her own hopeless passion for Deronda.[15] Obviously Theodora is not James's persona, but she represents one aspect of his criticism—the same aspect that was apparent in his almost religious admiration for Dorothea.

Pulcheria, who takes the negative position, is a far more complex figure. A connoisseur of Balzac, Sand, Mérimée, and French authors in general, she also admires Thackeray, Austen, Turgenev, and Hawthorne. Thus, she may be called the sophisticated reader, one who has little patience with oversimplified didacticism. From her point of view *Deronda* is "protracted, pretentious, pedantic": a novel marred by its bombastic style, its narrator's tendency to analyze the characters to death, its moralistic hero ("a dreadful prig"), and its uninteresting heroine (a figure "too light" to sustain "deep tragic interest"). These objections, of course, recall James's earliest criticism of Eliot. Moreover, Pulcheria dislikes the formlessness of the novel: "I never read a story with less current. It is not a river; it is a series of lakes. I once read of a group of little uneven ponds resembling, from a bird's-eye view, a looking-glass which had fallen upon the floor and broken, and was lying in fragments. That is what Daniel Deronda would look like, on a bird's-eye view."[16] Again, one hears the voice of James; compare the figure of the ponds with the image of the Irish stew.

But it is Constantius, the mediator between the two ladies, who bears the closest relation to the critic. Like James, he is a reviewer: "You know I must try to understand," he tells the women; "it's my trade." And he self-consciously admits to having written "*one*" novel—a sly reference to *Roderick Hudson*, published the previous year (1875). Furthermore, he resembles James in his ambivalence; though he says that he can "read nothing of George Eliot's without enjoyment," he admits that *Deronda* is "the weakest of her books." Supporting the latter contention, he repeats a number of Pulcheria's arguments, criticizing the idealized Jewish figures and the diffuseness of the novel. To these objections, he adds his own comments on Eliot's "loose" and "baggy" style—an indication of James's interest in the "mot juste."[17]

Ultimately, however, Constantius agrees more with Theodora than with her worldly antagonist. In the first place, he admires Gwendolen Harleth, not only because she suffers but because her conscience grows with her adversity: "The universe, forcing itself with a slow, inexorable pressure into a narrow, complacent, and yet after all extremely sensitive mind, and making it ache with the pain of the process—that is Gwendolen's story." Moreover, he joins Theodora in commenting favorably on the "poetic" figures in the novel, including Herr Klesmer, an idealistic musician, and Hans Meyrick, an irresponsible young artist. Such characters, he says, are "born out of the *overflow* of observation," making "the drama seem multitudinous, like life."[18] This statement may be contrasted with James's early criticism of Eliot, in which he argued that she was incapable of making "those great synthetic guesses with which a real master attacks the truth."[19] It is quite probable that James's acquaintance with the naturalists, all of whom emphasized exact observation, made him more appreciative of Eliot's inventive powers.

But James (or rather, his persona) carried his defense of the novelist one step further. To the extent that she lacked spontaneity, he argued—to the extent that she created wooden figures like Deronda, analyzing them too much and making them act too little—she merely reflected the spirit of the time: "If she had fallen upon an age of enthusiastic assent to old articles of faith, it seems to me possible that she would have had a more perfect, a more consistent and graceful development, than she has actually had."[20] Thus, though he still regarded the author's skepticism as detrimental to her art, he implied that it was scarcely avoidable. There was good reason for James to be sympathetic: his own *Roderick Hudson* had been criticized for its lack of plot, its scientific coldness, and its power to tax the attention "like metaphysics."[21]

Finally, Constantius sides with Theodora in preferring spirit to form: "I think there is little art in Deronda, but I think there is a vast amount of life. In life without art you can find your account; but art without life is a poor affair. The book is full of the world."[22] This statement suggests not only James's increased respect for Eliot, but also, as Cornelia P. Kelley has noted, his alliance with the British novelists against the French *cénacle*.[23] Yet Pulcheria's comments remind one that this alliance was not absolute, as does much of James's other criticism; when, for example, he reviewed Hardy's *Far from the Madding Crowd*—a novel dealing with an "inconsequential, wilful" heroine—he complained bitterly that English fiction lacked form.[24] Nonetheless, because he believed that character preceded form, he gave priority to "life," preferring Eliot to her more cynical contemporaries.

A second novelist whom James reassessed—one is tempted to say, rehabilitated—was Anthony Trollope. During the sixties, the critic had treated him as a superficial writer, a defender of truth to common life at the expense of "truth to nature"; yet in an 1883 essay, he praised the depth of his understanding, especially in the realm of characterization. Again, there were a number of reasons for James's change in attitude. Because he was writing a memorial essay, not a review, he probably made an effort to be laudatory; and because he was dealing with Trollope's works in general, he could focus on his earlier fiction—novels he preferred to those he had reviewed in the sixties, which in his judgment suffered from "a fatal dryness of texture." Furthermore, as a practicing novelist, the older James admired Trollope's "fecundity" even while noting that he "published too much." He had observed Trollope's dedication during a voyage they had both taken in 1875, when the latter had shut himself in his cabin each day to work on his book. Recalling the author's "stiff persistence" on that occasion, James added: "Trollope has been accused of being deficient in imagination, but in the face of such a fact as that the charge will scarcely seem just." Clearly, the critic regretted his youthful sarcasm. Still another reason for his shift in judgment was his identification of himself with the British, as evidenced by his closing reference to "Our English race."[25]

Most important, however, was the factor that initially caused James to establish himself in London—his belief that British "psychology" was better than French aestheticism. "There is perhaps little reason for it," he wrote, "but I find myself comparing [Trollope's] tone of allusion to many lands and many things, and whatever it brings us of easier respiration, with that narrow vision of humanity which accompanies the strenuous, serious work lately offered us in such abundance by the votaries of art for art who sit so long at their desks in Parisian *quatrièmes*." And he went on to describe the polarity between Trollope's breadth of subject-matter and the naturalists' concentration; between the former's "purity of imagination" and the French writers' lack of it; and between the "instinctive realism" of the British novelist and the French devotion to system. The advantage, to be sure, was not entirely on Trollope's side; James said that Flaubert and his countrymen were superior "in audacity, in neatness, in acuteness, in intellectual vivacity, in the arrangement of material, in the art of characterizing visible things." But once again he stressed the idea that the English, including Trollope, were "more at home in the moral world"—the world of "conscience" and the deeper psychology. And he argued that Trollope's "happy, instinctive perception of character" more than compensated for his lack of system, as it enabled him to depict "living figures" without taking the "scientific view" or engaging in "morbid analysis."[26] Thus, he placed Trollope in approximately the same category as Eliot, dealing with him as a psychological novelist, not as a superficial observer of manners.

Quite naturally James devoted much of his essay to Trollope's characters. Among these were the heroines whom he had first admired—Linda Tressel, Nina Balatka, and Lady Glencora. Yet while he still enjoyed the "poetry" of such figures, he devoted more attention to the author's typical heroines—girls like Mary Lowther (*The Vicar of Bullhampton*), who loves her cousin but has difficulty refusing his rival, whom her friends urge her to accept. To the early critic such figures seemed too dutiful, too little moved by passion; to the later James, however, they appeared delightfully refreshing: "Trollope settled down steadily to the English girl; he took possession of her; he turned her inside out. He never made her a subject of heartless satire, as cynical fabulists of other lands have been known to make the sparkling daughters of those climes."[27] The "cynical fabulists," of course, were the French; one thinks especially of Cherbuliez, whose *Miss Rovel* ridiculed the "British maiden." Aware of such writers, James reappraised Trollope as he had Eliot, stressing his portrayal of innocence and ignoring the dearth of strong feeling in his works.

Perhaps more interesting are James's comments on the author's fallible heroes. As he had praised Eliot's treatment of Casaubon, so he admired Trollope's characterizations of worldly yet moral figures such as Mr. Harding (*The Warden*), the quiet, modest old man who resigns his comfortable position when his conscience forbids him to keep it, and Fenwick (*The Vicar of Bullhampton*), an Anglican divine whose distaste for Methodist enthusiasm contrasts sharply with his charity toward a young man accused of murder and toward his sister, a prostitute. "[T]he most striking thing," said James, "is the combination, in the nature of Frank Fenwick . . . of the patronizing, conventional, clerical element, with all sorts of manliness and spontaneity." Similarly, he admired Trollope's sympathetic treatment of characters whose virtues were less than average: Archdeacon Grantley, Harding's foil, who regards the church as a "fat, social pasturage"; Jacob Brattle, the "half-brutal, half-spiritual" old farmer in *The Vicar of Bullhampton;* and Louis Trevelyan, the stiff-necked, jealous protagonist of *He Knew He Was Right*. In all these instances, he said, Trollope's characterizations were humane and just. Thus, though he noted the author's tendency to dwell too much on "vulgar people," he appreciated his breadth of sympathy— including his love of the commonplace—far more than he had as a young reviewer. His only criticism, in fact, was of Trollope's occasional lapses into satire, as in his portrayal of Slope and Mrs. Proudie, and into satiric allegory, as in his treatment of Mr. Sentiment and Dr. Pessimist Anticant (all of *Barchester Towers*).[28]

Aside from his comments on the merits of French technique, James had little to say against Trollope's artistry. No longer did he condemn the author's works for their lack of drama; instead, he credited Trollope with recognizing that "character in itself is plot, while plot is by no means character."[29] Like his remarks on Eliot, this statement may well have been prompted by other reviewers' comments on his own novels: *Roderick Hudson* and *The Portrait of a Lady* had both been criticized for their dearth of plot and for their abundance of psychological analysis.[30] Indeed, James's only real objection to Trollope's technique was that he "took a suicidal satisfaction in reminding the reader that the story he was telling was only, after all, a make-believe." Such intrusions, argued James, betrayed the novelist's role as "historian": "when Trollope suddenly winks at us and reminds us that he is telling us an arbitrary thing, we are startled and shocked in quite the same way as if Macaulay or Motley were to drop the historic mask and intimate that William of Orange was a myth or the Duke of Alva an invention."[31] This statement, of course, reveals the seriousness with which he viewed Trollope's figures and the extent to which he regarded him as a delineator of character.

But James's warmest praise was reserved for Ivan Turgenev, who in his view remained free from Gallic cynicism despite his affiliation with Flaubert's *cénacle*. Writing from Paris in 1876, James contrasted him with his colleagues, the "little rabble of Flaubert's satellites" who were "not worthy to untie Turgenev's shoelaces."[32] Undoubtedly this reaction was not only aesthetic but personal, as one may infer from a reading of James's memorial essay on the novelist (1884). There, he opposed Turgenev's cosmopolitan outlook to the naturalists' parochialism and his concern for morality to their exclusive preoccupation with art. All in all, he said, the Russian had impressed him as "a singularly complete human being"—a distinction not attained by "the new votaries of realism, the grandsons of Balzac."[33] As Dale Peterson has noted, Turgenev's status as a provincial in Paris—his being, like James himself, on the edge of the literary circle—enabled the critic to perceive him as an ally, a fellow defender of "the worth and validity of indigenous points of view."[34]

Yet as in the case of Flaubert and the Goncourts, James's prior knowledge of Turgenev's fiction may well have influenced his personal impressions. During the early seventies, the writer's works had been well-received in the United States, particularly by the critics and readers of the Eastern periodicals.[35] And even before his visit to France, James had joined the circle of admirers; his most important study of Turgenev is not his essay of 1884 (which is largely devoted to reminiscence), but rather the 1874 review which he later reprinted in *French Poets and Novelists*.

According to James, Turgenev belonged to a "limited class of very careful writers" notable for their "narrow observation": "To describe him in the fewest terms, he is a story-teller who has taken notes." Clearly, one perceives the novelist's relationship to the French note-takers, especially Taine and Flaubert. Nonetheless, added James, Turgenev did not advocate "art-for-art" but recognized the "intrinsic value of 'subject'": he "holds that there are trivial subjects and serious ones, that the latter are much the best, and that their superiority resides in their giving us absolutely a greater amount of information about the human mind."[36] This statement allies Turgenev with Eliot and Trollope as a believer in mind—in human as opposed to animal motives—and as a creator of interesting characters.

Among these, not surprisingly, were his heroines, especially Hélène (*On the Eve*) and Lisa (*A Nest of Noblemen*). The former, who somewhat resembles Trollope's Linda Tressel, rejects three fairly conventional suitors to marry a Bulgarian patriot. Such "spontaneity" and "independence," said James, were "quite akin to the English ideal of maiden loveliness." Moreover, he found her virtues enhanced by the stodginess of middle-class society and by "the orthodoxy of the people who surround her." There is an obvious similarity between this critique and James's comments on British fiction, although Hélène is more passionate than her English counterparts (one scene, in which she gives herself to the hero, is notable for its frankness)[37] and considerably more adventurous (when her husband dies, she leaves for Bulgaria to aid his comrades in their war against the Turks). Indeed, James called her "a heroine in the literal sense of the word; a young girl of a will so calmly ardent and intense that she needs nothing but opportunity to become one of the figures about whom admiring legend clusters."[38] Even more than Linda, she seems to have been the "heiress of all the ages" so admired by James and his contemporaries.

Whereas Hélène represented passion, Lisa embodied the purity that James thought lacking in French fiction. The second heroine is a deeply religious girl in love with a man whose wife is presumed dead; but upon learning that the woman is alive, she stifles her feelings, urges him to obey his marriage vows, and enters a convent. The critic found this figure appealing because she exemplified the "*ascetic* passion, the capacity of becoming dead to colors and odors and beauty, never dreamed of in the philosophy of Balzac and Flaubert, Octave Feuillet and Gustave Droz." Like Eliot's Dorothea, then, she served as a corrective to the French idea of women. Furthermore, she reminded James of his favorite character, the American heroine: "Russian young girls, as represented by Lisa, . . . have to our sense a touch of the faintly acrid perfume of the New England temperament,—a hint of Puritan angularity. It is the women and young girls in our author's tales who mainly represent strength of will—the power to resist, to wait, to attain." James noted, too, that Lisa's passion was "in its essence half renunciation."[39] These comments, foreshadowing his own creation of Milly Theale,[40] show the affinities of his art with Turgenev's "poetic realism"—a mode which Peterson has described as emphasizing "the power of human perception to extract felt value from even the most constricting . . . of circumstantial realities."[41]

Also significant was the critic's taste for Turgenev's male figures, who varied in complexity but who all suffered from "a fatal weakness of will" that rendered them helpless against circumstances. In his early criticism, one recalls, James showed little sympathy for such characters; but as he matured, he became more interested in these victims of modern life and praised the novelist for his understanding of them. For example, he admired the portrayal of Hélène's disappointed suitor in *On the Eve*, a man "condemned to inaction" by his mediocrity: "There is something in his history more touching than even in that of Hélène and Inssarow." A related figure is the protagonist of "The Hamlet," who realizes that in all his life he has accomplished nothing but has merely obeyed the will of others. Commenting on the "deep moral note" struck by this sketch, James called its anti-hero a "poor gentleman"[42]—the same term he applied, some thirty years later, to Marcher of "The Beast in the Jungle."[43] Perhaps it was Turgenev who first inspired the author's sympathy for those who had not *lived*. Equally fascinating, in his view, were the characters that failed through moral weakness, such as Ssanin (*Spring Torrents*), who allows himself to be seduced by a vicious woman, and Rudin (*Rudin*), who speaks eloquently of poetry, idealism, and the necessity of work but lacks the courage to marry the girl he loves or to translate his words into deeds. As Daniel Lerner has noted, both of these characters may be seen as prototypes of James's Roderick Hudson, another figure "strong in impulse, in talk, in responsive emotion, but weak in will, in action, in the power to feel and do singly."[44]

Then there were the characters whose tragedy was of a higher order, resulting from the conflict between their emotional and intellectual commitments. The most out-standing example was the hero of *Virgin Soil*, which James reviewed in 1877: "the 'aesthetic' young man" who "venturing to play with revolution, finds it a coarse, ugly, vulgar, and moreover very cruel thing."[45] In the end he commits suicide, leaving the heroine, a dedicated anarchist, to marry his rival, whose persuasions are stronger than his. The kinship of Turgenev's Neshdanoff and James's Hyacinth Robinson is, of course, commonly recognized,[46] as is the similarity of the writers' attacks on the "scientific," materialistic view of life.

Finally, James praised Turgenev's more humble figures, including Mashurina, the ugly midwife quietly in love with Neshdanoff;[47] the deaf-and-dumb serf in "Mumu"; and the protagonist of "The Brigadier," a pitiable figure rendered insane by the death of a woman who has cruelly used him but whose memory he cherishes nonetheless. Thus, in his breadth of sympathy, Turgenev differed sharply from the cynical French while recalling the more humane British: "He seems to us to care for more things in life, to be solicited on more sides, than any novelist save George Eliot."[48]

Yet so far as technique was concerned, James contrasted Turgenev's novels with British fiction in general and with Eliot's works in particular. The first difference was structural: whereas English novels were diffuse, the Russian's were notable for their concision.[49] Nevertheless, James also argued that Turgenev did not adhere to a given structural formula, but instead used his characters as centers, sacrificing "architecture" to human truth whenever necessary. Hence, while his concision set him apart from the British, his flexibility distinguished him from the French—especially from the Goncourts, who regarded the novel as "a structure built up of picture-cards," not as a means of conveying "life."[50] Apparently Turgenev's idea of structure greatly impressed James; decades later, in his preface to *The Portrait of a Lady*, he wrote that the author's technique set a precedent for his own use of Isabel as "center" and equally, for his seeming inattention to "architecture."[51]

As might be expected, he also liked Turgenev's practice of allowing plot to develop from character. "George Eliot," he noted, "has a weakness for making a rounded plot, and often swells out her tales with mechanical episodes, in the midst of which their moral unity quite evaporates."[52] Turgenev, on the other hand, never sacrificed moral unity to the construction of an exciting fable: "Story, in the conventional sense of the word, . . . there is as little as possible. The thing consists of the motions of a group of selected creatures, which are not the result of a preconceived action, but a consequence of the qualities of the actors."[53] In this respect, too, the author anticipated James's theory and practice.[54]

A third point discussed by the critic was Turgenev's

skillful narrative technique. Unlike Eliot, he did not "describe and analyze his characters to death"; rather, he dramatized his figures, permitting situations to "speak for themselves." As an example, James cited an incident in *A Nest of Noblemen:* "When Lawretsky reads in the *chronique* of a French newspaper that his wife is dead, there is no description of his feelings, no portrayal of his mental attitude. The living, moving narrative has so effectually put us in the way of feeling with him, that we can be depended upon." The novelist's dramatic method thus distinguished his work from both didactic English fiction and "scientific" French fiction, although he had learned much from Flaubert in his use of "picture" and the "mot juste": "he has no recognition of unembodied ideas; an idea, with him, is such and such an individual, with such and such a nose and chin, such and such a hat and waistcoat, bearing the same relation to it as the look of the printed word does to its meaning."[55] Turgenev, then, was one of James's most important literary models; not only did he devote primary attention to character (in the sense that the critic used the word), but he developed a technique organically related to his theme.

James's only negative criticism of the novelist was that he was "morbidly serious" and took life "terribly hard": "We go from one tale to the other in the hope of finding something cheerful, but we only wander into fresh agglomerations of gloom." Apparently, the irony in Turgenev's fiction—more pronounced, as a general rule, than that in Eliot's novels—impressed James as being too harsh. This was especially true, he contended, of such works as *Smoke* and "A Correspondence," treatments of the "belle dame" theme which lacked the moral interest of *Spring Torrents.* More generally, he sympathized with the novelist's ineffectual heroes but wondered why they should invariably be overcome by circumstances: "The author continues everywhere to imply that there is something essentially ridiculous in human nature, something indefeasibly vain in human effort." And he made a statement anticipating that of Howells in *Criticism and Fiction:* "we hold to the good old belief that the presumption, in life, is in favor of the brighter side, and we deem it, in art, an indispensable condition of our interest in a depressed observer that he should have at least tried his best to be cheerful."[56] To the twentieth-century reader, such pronouncements may seem naive; but they fairly represent the American reaction to the new determinism.

Indeed, James's criticism of Turgenev, more than of any other writer, reveals that he shared the taste of his time.

Especially evident are the parallels between his essays and various reviews by Howells and Thomas S. Perry. They, too, praised the "poetical half-mystery" of the author's women, the "bold tenderness" of Hélène, the "deep moral earnestness" of Lisa. They also appreciated the complexity of his heroes, especially Ssanin and Rudin, and agreed with James on technical issues, opposing the novel of character to that of incident and arguing for the virtues of concision and dramatic technique. And again like the critic, they wrote of the dangers of Turgenev's pessimism.[57] One infers, therefore, that James was culturally less isolated than he is sometimes supposed to have been.

James's essays on Eliot, Trollope, and Turgenev are among his most important criticism, for they discuss the matter that he always regarded as central—the delineation of character. In his earlier reviews, one recalls, his conception of the deeper psychology appeared rather narrow; he focused most of his attention on such heroines as Linda Tressel and Mlle. Cibot. During the next decade, however, his reading of the naturalists led him to see new depths in a variety of figures: the righteous heroes of Eliot, the bourgeois protagonists of Trollope, the "moral failures" of Turgenev, and the humble characters of all three of these novelists. Furthermore, he became less impatient with the British authors' technical failings, though his highest praise went to Turgenev, who combined an interest in character with a concern for form.

But there was one ingredient that James found lacking in the psychological novels—the quality he associated with romance. Eliot, he contended, was too ponderous; when she tried simply to tell a good story (such as Mirah's narrative in *Daniel Deronda*), her manner seemed strained. ("George Sand," says James's Constantius, "would have carried it off with a lighter hand.")[58] Trollope, of course, was devoted to the commonplace, writing in a "solid, definite" and "somewhat lumbering way."[59] As for Turgenev, his seriousness and pessimism made him the antithesis of the romancer: "He has not the faculty of rapid, passionate, almost reckless improvisation,—that of Walter Scott, of Dickens, of George Sand."[60] To understand the value James assigned to this faculty, we must turn to his criticism of romance—particularly to his essays on Sand and her American counterpart, Nathaniel Hawthorne.

Chapter VII

The Romancers:
Sand and Hawthorne

ALTHOUGH some critics believe that during the seventies, James turned against romance,[1] there is good evidence that his taste for "experience liberated" remained in conflict with his demands for "character," aesthetic form, and high seriousness. Sometimes, as in the sixties, he displayed contempt for romances and their writers, calling *Wuthering Heights* a "crude and morbid story"[2] and saying of Edgar Allan Poe: "With all due respect to the very original genius of the author of the 'Tales of Mystery,' it seems to us that to take him with more than a certain degree of seriousness is to lack seriousness one's self. An enthusiasm for Poe is the mark of a decidedly primitive stage of reflection."[3] More typically, however, he defended romantic stories and the pleasure derived from reading them—a pleasure afforded neither by naturalistic fiction, which jarred the reader's sensibilities, nor by the novels of Eliot and Turgenev, which upheld human dignity but reflected the bleak pessimism of the age.

One romancer whom James consistently admired was Prosper Mérimée. As a young writer in the sixties, he had translated several stories by the French author, using these as models for his own tales; [4] but not until 1874 did he have the occasion—or perhaps the desire—to discuss the virtues of Mérimée's "chiselled and polished little fictions," many of which had "a fantastic or supernatural element. . . thrown into startling relief against a background of hard, smooth realism." A case in point was his "Vénus d'Ile," the account of an animated statue which falls in love with a woman's fiancé and enraged by jealously, murders him on his wedding night. This tale, which James commended for "its admirable art,"[5] had been the source of his own "Last of the Valerii."[6] Another of his favorites was "Lokis," the story of a moody count whose mother was once carried off by a bear. From various details—the protagonist's fits of madness, the terror he inspires in animals, and his disappearance on his wedding night, when his bride is found clawed to death—the reader infers the truth: the count is half-human, half-ursine. Praising this "picturesquely unnatural" story, James recommended it to readers "not averse to a good stiff horror" and rather self-consciously defended his liking for such Gothic fiction: "Twenty years hence, doubtless, clever young men. . .will. . .be lending [Mérimée's] volumes to appreciative female friends, and having them promptly returned, with the observation that they are 'coarse.' Whereupon, we suppose, the clever young men will fall to reading them over, and reflecting that it is quite right, after all, that men should have their distinctive pleasures, and that a good story by Mérimée is not the least of these." To James, then, the author's fiction was a superior form of entertainment, the product of a talent which was "singularly perfect" but also "limited."[7] Nonetheless, he valued aesthetic pleasure even more than he had as a younger critic, probably because Flaubert and Zola were excessively scornful of it.

One finds similar criticism in his review of Victor Hugo's *Quatrevingt-treize,* a romance of the French Revolution. Although he had previously been contemptuous of the author, attacking the mannerism and the absurd plot of *Les Travailleurs de la mer,* his 1874 critique is unusually sympathetic. Not that Hugo had changed: on the contrary, James remarked, he was "himself again with a vengeance" and walked "escorted between the sublime and the ridiculous as resolutely as his own most epic heroes." Moreover, unlike Mérimée, he had little sense of structure or aesthetic form: "M. Hugo's manner is as diffuse as that of the young woman in the fairy tale who talked diamonds and pearls would alone have a right to be, and as shapeless and formless as if it were twenty times the 'grande improvisation' which is his definition of the French Revolution." But then—as in

James's early essays on Scott and Morris—the analytical
critic yielded to the lover of literature who judged works
"from the picturesque point of view": "We have a vision
of the vanity of remonstrance and of the idleness of criticism. . . . We are doubtless wrong in breaking our yardstick;
for what is to become of the true and the beautiful without
a 'high standard'? We only say that we are natural, and we
simply pretend that in this natural fashion we have been
enjoying 'Quatrevingt-treize.' "[8]

Indeed, James sometimes admitted to a taste for romances
by no means as good as those of Mérimée and Hugo. Writing
of Julian Hawthorne's *Idolatry*, for example, he acknowledged that its ridiculous plot—which hinges on the
machinations of an Egyptian priest living near the Hudson
River in a temple built by an American antiquary, a Dr.
Hiero Glyphic—is "a very easy story to give a comical account
of"; yet he also praised the younger Hawthorne for being
"a story-teller with a temperament," arguing that "as
matters stand just now, the presumption seems to us to be
rather in favor of something finely audacious in the line of
fiction."[9] And reviewing one of the many works of "Ouida"
(Louise de la Ramée), a popular author of Gothic thrillers, he
confessed that "she is not to our minds possible reading. But
then we know that we are fastidious, and we are tempted to
wish we were not, so that we might innocently swallow
her down and think her as magnificent as she pretends
to be."[10]

In these reviews, all written in 1874 and 1875, James's
defense of romance was little more than a plea for escapism.
In the sixties he had referred wistfully to the stories of Scott
and Morris; and now, ten years later, he seemed almost
willing to abjure his critical role and to accept the works
of far inferior writers. Clearly he was faced with a dilemma,
for although romance seemed increasingly less serious in a
scientific age, the works of the naturalists made the need
for entertainment—for escape—appear all the more urgent.
To resolve this conflict he needed to discover the deeper
values inherent in romance—values that a "philosophical"
critic might find acceptable. This he attempted to do in the
commentaries on George Sand which he wrote in 1876
and 1877.

Quite obviously he enjoyed the complex intrigues that
characterized Sand's fiction. *Flamarande*, for example,
deals with a misanthropic count who suspects that his wife's
baby has been fathered by his erstwhile friend and spirits
the child away with the aid of his trusty retainer. In the

end, of course, virtue proves triumphant, and Flamarande's son is recognized as his legitimate heir. Writing of the book in January, 1876, James called it a "capital romance of the old school," with a "fantastic" plot which gave the reader the sense of "gliding in a gondola past a painted landscape. But the painting is so facile and mellow and harmonious that he at last 'makes believe,' at least, that he is deceived."[11] Such comments are similar to his remarks on Hugo and "Ouida."

But in the conclusion of his essay on "The Minor French Novelists" (published one month after his notice of *Flamarande*), he claimed that Sand was something more than a "wonderful improvisatrice": "Five-and-twenty years ago, before the writers of whom these pages treat [Bernard, Flaubert, the Goncourts] had (with one exception) presented themselves to the public, Mme. Sand was the first of French romancers. Five-and-twenty years have elapsed: . . . and Mme. Sand is still unsurpassed. . . . She has the true, the great imagination—the metaphysical imagination. She conceives more largely and executes more nobly; she is easy and universal and—above all—agreeable."[12] Here, in contrasting Sand with Flaubert and his çénacle, James seems to have lapsed into hyperbole. That he found Sand "easy" and "agreeable" is evident enough, but one wonders whether he could seriously regard her as a "metaphysical" writer. In these comments there is a disturbing vagueness, as if he had avoided more specific terms for fear of revealing his own uncertainty.

This same vagueness appears in his letter on Sand in the *New York Tribune,* written on the occasion of her death the following June. There, he called her "an *improvisatrice,* raised to a very high power" and pitied those who had denied themselves the pleasure of reading her. But he also stated that "some of her stories will not bear much thinking over"; that she was "a decidedly superficial moralist," though "a born romancer"; and that her didacticism had always seemed to him "what an architectural drawing would be, executed by a person who should turn up his nose at geometry." Furthermore, he made a personal admission: "I have been refreshing my memory of some of George Sand's earlier novels, which I confess I do not find as easy reading as I once did." From these remarks one might conclude that James had dismissed Sand as a mere entertainer. Yet he persisted in contrasting her favorably with her successors:

Her novels have a great many faults; they lack three or four qualities which the realistic novel of the last thirty or forty years, with its great successes, has taught us to consider indispensable. They are not exact nor probable; they contain few living figures; they produce a limited amount of illusion. . . . [H]er people are usually only very picturesque, very voluble, and very "high-toned" shadows. But the shadows move to such persuasive music that we watch them with interest. . . . The recital moves along with an evenness, a lucidity, a tone of seeing, feeling, knowing everything, a reference to universal things, a sentimental authority, which makes the reader care for the characters in spite of his incredulity. . . . He feels that the author holds in her hands a stringed instrument composed of the chords of the human soul.[13]

Like the passage in "The Minor French Novelists," these remarks are less than convincing. Was Sand a serious musician, playing on the reader's soul, or a charlatan, playing on his credulity? James's dissatisfaction with this essay may be inferred from a letter he wrote to his brother several weeks later: "All desire is dead within me to produce something on George Sand; though perhaps I shall, all the same, mercenarily and mechanically—though only if I am forced."[14]

In fact, the following year (1877), James did publish a major critique of Sand which he subsequently reprinted in his *French Poets and Novelists* (1878). His thinking on the romancer and her works was undoubtedly stimulated by Hippolyte Taine, whose brief essay on the author appeared in the same month as James's *Tribune* letter. According to Taine, Sand was interesting not only as a psychological case study and an expert stylist, but also as a serious artist: "personne n'a plus continuellement, et avec plus de bonne foi, agité les questions graves; elle en était préoccupée jusqu'à en être obsédée, et l'on pourrait, en suivant ses romans, faire d'après eux l'histoire morale et physique du siècle." Moreover, he praised her idealized characters, her portrayal of a finer and better humanity than ours.[15] These comments must have attracted James's attention, for on July 27, 1876, he wrote a brief note in the *Nation* on Taine's "interesting" article. Though he cited several passages from the French critic's essay (including those quoted above), he added few remarks of his own. But he did agree with Taine's most important argument: namely, that "if George Sand's novels have not the solid realism of those of Balzac, their species is a higher one."[16] James was thus intrigued, if not fully convinced, by Taine's effort to establish Sand's position as a "philosophical" novelist of character and ideas.

Yet in his 1877 essay, James denied most of the claims that Taine had made for the romancer. To be sure, he cited the French critic as an authority, both on Sand's personal background and on her mastery of the French language,[17] but he challenged Taine's belief in her moral profundity. In the first place he discounted Sand's ideas on marriage, democracy, and the church, expressing doubt as to whether she took herself seriously as a woman of letters. More specifically, he attacked her fondness for "amatory disquisition" in defense of sexual freedom. Arguing that her works often contained "an odd mixture of the didactic and the irresponsible," he implied that in her "technically amatory novels," the latter prevailed over the former.[18] Among these books were *Mademoiselle Merquem*, which he had reviewed with disapproval in 1868, and *Lucrezia Floriani*, in which Sand had carried her feminism to still further extremes. Lucrezia, according to the moralizing narrator, is endowed with numerous virtues: she is "désintéressée," "sincère," "libérale," "modeste," and thoroughly democratic in her sympathies. She is even, after her own fashion, "honnête," though she has four children by three different lovers. But alas, her idealism and naiveté lead her to put too much trust in Karol, a young prince whose failing is "l'intolerance de l'esprit."[19] Madly in love with her at first, he becomes jealous when the fathers of her children appear; and eventually, worn out by his demands, Lucrezia dies the death of the righteous. Such romances, of course, were hardly calculated to appeal to James; he complained (with justice) that they presented passion as "too intellectual, too pedantic, too sophistical, too much bent upon proving its self-abnegation and humility, maternity, fraternity, humanity, or some fine thing that it really is not and that it is much simpler and better for not pretending to be." Sand, he added, was "a very high order of sentimentalist, but she was not a moralist."[20]

Related to these objections were James's comments on Sand's idealized figures, particularly her heroines. Not only were they "vague in outline, deficient in detail," but they were also unnaturally self-righteous, abandoning their lovers and lying to their husbands "from motives of the highest morality." In rejecting Sand's portrayal of "a higher and better humanity," James was tacitly taking issue with Taine; and at the close of his essay, he made the disagreement explicit: "M. Taine calls [Sand] an idealist; I should say, somewhat more narrowly, that she was an optimist. . . . George Sand's optimism, her idealism, are very beautiful, and the source of that impression of largeness, luminosity, and liberality which she makes upon us. But I suspect that something even better in a novelist is that tender appreciation of actuality which makes even the application of a single coat of rose color seem an act of violence."[21] So much, then, for Sand's "metaphysical" qualities, and for the efforts of Taine—and of James himself—to treat her as a serious novelist.

But despite his negative criticisms, James did not reject Sand as a mere entertainer; rather, he found that her "irresponsibility" had certain values of its own. For one thing, it enabled her to depict sexual love—the "ardent forces of the heart"—far more freely than had her Anglo-Saxon peers. Sand, James contended, "has portrayed a *passion*," whereas "Miss Austen, Walter Scott, and Dickens . . . appear to have omitted the erotic sentiment altogether, and George Eliot [seems] to have treated it with singular austerity."[22] The importance which James assigned to Sand's gift may be inferred not only from this essay but from his *Hawthorne* and "The Art of Fiction." In 1868, one recalls, he had written of the "delightful and intoxicating" effect of her works on the American Transcendentalists,[23] and now he implied that they might also have a tonic value for contemporary readers.

Of still greater significance to James was the facility displayed by Sand in her writings. Indeed, he found her romances less interesting for their own sake than for what they revealed of the author's mind. This explains his high regard for *Valentine*, the story of a Byronic hero, Bénédict, and the three women who love him. Its plot is melodramatic (in the end, Bénédict is shot by the jealous husband of a woman he has never loved, and the much-abused heroine dies of grief) and its style is characterized by rhetorical speeches and equally impassioned narrative. Writing of the romance, the critic dismissed its moral content, dwelling instead on its "passionate eloquence"; in it, he said, "there is proof of the highest literary instinct." The word "instinct" deserves special emphasis, for James was intrigued by the seeming effortlessness of Sand's writing: "She wrote as a bird sings." Even when he criticized the results of her lack of artistry— her improbable plots and the absence of "classical" form in her works—he nonetheless admired her creativity.[24]

In Sand's prefaces to her writings James found further evidence of her "extraordinary facility and spontaneity." Typically, Sand discussed the inspiration behind her romances, noting particularly that she had not transcribed the stories of actual persons but had used these to stimulate her own imagination. The preface to *Isidora*, for example, explains that she had not depicted the woman whose confession had prompted her to write the tale: "C'était une très-belle personne, extraordinairement intélligente, et qui vint plusieurs fois *verser son coeur à mes pieds*, disait-elle. Je vis parfaitement qu'elle *posait* devant moi et ne pensait pas un mot de ce qu'elle disait la plupart du temps. Elle eût pu être ce qu'elle n'était pas. Aussi n'est-ce pas elle que j'ai dépeinte dans *Isidora*."[25] Similarly, in her preface to *André*, Sand related that the conversations of her Italian servants had made her recall the details of village life in France, where the story takes place.[26] James cited these examples, and several others as well, with obvious approval.[27] Clearly it was Sand who led him to formulate the principle stated in his own prefaces: "the minimum of valid suggestion [serves] the man of imagination better than the maximum."[28]

Thus, the romancer's works acquired a significant value for James, not because they were serious in themselves but because they helped him prove an epistemological point. As Harold McCarthy has noted, the critic's insistence "that the artist should rely as much as possible upon his personal sense of things" ran "counter to the popular current in literary affairs."[29] Both the naturalists and the realists, of course, believed that the author should depend primarily on his observations; yet James stressed the importance of the imagination, especially as it was evidenced by man's love of story-telling. This issue, moreover, was a philosophical as well as a literary one, since Huxley, Spencer, and their school had advanced the idea that the human consciousness was merely passive, recording experience but having no impulses of its own. Interestingly enough, William James, in taking issue with such thinkers, used arguments closely related to those in his brother's criticism. In an article entitled "Are We Automata?" he answered the question negatively: "there is one thing which [consciousness] does, *suâ sponte* and which seems an original peculiarity of its own; and that is, always to choose out of the manifold experiences present to it at a given time some one for particular accentuation, and to ignore the rest."[30] And in another essay, he wrote: "the personal *tone* of each mind, which makes it more alive to certain classes of experiences than others, . . .is. . .the result of that invisible and unimaginable play of the forces of growth within the nervous system which, irresponsibly to the environment, makes the brain apt to function in a certain way."[31] Though Henry James went further than his brother in defending the spontaneity of the mind—he thought it creative as well as selective—there are evident parallels between these passages and his essay on Sand. Note especially that the philosopher's idea of the mind's functioning "irresponsibly to the environment" corresponds to the critic's admiration for "irresponsible" (romantic) fiction.

In James's later work, especially, one sees the results of his participation in this intellectual debate. Most obviously, he wrote his own prefaces, which are closely modeled on those of Sand in relating the "story of his story," the process through which he converted experience into art. Secondly, his later preoccupation with point of view—a matter to which he devoted scant attention in his early criticism—may well have derived from his interest in the artist's personal vision. (Most of his protagonists, after all, are either artists or the possessors of a strongly aesthetic consciousness.) Then, too, in practice as well as in theory, James continued to depart from the conventions of realism, not only in such romances as *The Turn of the Screw* but also in his major novels—especially *The Wings of the Dove* and *The Golden Bowl*, which are notable for their elements of fairy-tale.[32] And as we shall see, in later years his attention as a critic was focussed on the various means of synthesizing the romance and the realistic novel, allowing for the interplay of imagination and observation.

James's study of Hawthorne (1879) should be read in the light of his essays on other romancers, particularly George Sand. She and her English counterpart, Sir Walter Scott, shaped the critic's idea of romance as a genre characterized by its exciting plot and picturesque setting, and equally, by its lack of didactic content and serious psychological analysis. Obviously Hawthorne's romances, which were essentially American in their emphasis on the individual's self-discovery,[33] could hardly be placed in this European context. James therefore tried to account for the divergence between Hawthorne and his foreign peers and to define his peculiar strengths and weaknesses.

In the American environment itself he found the key to Hawthorne's inability to write conventional romance. Whereas George P. Lathrop (whose biography of the author James had consulted) stressed the merits of New England as a source of picturesque fiction,[34] the reader of Sand was more acutely aware of the "negative side of the spectacle on which Hawthorne looked out." James's recital of everything "absent from the texture of American life"—a recital based on Hawthorne's own preface to *The Marble Faun*—has often been quoted: "No sovereign, no court, no personal loyalty, no aristocracy, . . . no country gentlemen, no palaces, . . . nor manors, nor old country-houses, . . . nor ivied ruins."[35] To Howells, the realist, all this was "dreary and worn-out paraphernalia";[36] but to James, it was the very stuff of which fiction—and especially romance—was made. Repeatedly, therefore, he expressed pity for "[p]oor Hawthorne," who, "[h]ungry for the picturesque as he always was," found little to satisfy his appetite.[37]

Then too, James believed that the American people, especially those living before the Civil War, were less than friendly toward romance. Writing of the Transcendentalists, he noted: "Their usual mark . . . was that they seemed excellently good. They appeared unstained by the world, unfamiliar with worldly desires and standards, and with those various forms of human depravity which flourish in some high phases of civilisation; inclined to simple and democratic ways, destitute of pretensions and affectations, of jealousies, of cynicism, of snobbishness." To borrow Matthew Arnold's terminology, these New Englanders seemed Hebraic rather than Hellenic—notable for "strictness of conscience," not for "spontaneity of consciousness." Such persons, of course, hardly fostered the development of an "irresponsible" artist. Because of their moral seriousness and paucity of aesthetic sense, they were an inadequate audience for "a young man of beautiful genius";[38] and because of their democratic attitudes, they could not furnish him with a gallery of interesting social types. (As James commented in a review of Emerson's letters, the essayist described his peers "according to their morality," for "[t]here was nothing else to describe them by.")[39] James's short story "Benvolio" (1875) dramatizes the dilemma of the American artist: when he rejects the Countess (Europe) in favor of Scholastica (New England), he chooses virtue, but his poetry becomes "dismally dull."[40]

Hawthorne, in James's view, escaped Benvolio's fate, yet only by a rather narrow margin; though his moral seriousness did not ruin his romances, it was nonetheless responsible for their defects. One of these was the presence of allegorical symbolism, especially in *The Scarlet Letter*, *The Marble Faun*, and such stories as "The Birthmark" and "The Bosom Serpent." To James, the author's attempts to combine the didactic and the picturesque seemed infelicitous. On the one hand, he found Hawthorne's symbols too "stiff and mechanical," and therefore out of place in imaginative fiction; on the other, he thought such "picturesque conceits" unsuitable for conveying serious meaning. A second artistic flaw, which James attributed to the author's character as well as to his environment, was the lack of picturesque detail in his works. In *The Scarlet Letter*, for example, the critic believed the "historical colouring" to be "rather weak than otherwise"; and in *The House of the Seven Gables*, a romance having "greater richness and density of texture," he thought it "a pity" that the "old Pyncheon-qualities" had not been more adequately represented: because Hawthorne mistrusted "old houses, old institutions," and "long lines of descent," argued James, he had made "the mustiness and mouldiness of the tenants of the House of the Seven Gables crumble away rather too easily." Above all, the romancer's asceticism—a quality he shared with many of his countrymen—caused him to be unappreciative of the picturesque values of Europe. *The Marble Faun*, in James's opinion, was weaker than Hawthorne's American romances because it betrayed his ambivalence toward Italy: "he incurs that penalty of seeming factitious and unauthoritative, which is always the result of an artist's attempt to project himself into an atmosphere in which he has not a transmitted and inherited property."[41] Implicit in this statement, of course, is James's contrast between himself and his "simpler" predecessor.

In Hawthorne's characterization and plotting, James again detected the influence of American asceticism. The author's taste in women, he said, was decidedly conservative; hence his female figures (Zenobia aside) tended to be deficient in passion and spontaneity. Hester, for one, seemed cold-blooded; Priscilla, for another, had so many "Sibylline attributes" that she appeared unnatural. Writing of these heroines. the critic may well have contrasted them with Sand's women, who were nothing if not liberated. And so far as plotting was concerned, James could find little evidence of the author's facility, his story-telling gift. Indeed, he noted the absence of "progression" in *The Scarlet Letter*, the fragmentary nature of *The House of the Seven Gables*, and the inartistic narration in *The Marble Faun:* "The story straggles and wanders, is dropped and taken up again, and towards the close lapses into an almost fatal vagueness."[42] Whatever the merits of Hawthorne's romances, they lacked the improvised plots regarded by the critic as expressions of the artist's imagination.

James's contrast of *The Scarlet Letter* with John G. Lockhart's *Adam Blair* underscores the distinction between

American and European romance. The Scottish tale deals with a minister who, after the death of his wife, Isobel, commits adultery with her unhappily-married cousin, Charlotte Campbell. Like Dimmesdale, he makes a public confession of his guilt; but unlike Hawthorne's minister, he does penance and urged by his friends, returns to his pulpit. Throughout the book, there are numerous melodramatic touches: Charlotte's nocturnal visit to Isobel's grave, where she weeps passionately, wishing she were in the dead woman's place; her heroic rescue of Blair and his daughter when they are in danger of drowning; Blair's frantic chase after Charlotte when she is spirited away by her husband's lawyer; his suicide attempt following his sinful deed; and his anguished outburst when he regains consciousness, only to discover that his beloved has died (presumably of remorse).[43] Though James thought that the romance was "second-rate" and compared to *The Scarlet Letter*, "much more vulgar," he argued that Lockhart's strengths shed light on Hawthorne's weaknesses:

> Lockhart was struck with the warmth of the subject that offered itself to him, and Hawthorne with its coldness; the one with its glow, its sentimental interest—the other with its shadow, its moral interest. Lockhart's story is as decent, as severely draped, as *The Scarlet Letter;* but the author has a more vivid sense than appears to have imposed itself upon Hawthorne, of some of the incidents of the situation he describes; . . . his heroine in especial, though not in the least a delicate or a subtle conception, has a sort of credible, visible, palpable property, a vulgar roundness and relief, which are lacking to the dim and chastened image of Hester Prynne. . . Lockhart was a dense, substantial Briton, with a taste for the concrete, and Hawthorne was a thin New Englander, with a miasmatic conscience.[44]

Thus, the question arose: in what sense could Hawthorne's works, which bore little resemblance to those of Scott and Sand, be classified as romances? The answer lay in the author's treatment of the one resource left to the American artist—the "deeper psychology." In the United States, James wrote, the individual "counts for more" than in Europe, "and, thanks to the absence of a variety of social types and of settled heads under which he may be easily and conveniently pigeonholed, he is to a certain extent a wonder and a mystery." Heretofore, the critic had associated psychological depth with the moral seriousness of the novel, not with the picturesqueness of the romance; but in the American conception of character, he found the two elements combined. The pathetic young girls of Trollope and Eliot, the wronged heroines of Cherbuliez and Droz, the weak men and strong women of Turgenev, all bore a certain resemblance to one another; though they had their share of "poetry," they were, in a sense, predictable and conventional. But the American writer, deprived of social categories, could hardly create such types; instead, he had to focus on the individual consciousness, an uncharted territory which might well rival Europe in romantic interest. James's language as he wrote of Hawthorne reveals his preoccupation with this idea. At one point, he referred to the artist as a "confirmed *habitué* of a region of mysteries and subtleties"; and at another, he noted: "There was . . . among the cultivated classes, much relish for the utterances of a writer who would help one to take a picturesque view of one's internal possibilities, and to find in the landscape of the soul all sorts of fine sunrise and moonlight effects."[45] Thus, American self-consciousness, though it hindered the development of the "plastic sense," inspired a taste for a new kind of aesthetic pleasure.

The beauty and moral depth of the artist's "landscapes" were enhanced by his feeling for the darker side of life, for the realities of sin and evil. In this respect, the author differed from his optimistic countrymen—notably from Emerson, who, "as a sort of spiritual sun-worshipper, could have attached but a moderate value to Hawthorne's cat-like faculty of seeing in the dark."[46] True misanthropy, in the critic's opinion, was not conducive to romance; it led instead to the rigid moralism of Sunday-school fiction or to the bleak pessimism of the naturalistic novel. But James contended that Hawthorne's "quality of imagination," his "purity and spontaneity and naturalness of fancy," freed him from such limitations; unlike the Puritans, he was not weighed down by his consciousness of sin, and unlike the naturalists, he had no "morbid and bitter views and theories about human nature."[47] Rather, he "played with [sin] and used it as a pigment; he treated it, as the metaphysicians say, objectively." From this description, one infers the relationship between Hawthorne's creative gift and that of George Sand. Yet he differed from her as well, for he "combined in a singular degree the spontaneity of the imagination with a haunting care for moral problems."[48] Paradoxically, then, he was a *responsible* romancer, whose fiction was at once serious and picturesque.

T. S. Eliot has called Hawthorne "the one English-writing predecessor of James whose characters are *aware* of each other."[49] He exaggerates, of course; but herein lies the key to James's admiration for Hawthorne as a romancer and a moralist. Consider James's descriptions of the central themes of *The Scarlet Letter*, *The Blithedale Romance*, and *The Marble Faun:*

> The story goes on for the most part between the lover and the husband—the tormented young Puritan minister, . . . and the older, keener, wiser man, who . . . devises the infernally ingenious plan of conjoining himself with his wronger. . . . The attitude of Roger Chillingworth, and the means he takes to compensate himself—these are the highly original elements in the situation that Hawthorne so ingeniously treats.

> The most touching element in the novel is the history of the grasp that this barbarous fanatic [Hollingsworth] has laid upon the fastidious and high-tempered Zenobia, who, disliking him and shrinking from him at a hundred points, is drawn into the gulf of his omnivorous egotism.

> The character of Hilda has always struck me as an admirable invention—one of those things that mark the man of genius. . . . This pure and somewhat rigid New England girl . . . unacquainted with evil and untouched by impurity, has been accidentally the witness . . . of the dark deed by which her friends, Miriam and Donatello, are knit together. This is *her* revelation of evil, her loss of perfect innocence. She has done no wrong, and yet wrongdoing has become a part of her experience, and she carries the weight of her detested knowledge upon her heart.[50]

In each case a character's consciousness develops as he becomes aware of another: Dimmesdale, tormented by Chillingworth, feels the burden of his guilty secret; Zenobia, intrigued by Hollingsworth, senses the conflict between her need to dominate and her desire to be dominated; and Hilda, influenced by her friends' tragedy, arrives at the knowledge of evil. Clearly James was interested in the moral and psychological aspects of such relationships—in the victimizer's power over the victim, and in the effect of experience upon innocence. These, of course, were themes he developed in his own fiction; Marius Bewley has noted Verena Tarrant's kinship to Zenobia, and Milly Theale's to Hilda.[51]

Equally significant to James was the romantic and picturesque quality inherent in these same motifs. Superficially, there is little exciting action in Hawthorne's romances (Zenobia's suicide is a notable exception); but—as one readily observes from James's plot summaries—there is a great deal of *mental* drama in the characters' conflicts with each other and with their own consciences. Although the critic did not elaborate on this point, it is implied in his

reference to the "moral picturesqueness" of the relations
among Hawthorne's figures. Furthermore, James's comments in "The Art of Fiction" and his own practice as a
novelist reveal his preoccupation with the dramatic potential
of a character's situation. Hawthorne's example, then,
influenced James to a greater degree than did that of George
Sand. Whereas the French romancer's plots, despite their
imaginative appeal, seemed superficial and outmoded,
Hawthorne's fables were of serious interest to the modern
reader—the reader who had lost his antebellum innocence,
his faith in man's ability to perform marvelous deeds. Such
a person, himself destined to be "an observer,"[52] might easily
find more meaning in the drama of consciousness than in
that of action.

Hawthorne's romances were picturesque in another
respect as well: because his characters were aware of each
other—because, indeed, they *saw* each other—they generated
a large number of mental images. In the following passage,
which James cited for its "genius of style," Hester's observation of Dimmesdale during the Election Day procession
is colored by her own emotions: "And was this the man?
She hardly knew him now! He, moving proudly past, en-
veloped as it were in the rich music, with the procession
of majestic and venerable fathers; he, so unattainable in
his worldly position, and still more so in that far vista of
his unsympathising thoughts, through which she now beheld
him!" A second passage quoted by James was Coverdale's
description of Hollingsworth: "he would glare upon us from
the thick shrubbery of his meditations, like a tiger out of
a jungle, make the briefest reply possible, and betake himself
back into the solitude of his heart and mind." The metaphoric
language here seems to anticipate that in "The Beast in the
Jungle," another tale dealing with the "landscape of the
soul." Moreover, James admired the way in which Hawthorne's narrators describe the characters' states of mind,
especially their perceptions of one another. An example is
the "charming image" representing the influence of Phoebe's
"maidenly salubrity upon poor Clifford" (*The House of the
Seven Gables*): "this poor forlorn voyager from the Islands
of the Blest, in a frail bark, on a tempestuous sea, had been
flung by the last mountain-wave of his shipwreck, into a
quiet harbour. There, as he lay more than half lifeless on the
strand, the fragrance of an earthly rosebud had come to his
nostrils."[53] Again, one is reminded of James's later techniques, for his narrators also use extended metaphors
as a means of character delineation. In taking a "picturesque

view" of man's "internal possibilities," James surely followed the lead of his predecessor.

Thus, Hawthorne played an important role in James's critical development. His failings, stemming as they did from his asceticism and his lack of literary material, illuminated the problems facing all American writers; while his great triumph—his combination of romance and the "deeper psychology"—suggested a partial solution to these same difficulties. Unfortunately, James thought, the majority of Hawthorne's successors had neither his moral insight nor his imagination.

Chapter VIII
The American Scene:
Hawthorne's Successors

"FOR THE contemporary American novel," writes George DeMille, "or, indeed, for the American novel of any time, [James] seems to have had little regard."[1] As we have seen, the critic did admire Hawthorne, acknowledging his merits as well as his faults, but he paid little attention to his successors, the generation of realists who began writing in the 1870s. James's neglect of these authors set him apart from the Eastern critics and editors who welcomed the new writers and encouraged the development of American fiction. Under the editorship of William and Frank Church, the *Galaxy* became a national magazine designed to offset New England provincialism,[2] publishing the novels of DeForest and the humorous tales of Twain as well as James's travel sketches, stories, and essays on the French writers. And William Dean Howells transformed the *Atlantic*, once the bulwark of Brahmin conservatism, into a journal printing a wide range of American fiction. In its pages appeared John William DeForest's *Kate Beaumont* (1871) and his *Honest John Vane* (1873); Harriet Beecher Stowe's *Oldtown Fireside Stories* (1871); Mark Twain's *Old Times on the Mississippi* (1875-76); Sarah Orne Jewett's Deephaven sketches (1875-76); Bret Harte's Western tales (1871-72); Howells's *A Chance Acquaintance* (1873), *A Foregone*

Conclusion (1874), and *The Lady of the Aroostook* (1878-79); and finally, James's own novels: *Watch and Ward* (1871), *Roderick Hudson* (1875), *The American* (1876-77), and *The Europeans* (1878). Moreover, the reviewers of the *Atlantic*, including Thomas Wentworth Higginson, Clarence Gordon, Harriet W. Preston, and Howells himself, praised the realists warmly and looked forward to the writing of the great American novel.[3] Three decades later, Howells recalled the increasing scope of the journal: "The fact is that we were growing, whether we liked it or not, more and more American. Without ceasing to be New England, without ceasing to be Bostonian, at heart, we had become southern, mid-western, and far-western in our sympathies."[4]

But Howells's "we" did not include James. Though he surely was familiar with the works of his contemporaries, he himself remained an Easterner—a Europeanized Easterner, to be sure, but still a defender of culture and high seriousness. Significantly, all but one[5] of his essays on American novels were published in the *Nation*, whose other critics—notably Thomas S. Perry and George P. Lathrop—frequently disparaged the new fiction, calling attention to its crudity, dreariness, and vulgarity.[6]

James's concern for culture—his fear that Americans might be lapsing into Philistinism—explains his disregard of his greatest contemporary, Mark Twain, to whom he merely alluded in his study of Hawthorne. Noting the lack of texture in the national life, he conceded: "The American knows that a good deal remains; what it is that remains—that is his secret, his joke, as one may say. It would be cruel, in this terrible denudation, to deny him the consolation of his national gift, that 'American humour' of which of later years we have heard so much."[7] But the tone of his remarks indicates that such humor was almost foreign to him. Furthermore, one recalls, his *Hawthorne* dwelt chiefly on another "national gift," that of psychological penetration—a gift he associated with the introspection of the Easterners, not with the comic sense of their Western countrymen. A second reference, this one in a review of David Masson's essay on Milton, also suggests the critic's point of view: "In the day of Mark Twain, there is no harm in being reminded that the absence of drollery may, at a stretch, be compensated by the presence of sublimity."[8] Quite obviously James felt that America needed the sublime more than the ridiculous.

From the fiction of the lesser realists he derived even less pleasure, for he found it narrowly didactic as well as

vulgar. Charles Doe's *Buffets*, for example, was a forerunner of the Horatio Alger novel, the story of a man who
breaks with his rich and idle friends, settles down to work,
and devotes himself to charitable deeds, eventually
prospering when he befriends some orphaned children and
improves on the inventions of their late father. Reviewing
the book, James applauded Doe's efforts: "The author has
bravely attempted to write a characteristic American novel,
which should be a tale of civilization—be void of big-hearted
backwoodsmen and of every form of 'dialect.'" Unfortunately,
he continued, the writer's "design has been more commend-
able than his success." His "drama" seemed like "a story
written for children"; his hero appeared too "pedantic,"
too inflexible in his "manly virtue"; his minor figures spoke
in an objectionable dialect; and his *mise en scène*, New York
City, lacked "color and picturesqueness." In short, *Buffets*
had all the faults of Hawthorne's novels—a dull plot, rigid
characters, and a drab setting—but none of their virtues; its
figures, commonplace as they were, had no "deeper
psychology." Not surprisingly, James questioned the poten-
tialities of the author's *donnée:* "if this is the most that
local influences can do for the aspiring and confiding
American artist, he will not be encouraged to appeal
to them."[9]

A still less promising novel was Harriet Beecher Stowe's
We and Our Neighbors: Records of an Unfashionable Street,
whose protagonist turns her back on "society" in order to
do her Christian duty (saving her cook's wayward daughter,
conducting religious discussions, overseeing her sisters'
romances, and so forth). The moral implications of the
novel James found easy to ignore; what did interest him,
however, was the vulgarity of Stowe's figures, even those
belonging to "one of the first families of New York." Especially revealing is James's account of the episode in which
the Hendersons entertain a British guest at an informal
family dinner:

> "A real high-class English gentleman," under these circum-
> stances, the author goes on to remark. . . , "makes himself
> frisky and gamesome to a degree that would astonish the
> solemn divinities of insular decorum." In this exhilaration
> "soon Eva and he were all over the house, while she eloquently
> explained to him the working of the furnace, the position of the
> water-pipes, and the various comforts and conveniences which
> they had introduced into their little territories." They—who?
> The water-pipes? The phrase is ambiguous, but it is to be

supposed that this real high-class English gentleman understood everything.[10]

This was obviously an attack not only on the author's style but also on her conception of society and good breeding. Indeed, her characters resembled the American tourists whom James satirized in his European novels.

Buffets and *We and Our Neighbors* exemplified all that he disliked in American fiction—its moralism, its dearth of picturesque interest, and above all, its lack of refinement. Furthermore, he criticized those authors who did not celebrate the commonplace but who attacked American crudity by depicting it in their novels. DeForest, for example, in his *Honest John Vane*, satirized the popular ideal of the self-made politician, portraying a manufacturer turned congressman who is bribed to vote in favor of the Great Subfluvial Tunnel Road (a symbol of the Crédit Mobilier).[11] Conceding that DeForest's effects had been deliberate, James denied that the moral purpose of the novel compensated for its unpleasantness: "the reader . . . may be excused for wondering whether, if this were a logical symbol of American civilization, it would not be well to let that phenomenon be submerged in the tide of corruption."[12] This review, then, like James's earlier criticism, suggests that he regarded satires on vulgarity as being vulgar in themselves.

In contrast with DeForest's figures, the heroine of Helen Hunt Jackson's New England novel, *Mercy Philbrick's Choice*, is genteel and even artistic. An amateur poetess with a keen perception of right and wrong, she becomes enamored of an aesthetic young man who unfortunately falls short of her high moral standards; and saddened by his dishonesty and by the death of her mentor, Parson Dorrance (whom she had admired but refused to marry), she devotes the rest of her life to writing and to awaiting her heavenly reunion with the parson. James found no coarseness in the novel, but predictably, he criticized its "angular and pedantic" heroine and its author's moralistic viewpoint. And although he still considered such fiction to be preferable to the sensation novel (indeed, he compared the book favorably with Rhoda Broughton's *Joan*, which depicted "strapping young Guardsmen . . . who . . . profit by the occasion of presenting bedroom-candles to young ladies to keep hold of their hands"),[13] he undoubtedly wished that the American novel might be, if not more risqué, then at least more passionate and picturesque.

On the whole, he found that international novels, which portrayed American characters in a foreign milieu, transcended the limitations of those that treated them on their native soil. Such a setting not only afforded writers a picturesque *mise en scène*—an opportunity to describe more poetic objects than American plumbing fixtures—but also affected their characterization in ways that the critic thought desirable. As William Stafford has noted, James set his own novels in Europe so that he might deal with figures more interested in *each other* than in trade, politics, and so forth.[14] To preserve the tradition of Hawthorne and to explore the deeper psychology, the author and his peers had to leave a nation dominated by Doe's businessmen, DeForest's lobbyists, and Mrs. Stowe's charitable ladies. As for such figures as Mercy Philbrick, James found them rendered far more exciting by their experience abroad, for while retaining their American consciences, they lost their "angularity" and asceticism.

Kismet, by Julia Constance Fletcher, was in James's view "decidedly superior to the ordinary specimens of American fiction." Though this simple tale—the story of a young girl traveling in Egypt who rejects her fiancé in favor of another suitor—was "too slight" for the critic's taste, he nonetheless appreciated the "excellent intention in the figures of the heroine and the 'fastidious American' who wins her." These characters, interestingly enough, bear a close resemblance to those in *Daisy Miller*, published a year after the appearance of Fletcher's novel. The suitor in *Kismet*, Arthur Livingston, is in James's words "that *rara avis*, the American young man of the world and gentleman of leisure, who finds his native country a disagreeable place to live in and spends his melancholy prime in foreign lands." Perhaps James was being ironical in calling such a hero "the most beautiful and fascinating type in modern fiction," yet his own Winterbourne falls in the same category. Arthur also resembles Winterbourne in having a double standard respecting women; he is acquiescent when Bell desires to spend an unchaperoned evening with *him* but is shocked when she wants to visit a local café, and though he has had a romance with a married woman, he waxes indignant when Bell tells him of her fiancé. As for the heroine herself, James complained that her "morals" in breaking her engagement were "a trifle relaxed";[15] but in her naiveté, her immaturity, and her desire to please, she is surely akin to Daisy Miller and far removed from the rigid Mercy Philbrick. This review, then, suggests James's reasons for approving of "international" fiction. Not only did he admire "the author's pictures of the Egyptian landscape," but he also was interested in her characters, Americans abroad who were more complex than their provincial countrymen.

A second novel by Julia Fletcher, *Mirage*, impressed James as "a decided advance upon its predecessor." Once again, the author dealt with a young girl traveling abroad—this time in Syria and Palestine—who must choose between two men, an artist whom she prefers and a more common mortal whom she feels compelled to marry. In contrast with Bell, however, Constance Varley never informs her true love of her passion, but weds her faithful admirer and settles down to a conventional life. Superficially, this *donnée* appealed to James less than that of *Kismet;* he felt that Constance acted "gratuitously and unnaturally" in allowing her lover to remain in error, complaining also that the artist himself—"the aesthetic young man"—had a "rather shadowy and insalubrious air." On the other hand, he praised the delineation of the "prosaic, yet manly, personality of the accepted lover," Jack Stuart—a figure who, if placed in an American context, would hardly have attracted his notice. But he was obviously impressed by the psychological drama in Jack's encounter with a foreign culture and by his stubborn Americanism in the face of the unfamiliar.[16] In this respect, Fletcher's character foreshadowed some of his own minor figures, notably Caspar Goodwood.

Moreover, James admired the "great charm" of the author's descriptions, her rendering of her "fresh, personal impression of the country." Although he cited no examples, one infers his appreciation of such passages as this "picture" of some women in the graveyard: "It was a wonderful bit of effect—the wilderness of wan, gray stones, the sudden silence, the spectral, shrouded figures among those funereal trees." Or again, this portrait of Constance as she stands on an ancient tower in Jaffa: "The gray old stones behind her brought out in strong relief the delicate blonde coloring of her face and hair."[17] In these descriptions, the setting contributes to the charm of the human figures—an effect that James achieved in his own fiction.

The international novel *par excellence*, however, was William Dean Howells's *A Foregone Conclusion*. Like Fletcher's heroines, Florida Vervain is caught between two admirers; but one of these is an Italian priest, Don Ippolito, who desires to escape from tradition and to adopt American ways. Although she has encouraged him to do so, the unworldly Florida is shocked when he declares his passion for her and can only respond to it with pity. There-upon, Ippolito commits suicide; and Florida returns to the United States, where she marries an ordinary young man, Ferris, whom she also met on her Italian journey. Ironically, the two Americans, having settled down to a conventional life, soon forget about the poor priest whose plight had touched them both. More than Fletcher's novels, then, *A Foregone Conclusion* shows the interplay between the American and European characters and the conflicts which they experience in dealing with each other.

James's two essays on the novel (the first in the *Nation*, the second in the *North American Review*) suggest his keen interest in these figures. Don Ippolito, the priest with an incongruous "fancy for mechanics," impressed him as "a real creation": "The poor caged youth, straining to the end of his chain, pacing round his narrow circle, gazing at the unat-tainable outer world, bruising himself in the effort to reach it and falling back to hide himself and die unpitied,—is a figure which haunts the imagination and claims a permanent place in one's melancholy memories."[18] In the American hero—Doe's John Houldsworthy, for example—an interest in mechanical inventions hardly seemed a sign of imagination or sensitivity; but in the Italian priest, the same interest acquired a deeper significance, for it symbolized his desire to find a place for himself in the new world. (One thinks of Amerigo in *The Golden Bowl*.) And as James admired the priest for his vision of America, so he liked the heroine for her reaction to Europe—or more accurately, for her momen-tary response to Ippolito's passion. Throughout most of the story, Florida resembles Mercy Philbrick in her asceticism and unapproachability; as the critic noted, "she has an appearance of chilling rigidity and even of almost sinister reserve." But when the priest declares his love for her, she embraces his head and kisses it. This episode, said James, is the "finest scene in the book," the point at which Florida surpasses both the New England heroine and the woman of the sensation novel: "Her image is poetical, which is a con-siderable compliment, as things are managed now in fiction (where the only escape from bread-and-butter and common-place is into golden hair and promiscuous felony)."[19]

Because the novel focused on these characters, James also approved of its form, its "studied compactness." In the following passage, he praised Howells as a psychologist and an artist while referring to the issues that he was to deal with more fully in his *Hawthorne*:

[Howells] reminds us how much our native-grown imaginative effort is a matter of details, of fine shades, of pale colors, a making of small things do great service. Civilization with us is monotonous, and in the way of contrasts, of salient points, of chiaroscuro, we have to take what we can get. . . . All this refines and sharpens our perceptions, makes us in a literary way, on our own scale, very delicate, and stimulates greatly our sense of proportion and form. . . . "A Foregone Conclusion" puts us for the moment, at least, in good humor with the American manner. At a time when the English novel has come in general to mean a ponderous, shapeless, diffuse piece of machinery, "padded" to within an inch of its life, without style, without taste, without a touch of the divine spark, and effective, when it is effective, only by a sort of brutal dead-weight, there may be pride as well as pleasure in reading this admirably-balanced and polished composition.[20]

Clearly, James preferred psychological fiction—the novel of "fine shades" describing the nuances of character—to the English social novel, which he criticized for its diffuseness and its superficiality. But it should again be noted that the European setting of *A Foregone Conclusion* inspired his favorable response. Paradoxically, if Howells had not gone to Europe—if he had stayed at home with DeForest, Mrs. Stowe, and Mrs. Jackson—he would have found it difficult, in James's view, to practice his peculiarly American art, the picturesque delineation of character.

Indeed, James's only adverse criticism concerned the ending of the novel, which describes Florida and Ferris's return to the United States following Ippolito's suicide. In the first place, the critic felt that Howells had sacrificed the picturesqueness of the tale to his taste for American settings: the story, he said, "passes out of Venice and the exquisite Venetian suggestiveness, over to Providence, to New York, to the Fifth Avenue Hotel, and the Academy of Design. . . . It is a transition from the ideal to the real, to the vulgar, from soft to hard, from charming color to something which is not color."[21] The transition, moreover, involved the characters as well, for having left Europe, they prove to be typically American: Florida settles down to motherhood, losing herself in her "fierce devotedness" to her children; Ferris becomes a conventional family man, dismissing Ippolito as "a person of rather light feelings"; and when the couple revisit Venice, they discover that their married love has "exorcised all the dark associations of the place." Says the narrator, "People are never equal to the romance of their youth in after-life, except by fits."[22] This, of course, is the point of the story; given the characters' backgrounds, it is a foregone conclusion that events should happen as they do. James, however, found such cultural determinism highly unpalatable. The "story is Don Ippolito's," he wrote. "It is the poor priest's property, as it were; we grudge even the reversion of it to Mr. Ferris. We confess even to a regret at seeing it survive Don Ippolito at all, and should have advocated a trustful surrender of Florida Vervain's subsequent fortunes to the imagination of the reader." James's comment suggests why his own novels are written in a relatively romantic mode and why his Americans (his protagonists, at least) usually *are* transformed by their European experience, whether they remain abroad, like Isabel Archer, or return home, like Lambert Strether. One also understands why James never depicted Strether in Woollett, Massachusetts! Furthermore, there is good evidence that he perceived the divergence between Howells and himself. "The author," he conceded, "is thoroughly consistent, for in stamping his tale at the last with the American local seal he is simply expressing his own literary temperament."[23]

James's "temperament," obviously, led him away from local-color realism; but at times he joined Howells in defending the United States as a source of literary material. His most explicit statement on this subject may be found in an 1878 notice of a story by Laurence Oliphant, "The Tender Recollections of Irene Macgillicuddy." This British tale, originally published in *Blackwood's*, satirizes New York manners, especially (as James noted) "the eagerness and energy displayed by marriageable maidens in what is vulgarly called 'hooking' a member of the English aristocracy." The daughter of a self-made businessman, Irene relates how her mother had entertained two visitors, the Earl of Chowder and Lord Huckleberry, in the hopes of wedding her to one of them. But alas, Huckleberry married her cousin and rival, Flora; while Chowder, who had been interested in her, returned to England and prompted by his mother, broke off their relationship. Eventually, Irene says, she married an Englishman of no birth or breeding who has nonetheless become a famous scientist; and she is now telling her story for the improvement of her erstwhile countrymen. To the critic, this "slightly audacious *jeu d'esprit*" suggested

> that it is possible, after all, to write tales of "American society." We are reminded that there *are* types—that there is a good deal of local color—that there is a considerable field for satire. Only, why should it be left to the cold and unsympathetic stranger to deal with these things? Why does not native

talent take them up—anticipate the sneers of foreign irony, take the wind from its sails and show us, with the force of real familiarity, both the good and the evil that are to be found in Fifth Avenue and on Murray Hill? Are we then so dependent upon foreign labor that it must be left to the English to write even our "society stories"?[24]

Interestingly enough, it was James who accepted his own challenge, for his "An International Episode," published seven months later in *Cornhill Magazine*, may be called an American reply to "Irene Macgillicuddy." Like Oliphant's Chowder, James's Lord Lambeth comes to New York with his friend, Percy Beaumont. But it is *he* who pursues Bessie Alden and *she* who finally rejects him, realizing that his family is snobbish and that he himself (again like Oliphant's earl) is dull and stupid. Moreover, Mrs. Westgate, the counterpart of Irene's mother, hardly encourages Bessie's romance; rather, she warns her sister against English snobbishness, noting the unhappy fates of those Americans too naive to recognize it. Then, too, James tried to present his native country in an artistic manner. "The midsummer aspect of New York," he wrote in his first paragraph, "is not, perhaps, the most favorable one; still, it is not without its picturesque and even brilliant side." And he went on to describe "the comfortable animation of the sidewalks, the high-colored, heterogeneous architecture . . . the general brightness, newness, juvenility, both of people and things."[25] From these details, one infers James's desire to depict American local color and to join Howells in defending the United States from the "sneers of foreign irony." But one must also note that this tale, even more than "Irene Macgillicuddy," is truly "international"; not only does James contrast his Americans with his Englishmen, but in the second part of his *nouvelle* he shifts his scene to London. Thus, Bessie (unlike Irene) may directly observe her suitor's Philistinism and the insupportable attitude of his mother and sister. James's practice, then, bears out the implication of his essays on *A Foregone Conclusion*: the "fine shades" of the national character might best be portrayed against a European background.

In the romances of Hawthorne and the novels of Fletcher and the early Howells, James found a double interest—on the one hand, the "deeper psychology," and on the other, picturesque description. In the fiction of the American realists, however, he took little satisfaction, for its authors favored commonplace characters over heroes and heroines and everyday scenes over poetic ones. The modern reader may regret James's parochialism; if he had appreciated Twain, he might have seen the parallels between that author's humor and his own international themes,[26] and if he had paid attention to the tales of Sarah Orne Jewett, he might have approved of the psychology in them. Again, if he had remained in the United States throughout the 1880s, reading such novels as *Huckleberry Finn* and George Washington Cable's *The Grandissimes*, his opinion of American fiction might have changed. But during the 1870s, his hopes for a national literature seem to have been frustrated by a series of bad novels—novels notable for their shallow moralizing, their wooden characters, and their manipulated plots. James's reviews of these works suggest why he chose Europe over America, and why, in his "Art of Fiction," he implied that the failings of his countrymen were as much to be avoided as those of the naturalists.

Chapter IX

"The Art of Fiction"

IF READ as a statement of theory—a prototype of the works of Wayne Booth, Rene Wellek, or Austin Warren—"The Art of Fiction" (1884) seems confusing and self-contradictory; James stressed so many different points, often without defining his terms, that the reader may easily lose his way.[1] But if studied in conjunction with James's reviews, the essay becomes far more illuminating. In large measure, it is a response to specific questions—an attempt, as Robert Falk has noted, to mediate "between the extremes of American moral soundness and French scientific realism."[2] More directly, of course, it is a reply to Sir Walter Besant, whose own "Art of Fiction" expressed the opinions of the typical English writer of historical romances and melodramatic social novels. Within the context supplied by his peers, James tried to define his own position, both as a critic and as a novelist considering fiction from the viewpoint of the "producer."[3]

The initial part of James's essay is largely an elaboration of Besant's "first proposition": "That Fiction is an Art in every way worthy to be called the sister and the equal of the Arts of Painting, Sculpture, Music, and Poetry." The general public, continued Besant, had failed to honor the novelist as an artist, wrongly dismissing him as a story-teller, an inferior kind of entertainer.[4] In James, whose novels had already met with adverse criticism, this argument must have struck a responsive chord. Especially revealing are his comments on the aesthetic views held by various members of "our Protestant communities":

> They would argue, of course, that a novel ought to be "good," but they would interpret this term in a fashion of their own, which, indeed, would vary considerably from one critic to another. One would say tnat being good means representing virtuous and aspiring characters, placed in prominent positions; another would say that it depends [on] a "happy ending." . . . Another still would say that it means being full of incident and movement. . . . But they would all agree that the "artistic" idea would spoil some of their fun. One would hold it accountable for all the description, another would see it revealed in the absence of sympathy.[5]

Although at first glance, James's catalogue of vulgar errors might appear haphazard, it actually reflects his readers' attitudes toward his own works. A number of critics had complained of his perverse fondness for unhappy endings, as evidenced especially by the conclusion of *The American*;[6] others had noted the lack of exciting incidents in his novels;[7] and still others, including William Dean Howells, had chastized him for his "offensive want of compassion."[8] The truth of the matter was that American reviewers, accustomed to romances, to humorous tales, and to realistic fiction stressing (as Howells later said) the "smiling aspects" of the national life,[9] found James's novels rather heavy reading. Because his books emphasized character analysis, some critics went so far as to identify them with the fiction of the "French school";[10] and because they dealt with cultured figures, not with vernacular heroes, some thought that they revealed a lack of human warmth and democratic feeling on the part of their author. To James, who linked the deeper psychology with the higher culture, such objections seemed frivolous. The true artist, he stated, could hardly compromise with those wishing to be amused by a pleasant novel or moved by a sentimental one. He could not manufacture happy endings, exciting plots, and sympathetic figures at will; rather, he had to make his works "compete with life."[11]

The word "life" presents problems; indeed, it seems to beg the question, for any author must select his materials. Robert Louis Stevenson's "A Humble Remonstrance," written in response to "The Art of Fiction," raises a valid objection to James's argument: "Life is monstrous, infinite, illogical, abrupt, and poignant; a work of art, in comparison, is neat, finite, self-contained, rational, flowing, and emasculate."[12] But James, his apparent vagueness notwithstanding, had a fairly definite idea of what constituted "life," as one may infer from his own practice and from a digression in his 1883 article on Daudet. Objecting to Charles Dudley Warner's dictum that "the main object of the novel is to entertain,"[13] he wrote: "I should say that the main object of the novel is to represent life. . . . The success of a work of art, to my mind, may be measured by the degree to which it produces a certain illusion; that illusion makes it appear to us for the time that we have lived another life—that we have had a miraculous enlargement of experience." His statements on "life" thus constitute a defense of "character" as he found it in the works of Eliot, Turgenev, Hawthorne, Cherbuliez, and Droz. True, he acknowledged that the tastes of others might differ from his own. "I am perfectly aware," he continued,

> that to say the object of a novel is to represent life does not bring the question to a point so fine as to be uncomfortable for any one. It is of the greatest importance that there should be a very free appreciation of such a question, and the definition I have hinted at gives plenty of scope for that. For, after all, may not people differ infinitely as to what constitutes life— what constitutes representation? Some people, for instance, hold that Miss Austen deals with life, that Miss Austen represents. Others attribute these accomplishments to the brilliant "Ouida." Some people find that illusion, that enlargement of experience . . . in the novels of Alexandre Dumas. Others revel in them in the pages of Mr. Howells.[14]

In this passage and in his major essay, James obviously tried to transcend his own point of view. The reader of his criticism, however, should be aware that he found Jane Austen's characters excessively ordinary, that he thought "Ouida's" figures devoid of depth, and that he discovered the "illusion" he desired in Dumas' *Affaire Clémençeau* and in the romantic novels of Howells.

In "The Art of Fiction" itself, James's concern for the deeper psychology is suggested by the series of analogies he used to describe the novel. Fiction, he argued initially, is like painting: "When it ceases to compete [with life] as the canvas of the painter competes, it will have arrived at a very strange pass." Again, he said, "as the picture is reality, so the novel is history"; like the historian, the writer of fiction must deal with "the past, the actions of men." (And he went on to criticize Anthony Trollope for betraying his "sacred office" by telling his readers that his stories were only make-believe.) Finally, he identified the historian with the "philosopher": "It seems to me to give [the novelist] a great character, the fact that he has at once so much in common with the philosopher and the painter; this double analogy is a magnificent heritage."[15] One notices a progression in these definitions—a movement from surface to substance, from external to internal reality. Gautier, in James's parlance, was a painter; that is, he was primarily concerned with the picturesque qualities of objects and persons. So, too, were Flaubert and the Goncourts, who depicted their characters solely "from the outside." Balzac, however, was an historian; interested though he was in the picturesque, he differed from the other Frenchmen in his awareness of the human elements of the spectacle he described. But only Eliot and novelists like her could be called philosophers—historians who not only portrayed the "actions of men" but also fathomed the depths of the individual personality.

The first part of James's essay is thus an expression of the principles he had set forth in his reviews: the value of literary culture, the status of the novelist as an artist, and the importance of "character" or "life." So far as these matters were concerned, he had no quarrel with Besant, though he gave the Englishman's arguments his own peculiar twist. But he had reservations concerning Besant's "second proposition": that fiction, like "Painting, Sculpture, Music, and Poetry," is "governed and directed by general laws; and that these laws may be laid down and taught with as much precision and exactness as the laws of harmony, perspective, and proportion."[16] This principle probably reminded James of the views of Flaubert and his school, who compared the writing of fiction to painting and who believed that "precision and exactness" were to be sought in both. The craft of fiction, countered James, is not an exact art, much less an exact science; its "grammar" is less "definite" than that of painting, and its laws, while "suggestive" and "even inspiring," are never absolute.[17] In particular he took exception to Besant's "Rule" that "everything in Fiction which is invented and is not the result of personal experience and observation is worthless,"[18] arguing instead for the role of the creative imagination: "Experience is never limited and it is never complete; it is an immense sensibility, a kind of huge spider-web, of the finest silken threads, suspended in the chamber of consciousness and catching every air-borne particle in its tissue. It is the very atmosphere of the mind;

and when the mind is imaginative . . . it takes to itself the faintest hints of life, it converts the very pulses of the air into revelations." This, of course, is precisely the point that James had made in his essay on Sand: one recalls his admiration of her prefaces, in which she had shown how "the faintest hints of life" had served as the inspiration for her romances. Thus, he repeated his epistemological argument, admonishing the would-be artist: "Try to be one of the people on whom nothing is lost!"[19]

At this juncture, James had to face a problem, for as he well knew, his comments on inspiration might easily be interpreted as a defense of the "irresponsible" romance. In writing of the author's freedom, he insisted that "The only obligation to which in advance we may hold a novel . . . is that it be interesting," yet ultimately, he expected much more than this. To avoid giving undue praise to the rose-colored romances of Sand and her followers, he thus shifted his point of view rather abruptly: "I am far from intending by this to minimise the importance of exactness—of truth to detail. . . . [T]he air of reality (solidity of specification) seems to me to be the supreme virtue of a novel—the merit on which its other merits (including that conscious moral purpose of which Mr. Besant speaks) helplessly and submissively depend. If it be not there, they are all as nothing, and if these be there, they owe their effect to the success with which the author has produced the illusion of life." Here, then, was James's plea for realism. Yet he added that the novelist should render not merely "the look of things" but "the look that conveys their meaning," and not only the "surface" but also "the substance of the human spectacle."[20] Hence, in "The Art of Fiction" as in his reviews, he implied his preference for the romantic realism of Balzac over the scientific realism of his "grandsons."

Because James believed that art should be evocative as well as descriptive, he was rather skeptical of Besant's second rule: that the novelist must render his characters "clear in outline."[21] James agreed; "but how he shall make them so," he added, "is a secret between his good angel and himself. It would be absurdly simple if he could be taught that a great deal of description would make them so, or that, on the contrary, the absence of description and the cultivation of dialogue, or the absence of dialogue and the multiplication of 'incident,' would rescue him from his difficulties."[22] In thus commenting on narrative technique, he indicated that no single method insured the depiction of "living" characters. His reasons for thinking so may be

inferred from his reviews, in which he had noted the
successes and failures of specific authors. The Goncourts, he
had said, relied heavily on description, yet their figures
seemed cold and unnatural; Thomas Hardy cultivated
dialogue, but his Bathsheba Everdene was "inconsequential"
and "artificial"; Sand multiplied incident, but her characters
were nothing but picturesque shadows.[23] Conversely, Eliot,
using a descriptive technique, managed to make her characters live; so, too, did Turgenev, by means of a dramatic
method; so also did Cherbuliez and Droz, through the use
of incidents as striking as those in Sand's romances.[24] Little
wonder, then, that James found no simple correlation between
technique and the deeper psychology. As he stated in his
essay, description, dialogue, and incident all derived their
interest from "the general and only source of the success of
the work of art—that of being illustrative" (illustrative of
"life"). Furthermore, he added, "A novel is a living thing
all one and continuous, like every other organism, and in
proportion as it lives will it be found, I think, that in
each of the parts there is something of each of the other
parts."[25] He thus stressed the importance of organic form
without attempting to be prescriptive.

As his concern for character led him to minimize technical
distinctions, so it also caused him to deny the differences
between genres. In "The Art of Fiction," he specifically
refused to separate the romance from the novel, or as he
said, the "novel of incident" from the "novel of character. . . .
What is character," he asked, "but the determination of
incident? What is incident but the illustration of character?
What is a picture or a novel that is *not* of character?" This
represents a fairly important shift in James's viewpoint,
for as late as 1879, he did make the discrimination to which
he referred. Certainly, he never claimed that the works of
Scott, Sand, or Hugo were studies "of character" or that
their manifold incidents had any psychological implications.
In 1884, however, he chose to ignore the fiction of these
writers, even though he still valued the "irresponsibility"
of the artist and even though (as becomes evident later in
the essay) he still retained his liking for a good story. Quite
clearly, the problem was that he could not fit such romances
into his critical framework. From the European authors,
therefore, he turned to Hawthorne, who, he said, had called
his "story of Blithedale" a "romance . . . simply for the
pleasantness of the thing."[26] One sees James's logic here:
since Hawthorne's romances did deal with the "deeper
psychology," might they not be judged by the same standards
as the novels of Turgenev and Eliot? Of course, as Stevenson

noted, James was hardly justified in assuming that all fiction should be concerned with "character."[27] But once again, he was less an abstract theorist than a "producer" trying to define his views *vis-a-vis* those of his contemporaries Significantly, the later critic again recognized the romance as a legitimate genre,[28] although, as we shall see, he continued to be interested in works which defied easy categorization.

Being a "producer," James was equally wary of those who sought to restrict an author's choice of subject matter: "I can think of no obligation to which the 'romancer' would not be held equally with the novelist; the standard of execution is equally high for each. Of course it is of execution that we are talking—that being the only point of a novel that is open to contention. . . . We must grant the artist . . . his *donnée;* our criticism is applied only to what he makes of it." Clearly James wanted to allow the artist his freedom *before* he wrote the novel but to judge the work *after* it had been completed. Yet there is an inconsistency between this pronouncement and his belief—stated time and time again in his criticism of the naturalists—in the inherent importance of the *donnée.* The reason for his assuming a more liberal stance was that some of his favorite authors—notably Eliot, Trollope, and Turgenev—had dealt successfully with unpromising themes. In the sixties his idea of "truth to nature" had been so narrow that he praised few characters except the dark heroine; yet in the seventies, he perceived the deeper psychology in a variety of figures, especially in those of the authors just mentioned. He was therefore reluctant to impose limitations on the superior writer: "Art derives a considerable part of its beneficial exercise from flying in the face of presumptions, and some of the most interesting experiments of which it is capable are hidden in the bosom of common things." As an example he cited Turgenev's "Mumu," the story of a deaf and dumb serf whose only comfort is the stray puppy he has nurtured. Although the simple-hearted protagonist did not fit James's conception of the ideal fictional hero, he nonetheless called the story "touching, loving, a little masterpiece." But adding that not everyone had Turgenev's gift, he contrasted "Mumu" with Flaubert's "Un Coeur Simple," the tale of a servant girl who develops an irrational obsession for a giant parrot. Upon its death she has it stuffed, virtually turning it into an idol; and as she herself dies, she clutches its decaying, worm-eaten carcass. This "production," said James, "highly finished as it is, cannot on the whole be called a success."[29]

Not surprisingly, then, he modified his position in the

next paragraph, for in granting liberty to Turgenev he did not wish to give license to Flaubert: "Nothing, of course, will ever take the place of the good old fashion of 'liking' a work of art or not liking it; the more improved criticism will not abolish that primitive, that ultimate, test. I mention this to guard myself from the accusation of intimating that the idea, the subject, of a novel or a picture, does not matter." In stressing the role of taste, James was again attacking the naturalists—especially Zola, who erred, he said, in "thinking that there are certain things that people ought to like, and that they can be made to like." And he proceeded to lecture the would-be author of obscene novels while trying to maintain a liberal posture: "Oh, I grant you your starting-point, because if I did not I should seem to prescribe to you, and heaven forbid I should take that responsibility. . . . Of course I may not care for your idea at all; I may think it silly, or stale, or unclean; in which case I wash my hands of you altogether."[30] This, undoubtedly, is James at his most priggish, and one may easily prefer the righteous anger in his reviews to such equivocation. But unlike his essays on specific authors, "The Art of Fiction" was his attempt to reconcile opposites, even if he had to strain in order to do so.

Having escaped Scylla, the unclean naturalists, James struggled against Charybdis, the prudish Anglo-Saxons. In his essay, Besant emphasized the importance of "selection" as well as "observation," arguing that "The daily life of the world is not dramatic—it is monotonous; the novelist makes it dramatic by his silences, his suppressions, and his exaggerations."[31] This statement allied him (at least in James's opinion) with such American critics as Charles Dudley Warner, who defined art as "selection and idealization, with a view to impressing the mind with human, or even higher than human, sentiments and ideas."[32] Predictably, James attacked both Besant, whom he found superficial, and his own countrymen, whom he thought moralistic as well: "Catching the very note and trick, the strange irregular rhythm of life, that is the attempt whose strenuous force keeps Fiction upon her feet. . . . Art is essentially selection, but it is a selection whose main care is to be typical, to be inclusive. For many people art means rose-coloured windows, and selection means picking a bouquet for Mrs. Grundy." And he went on to castigate those who "rattle off shallow commonplaces about the province of art and the limits of art," urging the "young aspirant in the line of fiction" to trust his own taste instead of yielding to public opinion.[33] At this point, then, one discerns yet another polarity in the essay. When

James argued against the naturalists, he stressed the role of the critic and the need for an acceptable *donnée;* but when he attacked the "Anglo-Saxons," he dwelt on the role of the artist as his own best judge and on the need for "inclusion." Indeed, the passage quoted above seems to evoke the image of Balzac, the "historian" and precursor of Zola, who risked "vulgarity" in order to attain comprehensiveness.

So much, then, for "moralism." But Besant, in commenting on "selection," did not really suggest that the artist pick "a bouquet for Mrs. Grundy"; rather, he advocated that the novelist *amuse* the reader, even at the expense of verisimilitude. "Why, the story is everything," he wrote. "I cannot conceive of a world going on at all without stories, and those strong ones, with incident in them, and merriment and pathos, laughter and tears, and the excitement of wondering what will happen next."[34] To James this statement seemed to trivialize fiction as an art and also to attack his own novels, notable as they were for their absence of plot. He therefore reasserted the connection between character and incident:

> [W]hat *is* adventure, when it comes to that, and by what sign is the listening pupil to recognise it? It is an adventure—an immense one—for me to write this little article; and for a Bostonian nymph to reject an English duke is an adventure only less stirring, I should say, than for an English duke to be rejected by a Bostonian nymph. I see dramas within dramas in that, and innumerable points of view. A psychological reason [i.e., motive] is, to my imagination, an object adorably pictorial; to catch the tint of its complexion—I feel as if that idea might inspire one to Titianesque efforts.[35]

One notices both the reference to "An International Episode" and the parallels between James and Hawthorne, who each preferred psychological drama to the drama of incident and considered the portrayal of character to be picturesque.

Yet James could hardly conceal his uncritical liking for the "strong" story. In the next few sentences, he confessed his enjoyment of Stevenson's *Treasure Island,* contrasting it favorably with Edmond de Goncourt's *Chérie,* the tale of a young French girl whose elders prepare her for nothing except a fashionable marriage and who thus commits suicide when she cannot find a husband:

> I call *Treasure Island* delightful, because it appears to me to have succeeded wonderfully in what it attempts; and I venture to bestow no epithet upon *Chérie,* which strikes me as having failed in what it attempts—that is, in tracing the development of the moral consciousness of a child. But one of these productions strikes me as exactly as much of a novel

as the other, and as having a "story" quite as much. . . . For myself . . . the picture of the child's experience has the advantage that I can at successive steps . . . say Yes or No . . . to what the artist puts before me. I have been a child, but I have never been on a quest for buried treasure, and it is a simple accident that with M. Goncourt I should have for the most part to say No.[36]

This passage illustrates two important points. First, James obviously liked *Treasure Island*, yet it made him almost uneasy because he could not criticize it—could not say "Yes or No" to it. Having failed, in his study of Sand, to find any serious qualities in romance, he relegated the genre to a kind of limbo and even denied its existence altogether, though his taste often reasserted itself. Secondly, like many of his comments on the naturalists, his critique of *Chérie* is decidedly misleading. With the girl's "moral consciousness" Goncourt had nothing to do; the narrator, indeed, states that she has none.[37] Rather, he treated the development of her *sexual* consciousness, from her childish "passionette" for her grandfather's secretary, through her first menstrual period and her awakening to the realities of courtship, to her despair as she watches her friends find husbands while she does not. James's comments must therefore be read as a gloss on his own *Maisie*, not on Goncourt's novel.

From the question of "story," James turned his attention to the last of Besant's principles—that the "modern English novel, whatever form it takes, almost always starts with a conscious moral purpose." This, he added, "is a truly admirable thing, and a great cause for congratulation."[38] As James had disagreed with Besant's remarks on "selection" so he now took him to task for sanctioning the "moral timidity" of the English and American novelist: "The essence of moral energy is to survey the whole field, and I should directly reverse Mr. Besant's remark, and say not that the English novel has a purpose, but that it has a diffidence." True morality, he argued, was less a function of popular taste than of "the quality of the mind of the producer. In proportion as that mind is rich and noble will the novel . . . partake of the substance of beauty and truth." The aspiring novelist, in other words, ought to follow neither the "Anglo-Saxons" nor the French but to cultivate his own insight. And "The Art of Fiction" ends with an address to the hypothetical young writer, a plea that he avoid both Scylla and Charybdis:

Don't think too much about optimism and pessimism; try and catch the colour of life itself. In France to-day we see a prodigious effort . . . vitiated by a spirit of pessimism on a narrow basis. M. Zola is magnificent, but he strikes an English reader as ignorant; . . . if he had as much light as energy, his results would be of the highest value. As for the aberrations of a shallow optimism, the ground (of English fiction especially) is strewn with their brittle particles as with broken glass. . . . Remember that your first duty is to be as complete as possible— to make as perfect a work. Be generous and delicate, and then, in the vulgar phrase, go in![39]

Appropriately, perhaps, James's essay ends on a paradoxical note. The ideal artist had to combine Balzac's completeness with Turgenev's generosity and Hawthorne's delicacy—truly a large order for one novelist to fill.

"The Art of Fiction" is not James's most lucid work, partly because he followed Besant's essay (itself a confusing piece of writing) but mainly because he tried to deal with too many adversaries at once—the English critic, the Mrs. Grundys, the reviewers of his own novels, the "irresponsible" romancers, and of course, his French colleagues. At the same time, however, the essay is fascinating proof of his eclecticism. From Matthew Arnold and from his American counterparts, Charles Eliot Norton and James Russell Lowell, he derived his preoccupation with culture, which he translated into a concern for character—for "life"—and for "classical" form. From Turgenev, and from Eliot and Trollope as well, he attained a broader conception of "truth to nature" and human dignity. From Balzac, he acquired a taste for the picturesque qualities in the *comédie humaine*—for the excitement of even the vulgarity in the "strange irregular rhythm of life." From Hawthorne, the responsible romancer, he learned that psychology, too, had its picturesque interest. And from Sand, the irresponsible romancer, he derived his fascination with the artist's freedom of consciousness.

Moreover, the essay marks a transition in James's career as a critic. As we shall see, after 1884 he became far less dogmatic in his views, even to the point of accepting authors whom he had previously condemned. And although "The Art of Fiction" echoes many of his earlier statements, it also foreshadows the more liberal attitude he assumed in his later writings. One notices, for example, that it begins with a defense of fiction as an art yet ends with an exhortation urging the writer to ignore all preconceived standards— an indication that the critic was unwilling to stress theory at the expense of practice. Then, too, as James Miller has suggested, his interest in the author's unique vision of life led him to avoid making *a priori* statements, to reject the formulae of those who insisted that novels be grounded in objective "reality," and to respect writers whose practice differed from his.[40] True, he was still less than appreciative of Flaubert and Zola; but in his later essays, if not in "The Art of Fiction" itself, he did follow his own advice, paying less attention to questions of subject-matter and moral purpose and focussing instead on the "intensity of impression"[41] created by individual works of literature. One also notes James's effort to establish his independence as a critic, including his right to change his mind. In this respect he seems to have emulated Sainte-Beuve, whom he had formerly criticized for his excessive pragmatism but whom he had come to regard as a defender of "liberty of appreciation" in "a society that swarmed with camps and coteries."[42]

Finally, one must consider James's own comment on "The Art of Fiction"—his remark, in a letter to Stevenson, that it was "simply a plea for liberty."[43] It may, of course, be construed as more than this, but one can hardly overlook an interesting paradox: that the critic's sole attempt to summarize the principles of his art made him less of a theorist and more of an open-minded "observer." The results of this development in his attitude will be seen in subsequent chapters. First, however, we must turn to his reviews of poetry—essays showing the conservatism of his sensibility, which coexisted with his desire to accept modern fiction.

Chapter X
The Elegiac Impulse

As a CRITIC of poetry, the early James was more dogmatic than perceptive. Whitman, in his judgment, was crude; so, too, was the later Browning, whom he thought "barely comprehensible"; and Baudelaire, he said, seemed like "a gentleman in a painful-looking posture, staring very hard at a mass of things from which we more intelligently avert our heads."[1] Clearly such comments reflect the genteel opinion of the post-War decades, suggesting that in his poetic tastes, James was hardly ahead of his time. This impression is also borne out by his positive statements; when one reads, in his review of Howells's *Poems*, that these verses are "all really classic work,"[2] one is tempted to dismiss him as a typical magazine-writer. Like his other reviews, however, his critiques of poetry are important to an understanding of his development. Specifically, they reveal the nature of his sense of the past and the origin of the nostalgia expressed in his later writings.

Roger Salomon has noted that realism was the "aesthetic of disinheritance." In the latter part of the nineteenth century, many artists (including such poets as Yeats and such novelists as Howells and Twain) felt themselves cut off from the past, unable to bridge the gap between their memories and their artistic principles, caught between their belief in contemporary subject-matter and their dislike of the situation in which they found themselves. Their nostalgia, moreover, was all the greater because it was thought to be illegitimate.[3] As we have seen, James was no realist in the ordinary sense of the word, but he too suppressed his sensibility as he tried to deal with subjects that seemed pertinent to the modern age. One perceives this tension in his criticism of romance and even more in his comments on elegiac poetry, which lamented the passing of the simpler world where romance was still possible.

The verses of Howells gratified James's taste precisely because of their elegiac character. "Poetry," he wrote in his laudatory review, "was made to talk about vague troubles and idle hopes, to express the thinnest caprices of thought, and when sensitive people meddle with it it is certain to be charged with the more or less morbid overflow of sadness." And he related Howells's poems to his cultural situation: "They speak of the author's early youth having been passed in undisturbed intimacy with a peculiarly characteristic phase of American scenery; and then of this youthful quietude having expanded into the experience, full of mingled relief and regret, of an intensely European way of life."[4] That James shared this experience and the feeling which accompanied it is evident enough. Like Howells, he remembered his "Lost Beliefs"—the subject of a poem which he cited for its "permanent" charm:

> One after one they left us;
> The sweet birds out of our breasts
> Went flying away in the morning:
> Will they come again to their nests?
>
>   .   .   .
>
> O my life, with thy upward liftings,
> Thy downward-striking roots,
> Ripening out of thy tender blossoms
> But hard and bitter fruits!
>
> In thy boughs there is no shelter
> For the birds to seek again.
> The desolate nest is broken
> And torn with wind and rain![5]

According to James, this poem and others like it ("The First Cricket," "The Mulberries," "Bubbles," and the "Elegy on John Butler Howells") could be recommended to "all lovers of literary pleasures." Obviously he based his judgment not on the technical merits of Howells's verses, but on their appeal to the *mal du siècle*. Transcendentalism was dead; so also was conventional religion; and in their place, James and

Howells could only cling to a sad humanism, a belief in "life" that did not always provide an adequate defense against the new science. Not surprisingly, the authors yearned for the old simplicities. Howells, incidentally, recognized that he and his friend shared such feelings; he wrote James to thank him for treating his "poor little book with the first real discernment that has been shown by its critics."[6]

Predictably, James also admired Matthew Arnold, whom he called "the poet of his age, of the moment in which we live, of our modernity." Arnold's verse, he continued, "has a kind of minor magic and always goes to the point—the particular ache, or regret, or conjecture, to which poetry is supposed to address itself." Though James's essay (1884) cites no specific examples, one recalls that nearly all of Arnold's poems ("Resignation," "Thyrsis," "The Buried Life," "The Scholar Gipsy") deal with the conflict between reason and emotion in the post-Romantic age. To James, who had first noted this dichotomy in 1865, these poems may have taken on a more personal meaning as time progressed and as he himself tried to control his romantic, lyrical impulse— his impulse to retreat from the world—so that he might "see life steadily and see it whole." Unlike the Englishman, however, he did not insist that poetry be judged by the same standards as other writing: "Mr. Arnold . . . is content to describe poetry by saying that it is a criticism of life. That surely expresses but a portion of what poetry contains—it leaves unsaid much of the essence of the matter. Literature in general is a criticism of life—prose is a criticism of life. But poetry is a criticism of life in conditions so peculiar that they are the sign by which we know poetry."[7] Whereas Arnold, at least in theory, believed that poetry ought not to treat "the dialogue of the mind with itself," James thought it an appropriate vehicle for dealing with emotions that could hardly be expressed elsewhere.

For this reason, he also liked the poems of George Eliot, particularly those that were "less intellectualized" than *The Spanish Gypsy*. Reviewing *The Legend of Jubal and Other Poems* (1874), he devoted special attention to "Brother and Sister," verses celebrating the author's lost youth. Quite clearly, he approved of the "sentimental" note on which the poem concluded: "But were another childhood-world my share, / I would be born a little sister there!" Similarly, he praised Eliot's title-poem, the story of a musician whose songs have become famous but who himself is thought to be a lunatic. Poems such as these convinced James that Eliot's novels failed to reflect her true outlook: "the author of

'Romola' and 'Middlemarch' has an ardent desire and faculty for positive, active, constructive belief of the old-fashioned kind, but she has fallen upon a critical age and felt its contagion and dominion. If, with her magnificent gifts, she had been borne by the mighty general current in the direction of passionate faith, we often think that she would have achieved something incalculably great."[8]

Although this comment reveals James's desire to turn back the clock, he too felt the "contagion" of his age and hence was wary of nostalgia. As he had attacked the "irresponsible" romancers, so he also criticized the poets who indulged their sensibilities to excess, allowing the elegiac mood to absorb their other creative energies. Howells, in his opinion, was saved from this error by his "mild good humor" and by his aesthetic sense: "Before his sorrow is nine days old he is half in love with its picturesqueness."[9] As for Eliot and Arnold, both suppressed their feelings to become critics of the age, writers of prose as well as of verse. But other poets, if more passionate and lyrical, were also less versatile.

A case in point—at least to a certain degree—was Tennyson. In reviewing his drama *Queen Mary* (1875), James praised his earlier works, especially *The Idyls of the King:* "He depicts the assured beauties of life, the things that civilization has gained and permeated, and he does it with an ineffable delicacy of imagination." Even so, as he confessed his own taste for Tennyson, he became somewhat defensive:

> That King Arthur . . . is rather a prig, and that he couldn't have been all the poet represents him without being a good deal of a hypocrite; that the poet himself is too monotonously unctuous, and that in relating the misdeeds of Lancelot and Guinevere he seems . . . to "protest too much" for wholesomeness—all this has been often said, and said with abundant force. But there is a way of reading the "Idyls," one and all, and simply enjoying them. . . . If one surrenders one's sense to their perfect picturesqueness, it is the most charming poetry in the world.

These comments, obviously, bear a close resemblance to James's critiques of Sand. True, he found the *Idyls* enjoyable, but to appreciate them he had to stifle his critical sense and his belief that Tennyson had romanticized the past: "It is as an entertaining poet I chiefly think of him; his morality, at moments, is certainly importunate enough, but elevated as it is, it never seems to me of so fine a distillation as his imagery."[10] Nonetheless, his opinion that idealism was the poet's prerogative led him to approve of Tennyson—as a poet. But Tennyson the dramatist was open to criticism. "In a play," James argued, "the subject is of more importance than in any other work of art. Infelicity, triviality, vagueness of subject, may be outweighed in a poem, a novel, or a picture, by charm of manner, by ingenuity of execution; but in a drama the subject is of the essence of the work—it *is* the work." By "subject," he meant the exposition of character and the moral seriousness that accompanies it; his main objection to *Queen Mary* was that the anti-heroine, "a subject made to the hand of a poet who should know how to mingle cunningly his darker shades," had become in Tennyson's hands "a mere picturesque stalking-horse of melodrama." And again showing his bias in favor of psychological portrayal, he argued that the history play lacked structure. In brief, then, he implied that Tennyson's merits as a poet were also his defects as a playwright. Moreover, he clearly expressed his preference for the drama, stating that "The dramatic form seems to me of all literary forms the very noblest"; that "a real drama . . . more than any other work of literary art . . . needs a masterly structure"; and that to "work successfully beneath a few grave, rigid laws, is always a strong man's ideal of success."[11] In these passages James appears to have established a hierarchy of genres. At the top was drama, the direct, unsentimentalized presentation of the "subject"; at the bottom was poetry, the lyrical expression of the author. (The novel, as the writer's portrayal of the subject, lay somewhere between the two extremes.) A poet, therefore, if he followed his lyrical impulse, could achieve a minor perfection but could hardly become a "strong" artist. Such was the scheme of the "philosophical" critic—the critic who tried to check his own nostalgia and whose experiments with the drama may have been motivated by a need to escape from subjectivity.

Alfred de Musset, the French lyric poet, presented a more extreme case than did Tennyson. One one level, James admired him for his "accent of genuine passion" and for his treatment of those feelings referred to by Matthew Arnold as "the buried life": "What makes him valuable is just this gift for the expression of that sort of emotion which the conventions and proprieties of life, the dryness of ordinary utterance, the stiffness of most imaginations, leave quite in the vague, and yet which forms a part of human nature important enough to have its exponent." As examples, he cited passages from Musset's "Lettre à Lamartine," in which the speaker links the poetic gift to personal suffering ("Puisque tu sais chanter, ami, tu sais pleurer"), and from "Nuit de mai," which likens the poet writing for his audience to a pelican opening his breast to feed his starving young ("Les plus désespérés sont les chants les plus beaux, / Et j'en sais d'immortels qui sont de purs sanglots"). Such poems, said James, are "full of imaginative splendor and melancholy ecstasy." But as he had noted Tennyson's limitations, so he remarked on those of Musset. Predictably, he believed that the poet's concern for passion was hardly a moral one and that he lacked the discipline of the "strong" novelist or dramatist: "Musset's simple devices and good-natured prosody seem to belong to a primitive stage of art. . . . If people care supremely for form, Musset will always but half satisfy them." This weakness in "construction," added James, was especially apparent in the author's plays, the merit of which lay "not in their plots, but in . . . their sentimental perfume." Above all, he believed that Musset's life was almost "wasteful"— that in cultivating his feelings, he relinquished the chance to accomplish other things. Dwelling particularly on the poet's thwarted passion for George Sand, he concluded his essay by observing that Musset's "pangs and tears, his passions and debaucheries" were all "necessary in order that we should have the two or three little volumes into which his *best* could be compressed. It takes certainly a great deal of life to make a little art! In this case, however, we must remember, that little is exquisite."[12] The example of Musset thus posed a dilemma. On the one hand, he could scarcely have been the poet he was had he not yielded to his emotions; yet on the other, his way of life produced "little" art—little in quantity, to be sure, and little in kind as well. It seems safe to conclude that James, as an aspiring novelist and dramatist, hardly wished to follow in his footsteps. Indeed, *Roderick Hudson* may be read as a parable on the artist whose emotions destroy his "constructive faculty."

Thus, in many respects, James classified the poets with the romancers, believing that both indulged their feelings, and especially their nostalgia, to a dangerous degree. But there was a subtle difference between the two. Whereas the romancers were escapists—optimists living in the past, writing the stories of a simpler age—the poets were men of their time who regarded history from their own vantage point. Salomon has noted that for James, this historical consciousness was potentially a unifying force, for if one remembered the past he might incorporate it into the present.[13] In the writings of the poets, however, James failed to discover such cohesion. Arnold and Eliot, he thought, each suffered from a divided sensibility; their verse was written in one mode, their prose in another. As for Tennyson and

Musset, the former was too sentimental and the latter too much absorbed in his elegiac mood to address himself to larger concerns. But in the works of Ernest Renan, the French philosopher whom he met on his visit to Paris in 1876,[14] James did find the unity he was seeking. The elegiac impulse, if properly controlled, might evolve into a critical sense—a sense that would be useful to the observer of contemporary life.

Richard Blackmur has noted that James "was an example of what happens to a religious man when institutional religion is taken away."[15] The same was true of Renan, whose *Life of Jesus* (1864) had shaken conventional orthodoxy but whose sensibility had remained that of a Catholic priest. His *Souvenirs d'enfance et de jeunesse* (1876) describes the effect of his religious upbringing and education upon his mature outlook. "[L]e pli était pris," he wrote. "Je ne fus pas prêtre de profession, je le fus d'esprit."[16] Reviewing the book, James cited this statement with obvious pleasure, as well as a lengthier passage in which the French author compared his lost faith to a city submerged beneath the sea: "It seems to me often that I have in the bottom of my heart a city of Is, which still rings bells that persist in gathering to sacred rites the faithful who no longer hear."[17] James, of course, was translating Renan, but as one may infer from his comments on Howells's "Lost Beliefs," he might equally have been writing about himself. Clearly he sympathized with Renan as an elegiac writer, a poet of prose.

Yet to James, the philosopher was not only a man of feeling but also "a most discriminating critic of life," especially of democracy. As an example, he quoted Renan's complaint that "our great democratic machines exclude the polite man" and his confession that he had given up using the omnibus because the conductors had not shown him the proper respect. "There is a certain dandyism of sensibility ... in that," James conceded, "but the author's perfect good-humour carries it off, as it always carries off the higher flights of his fastidiousness."[18] Again, he liked the philosophic attitude expressed in Renan's comment that "The world moves toward a sort of Americanism, which wounds our refined ideas, but which, once the crisis of the present hour is passed, may very well be no worse than the old *régime* for the only thing that matters . . . the emancipation and the progress of the human mind." This, said the critic, was the belief of a *raffiné*, but of "a raffiné without bitterness";[19] Renan had accepted his age. The Frenchman thus had two virtues: his refinement, the result of his past experience, which enabled him to criticize modern life, and his stoicism, the gift of time, which permitted him to do so without becoming embittered. Undoubtedly James would have agreed with the author's dictum: "Les vrais hommes du progrès sont ceux qui ont pour point du départ un respect profond du passé."[20]

As a philosopher, however, Renan carried his ideal of consciousness much further than this. The man of "progress," he believed, not only criticized his age but also understood it and felt it, for his superior awareness allowed him to enter into the minds of others and to participate in all human experience, past, present, and future. Such a person would become god-like; indeed, a perfectly conscious being (who Renan hoped might evolve in the course of history) would become God, thus replacing the deity of his lost faith. These ideas are set forth in the author's *Dialogues et fragments philosophiques* (1876), which substitutes a religion of consciousness for Christianity, treating "la conscience" as the goal of the universe.[21] Though there is little evidence that James valued Renan as a systematic thinker, his account of the *Dialogues* in one of his *Tribune* letters suggests his interest in the Frenchman's ideas. In particular, he quoted Theoctistes, one of the philosopher's personae, who speculates that God might be realized in "un seul centre conscient":

For myself [James translated], I relish the universe through that sort of general sentiment to which we owe it that we are sad in a sad city, gay in a gay city. I enjoy thus the pleasures of those given up to pleasure, the debauchery of the debauchee, the worldliness of the worldling, the holiness of the virtuous man, the meditations of the savant, the austerity of the ascetic. By a sort of sweet sympathy I imagine to myself that I am their consciousness. . . . I should be sorry that anything should be missing in this world, for I have the consciousness of all that it contains. My only displeasure is that the age has fallen so low that it no longer knows how to enjoy. Then I take refuge in the past . . . everything that has been beautiful, amiable, noble, just, makes a sort of paradise for me. With this I defy misfortune to touch me; I carry with me the charming garden of the variety of my thoughts.

"This paragraph," commented James, "seems to me magnificent; one would like to have written it." In part, he was intrigued by the author's manner, his "charm . . . of style";[22] but one also infers his interest in Renan's subject—the conversion of sensibility, especially one's feeling for the past, into a "general sentiment" that spans all ages and encompasses all persons. Unlike Musset, Renan did not remain trapped within himself.

Brief though they are, James's comments are of interest because of their relationship to his late fiction. One thinks, for example, of "The Great Good Place" (1900): its protagonist, an overburdened writer, retreats to a "great cloister," where he discerns "as from a distance the sound of slow sweet bells." Further, he perceives that "the whole thing [is] infallibly centred at the core in a consciousness"; and submerged (as a "Brother") in this collective identity, he can, for a time, divest himself of the burden of "personal publicity," the "vulgarity . . . of credit or claim or fame."[23] But the retreat is only temporary: like James and Renan, the fictional George Dane must eventually return to the fragmented world, where he must rely on his own consciousness as a unifying force. Similarly, Renan anticipated James in regarding "la femme" as a symbol of the past within the present and as a substitute for man's lost beliefs. In the preface of his *Souvenirs*, he wrote: "Le cerveau brûlé par la raisonnement a soif d'eau pure. Quand la refléxion nous a menés au dernier terme du doute, ce qu'il y a d'affirmation spontanée du bien et du beau dans la conscience féminine nous enchante et tranche pour nous la question . . . . La femme belle et vertueuse est le mirage qui peuple de lacs et d'allées de saule notre grand désert moral."[24] F. O. Matthiessen has noted that for James, such women as Milly Theale had much the same significance.[25] Renan thus provided an analogue, and perhaps a source, for the works of the novelist's "major phase."

In addition to suggesting his subsequent themes, James's citations of Renan also anticipate his mature techniques. Upon reading the statement of Theoctistes, one is struck by the resemblance of this figure to the author's third-person narrators, who enter the minds of his major characters and display sympathy for nearly all of them. Indeed, James's typical persona has the ability to "become" each character's consciousness while retaining his sense of beauty and his appreciation of all that the world contains. If the later novelist, as Wayne Booth has argued, fashioned a "seamless web of subject and treatment,"[26] he did so by creating a narrator not unlike Renan's hero of sensibility. Moreover, James's concern for stylistic beauty, which increased as time went on, was aroused by the works of the philosopher. Renan's style, he wrote in his *Tribune* letter, is "above all things urbane, and, with its exquisite form, is suggestive of moral graces, amenity, delicacy, generosity."[27] Undoubtedly, James was impressed by the author's use of metaphor (as in his equation of a beautiful woman with a mirage in a desert) and his love of rhetorical balance. This style was the natural correlative of Renan's philosophy, for it imposed the order and beauty of the past upon the chaos and ugliness of the present. The same, of course, might be said of James's later writing.

Even more significant are James's remarks on the style of Tennyson. Referring to his poetry, he noted that the "immobility . . . of his phrase would always defeat the dramatic intention" and cited as an example the verse describing Vivien's temptation of Arthur in the idyl "Merlin and Vivien":

> For once when Arthur, walking all alone,
> Vext at a rumor rife about the Queen,
> Had met her, Vivien being greeted fair,
> Would fain have wrought upon his cloudy mood
> With reverent eyes mock-loyal, shaken voice,
> And fluttered adoration.

Such a "picture," James argued, presents

> not the action itself, but the poet's complex perception of it; it seems hardly more vivid and genuine than the sustained posturings of brilliant *tableaux vivants*. With the poets who are natural chroniclers of movement, the words fall into their places as with some throw of the dice. . . . [W]ith Tennyson they arrive slowly and settle cautiously into their attitudes. . . . In consequence they are generally exquisite, and make exquisite combinations; but the result is intellectual poetry and not passionate—poetry which . . . one may qualify as static poetry. Any scene of violence represented by Tennyson is always singularly limited and compressed; it is reduced to a few elements—refined to a single statuesque episode.

Surely, this passage might equally refer to James's later manner. Through his use of poetic imagery, his reliance upon complex syntax, and his practice of piling phrase upon phrase and clause upon clause, the author, like Tennyson, created a realm of art, a representation of "repose and stillness, and the fixedness of things."[28] And although he wrote of sexual temptation in modern society, not in Camelot, he retained the sense of beauty associated with the past, treating even the sordid aspects of life in a style that provided him (to use Lawrence Leighton's metaphor) with an "armor against time."[29] Again, one notes the parallel between James and Renan.

The relationship of these reviews to James's later work is obvious enough, but the fact remains that he distrusted his own nostalgia. Significantly, he elevated the drama above all other genres—the drama, which required the objective presentation of character, not the expression of the author's sensibility. Moreover, as we have seen, he implied that poets (and perhaps poetic novelists as well) had a certain weakness of will which they indulged at their peril. Even Renan, a comparatively "strong" writer, did not quite escape his censure, as one discovers from a letter to his brother William. The latter, too, had reviewed the philosopher's *Dialogues,* but his comments were hardly sympathetic: he accused Renan of "priggishness," of "dandified despair," and of a "nerveless and boneless fear of what will become of the universe if 'l'homme vulgaire' is allowed to go on." In the future, the pragmatist argued, "not the man of the most delicate sensibility but he who on the whole is the most *helpful* man will be reckoned the best man."[30] Responding to this article, the critic wrote his brother:

> Your remarks on Renan were most refreshing, and (strange as it may appear to you after my worthless account of his book in the *Tribune*) quite in accordance with my own sentiments. I suspected what you say, but as it was only a vague feeling (mingled with a great admiration of his artistry) I attempted to make nothing of it (since I could make so little), and chose the tack of rather wholesale and general praise. But I am ready to believe anything bad of him. The longer I live in France the better I like the French personally, but the more convinced I am of their bottomless superficiality.[31]

Was James simply attempting to be tactful? Or was he honestly convinced that he had been mistaken? Neither is entirely true; though in the light of his later essay on Renan's *Souvenirs,* one suspects that he was hardly ready to "believe anything bad" of the writer, one receives the impression that he was desperately trying to lay the ghosts within himself and to win the approval of the brother who could more easily accept the new age. This, perhaps, explains his venture as a dramatist, his attempt to reach a contemporary audience. It also accounts in part for the more positive tone of his later essays, in which he made a concerted effort to do justice to the authors who had offended his sensibilities: the vulgar Balzac, the materialistic Flaubert, and the unclean Zola. And unlike his dramatic experiments, his critical effort was rewarded, for each of these writers contributed to his development as a novelist. But his own unique manner—the style we identify as peculiarly Jamesian—was largely the result of his sense of the past, which had been enhanced by his reading of Tennyson and Renan.

Chapter XI
Toward a New Perspective

ALTHOUGH it is sometimes believed that James became more dogmatic as his career progressed, the later critic was in fact far more liberal than the young reviewer. Indeed, by the early 1890s, James had abandoned his efforts to judge fiction according to a single set of standards and had begun to appreciate authors whom he had previously attacked. There were a number of reasons for this change in his perspective. First was his sense that he himself had entered his "middle years" and that his early critical efforts had been but partially successful. With this sense, as we have seen, came a feeling of nostalgia, apparent not only in his comments on the poets and Renan but also in his essays commemorating the New England writers who had first shaped his ideals. In 1887 he praised Emerson for having exemplified "a kind of high, vertical moral light, the brightness of a society at once very simple and very responsible";[1] in the nineties, he honored Lowell as "the last of the literary conservatives"[2] who delighted in "a quiet fireside, a quiet library, a singularly quiet community";[3] and immediately before his death, he recalled the founders of the *Nation* and the *Atlantic*, writing of the 1860s as "a page of romance"[4] and "a golden age that has left a precious deposit."[5] But this nostalgia also indicates James's dissociation of himself from the older generation, as well as his belief that the society for which he wrote was no longer "simple" or "quiet." Moreover, his sense of the past did not preclude his appreciation of the present, and especially of the new life he had made for himself in Europe. Writing of James after his trip to Italy in 1886-87, Leon Edel notes that he "had undergone the last stages of an almost imperceptible evolution begun years before—a process which had converted this hard-working, pleasure-loving duty-haunted sentient American, with his large and generous gifts, from an old Calvinistic inheritance of codes and rules and rigidities into a more relaxed (though still laborious) Americano-European. From this new attitude he discovered new meanings in the word *flexible*."[6] And flexibility was to be the hallmark of James's later criticism.

Then, too, as stated in Chapter IX, the writing of "The Art of Fiction" (1884) seems to have marked a turning point in the author's career. The title of that essay, echoing Besant's, leads one to anticipate a theoretical statement, a formulation of general principles; and it seems probable that James was trying, at least tentatively, to attain that end. But the reader soon recognizes the vagueness of James's ideas, concluding that he was at his best when dealing with specific examples—an insight that he himself seems to have gained once "The Art of Fiction" was written. This would account for his dismissal of the essay, in his letter to Stevenson, as "simply a plea for liberty,"[7] and for his apparent unwillingness in subsequent years to deal with fiction so comprehensively; all his later essays are far more limited in scope. Above all, this would explain the mature critic's efforts to deal with authors on their own terms—to regard them as interesting "cases" instead of scrutinizing them in the light of preconceived standards.

The word "case" is important, for it recurs as a leitmotif in many of James's later essays, beginning with his 1888 study of Guy de Maupassant. For some of the French writer's views, as set forth in the preface to his novel *Pierre et Jean*, James had little use; he was especially puzzled by Maupassant's preference for novels in which the characters' psychology was "hidden." But Maupassant was more liberal than the other naturalists in his refusal to raise his preferences to the level of theories. Instead, he defended the right of all novelists to follow the dictates of their individual temperaments, arguing (as James noted) that "any form of the novel is simply a vision of the world from the stand-point of a person constituted after a certain fashion and that it is therefore absurd to say that there is, for the novelist's use, only one reality of things." This defense of the writer's unique point of view met with James's approval, as did Maupassant's contention that the critic should judge an author on his own grounds. An artist's "particular organism," said James, "constitutes a *case*, and the critic is intelligent in proportion as he apprehends and enters into that case."[8] One finds these ideas repeated in James's 1891 introduction to Rudyard Kipling's *Mine Own People;* here he described the ideal critic as one who appreciates "freshness," who delights in the diversity of art produced by "innumerable natures," and "who has, *a priori*, no rule for a literary production but that it shall have genuine life."[9]

Thus, despite his increasing interest in technique, James became less preoccupied with theoretical formulations and more tolerant of aesthetic diversity. Even in his "major phase," after he had resolved some of the doubts that had beset him in the '80s and '90s, he was neither the dogmatist nor the theorist that his interpreters have often thought him to be. As a further example of his flexibility and of his preference for the "case" over the general rule, the introduction to his 1903 essay on Zola is of particular importance. Noting the widespread popularity of the novel, James posed a question: "What does it do for our life, our mind, our manners, our morals,—what does it do that history, poetry, philosophy, may not do, as well or better....?" And James confessed that he did not know "why people should like anything so loose and cheap as the predominant mass of the 'output.'" But he continued: "An abstract solution failing, we encounter it in the concrete. . . . We become conscious, for our profit, of a *case*, and we see that our mystification was in the way cases had appeared, for so long, to fail us. None of the shapeless forms about us, for the time, had attained to the dignity of one."[10] This passage, of course, suggests James's disappointment with popular fiction; but it also illustrates his reluctance to formulate theory, his dependence on the "case," and his later willingness to be open-minded about any serious artist—including Emile Zola. One might also note that James's Prefaces, though they have been rigidly interpreted by Percy Lubbock and others, constitute his presentation of his own case, not a set of formulae to be applied to the works of other novelists.

As James's youthful seriousness had led him to value "philosophy," and hence "character," in the novel, so his later acceptance of diversity led him to search for evidence of each author's uniqueness, his fidelity to his own impressions. One of the first signs of this change in the critic's outlook was his 1885 review of George Eliot's biography. Although he expressed his high regard for Eliot, he commented at length on her "absence of free aesthetic life": "We feel in her, always, that she proceeds from the abstract to the concrete; that her figures and situations are evolved, as the phrase is, from her moral consciousness, and are only indirectly the products of observations." And quoting Alphonse Daudet on the importance of the artist's personal impression ("nous périssons par les livres!"), James concluded by wondering whether Eliot's fiction would not have been better had she not met the intellectual George Henry Lewes.[11] Quite obviously, some of these comments echo James's earlier critiques of the English novelist; one recalls his preference for her dark heroines over her more virtuous characters and his dislike of her narrators' sermonizing. But one easily observes the difference in emphasis between this review and James's 1876 essay on *Daniel Deronda*, in which he had concluded, after some debate with himself, that Eliot's novels had "life," if not "art."

For the most part, however, James's critiques became more positive as his demands for high seriousness became less stringent. A case in point is his 1886 essay on William Dean Howells. That author's international novels, one recalls, had been warmly praised by James; but since writing *A Foregone Conclusion*, Howells had espoused realism, devoting his works to the commonplace and (from James's earlier point of view) the vulgar aspects of life. The critic's essay begins with a frank recognition of this fact: "There is nothing in *Silas Lapham*, or in *Doctor Breen's Practice*, or in *A Modern Instance*, or in *The Undiscovered Country*, to suggest that its author had at one time either wooed the lyric Muse or surrendered himself to those Italian initiations without which we of other countries remain always, after all, more or less barbarians." But instead of lamenting Howells's lapse into barbarism, James praised him for "painting what he [saw]." True, he cautioned his friend against "looking askance at exceptions and perversities and superiorities," and against holding style and composition "too cheap"; but the tone of the essay is cautiously favorable: "Mr. Howells's standpoint is an excellent one for seeing a large part of the truth, and even if it were less advantageous, there would be a great deal to admire in the firmness with which he has planted himself."[12] Here again, one can see James's increased respect for artistic freedom, noting too that he no longer insisted on the American artist's duty to improve his country's culture by avoiding commonplace subjects.

If James's tolerance had extended only to the work of his old friends, it would have been less significant; but it also affected his view of younger writers whose fiction he might not have been expected to admire. For an example, we can return to his essay on Kipling, the same essay in which he had redefined his own role as a critic. Leon Edel has stated correctly that James was "hedging" in this piece and that his admiration for Kipling diminished as the author's works became more violent;[13] yet the critique is still noteworthy for its sympathetic tone. Yes, James conceded, the voice of "the civilized man" and woman is absent from Kipling's work; "[b]ut this is an element that for the present one does not miss—every other note is so articulate and direct." And he went on to praise such tales as "The Courting of Dinah Shadd," a half-humorous, half-sentimental narrative by an Irish soldier, Mulvaney, and "The End of the Passage," the story of a British engineer who dies a terrible death in India, perhaps as a result of some unnamed supernatural force. James's liking for such tales is rather reminiscent of his earlier criticism; one recalls his taste for picturesque characters and for horror stories that depended more on subtle mystery than on "what is clumsy and tasteless in the time-honored practice of the 'plot.'" But in this essay, one also notes James's efforts to lay aside his prejudices in favor of "civilized" characters, his praise of Kipling's "freshness" and "disinterested sense of the real," and above all, his attack on "the old stupid superstition" that the vulgarity of an author's characters resulted from a similar defect in their creator. This "infantine philosophy," he added, had been disproven by Howells, who had handled "some of the clumsiest, crudest, most human things in life" with "the most distinguished dexterity and all the detachment of a master."[14] As James had earlier fallen prey to this "superstition," it seems evident that he was now making a conscious attempt to change his methods.

Perhaps the most telling example of James's change of outlook is his essay on Maupassant, in which, more than in the pieces on Howells and Kipling, there is a visible struggle between the old critic and the new. Notwithstanding his

defense of artistic freedom, James obviously found it difficult to accept Maupassant, whom he called an "interesting
case" but also "an embarrassing one, embarrassing and
mystifying for the moralist." Much of the essay, moreover,
is in the same vein as his earlier criticism of Flaubert and
his school. Predictably, he attacked Maupassant for dwelling too much on the sexual nature of his figures to the
exclusion of "that reflective part which governs conduct
and produces character," adding that "the impression of
the human spectacle for him who takes it as it comes has less
analogy with that of the monkeys' cage than this admirable
writer's account of it." And again predictably, James
expressed his distaste for Maupassant's more "brutal" and
"cynical" works: *Bel-Ami,* a novel concerning a ruthless
journalist who succeeds largely through his sexual conquests;
"Monsieur Parent," the portrait of a cuckold; and
"L'Héritage," the satirical story of a man who permits his wife
to have a child by his friend so that she will gain an inheritance promised to her by her aunt. The latter tale, said James,
"is a model of narration, but it leaves our poor average
humanity dangling like a beaten rag." Here, as in so many
of his early reviews, James was obviously taking the part of
the "Anglo-Saxons," whom he commended for their "mixture
of good humour and piety."[15]

But at the same time, James acknowledged that
Maupassant was a good writer, one "with whom it was
impossible not to reckon." Even as he dealt with the fiction
he disliked, James admired its author's visual sense and
his powers of selection; and in other parts of his essay, he
commended those tales in which the French author's weaknesses were less apparent—"genial" stories such as "La
Maison Tellier," a bawdy account of a madam who takes her
girls to her niece's confirmation service, and "tender"
stories such as "Miss Harriet," the history of an English
spinster who falls in love with a young artist, committing
suicide when she sees him kissing the maidservant. Above
all, James praised the novel *Pierre et Jean,* whose protagonist
jealous at first of his brother's inheritance, becomes painfully
conscious of the rival's illegitimacy and their mother's disgrace. This, said the critic, was an excellent novel, first
because Pierre was a complex figure and not "a mere bundle
of appetites," and also because Maupassant had dealt so
effectively with the bourgeoisie, "that vast, dim section of
society" often neglected by English authors. Such comments,
of course, still reflect James's personal bias, but they also
show his new determination to accommodate the naturalists.

The essay, moreover, ends on a conciliatory note: "Let us not be alarmed at this prodigy (though prodigies are alarming) of M. de Maupassant, who is at once so licentious and so impeccable, but gird ourselves up with the conviction that another point of view will yield another perfection."[16] Maupassant's perspective clearly was not James's; but then again, the critic was past the point of demanding that it should be.

In these essays, written in the late eighties and early nineties, one can indeed see a new flexibility, the result of James's desire to study "cases" instead of adhering to set standards. And this flexibility was to lead him toward a renewed appreciation of many kinds of fiction: the realistic novels of Howells, the picturesque but unrefined tales of Kipling, the naturalistic works of Maupassant, and (as we shall see) the romances of Sand and Stevenson. It should not be assumed, however, that James found "cases" wherever he looked; it was their rarity that made him value them all the more. One infers this not only from his 1903 essay on Zola, but also from a much earlier piece of writing—a letter, written in 1889, to a summer school on "The Novel" in Deerfield, Massachusetts. In advising the "young nymphs and swains," he urged them not to talk too much about fiction, but to produce "something from [their] point of view," an "ounce of example" being "worth a ton of generalities." And he added that he exhorted them "to consider life directly and closely" because the English novel was "in a bad way," and "nothing but absolute freedom . . . [could] restore its self-respect."[17] Obviously James believed that theorizing was premature, and that the poor quality of popular fiction justified his encouraging any "producer" who might raise its standard.

Early in his career, of course, James showed his distaste for most popular novels, especially in the United States; and later in the century, various circumstances made exceptional works even more difficult to find. One of these conditions, as Larzer Ziff has noted, was the increasing power of women readers; authors publishing their fiction in magazines had to be particularly mindful of their female audience.[18] The result, unfortunately, was a proliferation of the sentimental novels that James had attacked in his "Art of Fiction," at the expense of works dealing more honestly with "the great relation between men and women."[19] That the critic was aware of this development can be inferred from his sketch entitled "An Animated Conversation," published by *Scribner's* in 1889. In this piece, representing a literary discussion among a group of British and Americans, the part of James is played by a figure named Darcy. Darcy is something of an optimist, at least so far as the future of art is concerned; he speaks hopefully, for example, of the "grand" opportunity for the "two great peoples" to "tackle the world together" and to "make life larger and the arts finer, for each of them." And on the subject of the new prevalence of women writers and readers, which he calls a "portentous fact," he tries to maintain a balanced view; noting that "it is fatal" to write for the women, he nonetheless disagrees with a character who predicts a great battle of the sexes: "Excuse the timidity of my imagination," he says, "but it seems to me that we *must* be united."[20] During the 1890s, however, James found this unification more difficult than he had first imagined it to be. His 1899 essay on "The Future of the Novel," though still hopeful in tone, is far more severe concerning "the vulgarization of literature in general" resulting from "the presence of the ladies and children . . . the reader irreflective and uncritical." And while he offered the hope that the liberation of women might lead to the liberation of the novel, he insisted that the aritist ought not to succumb to the current demands of his youthful, female audience—especially in his treatment of sexual relations.[21]

If James seems biased in his strictures against women, one must nonetheless admit that many ladies' novels were marred by prudishness and sentimentality. Moreover, the critic did make some effort to give such fiction its due. In 1887, for example, he wrote a friendly essay on the works of Constance Fenimore Woolson, who specialized in depicting heroines with a predilection for self-sacrifice; and in 1892 he published a brief but favorable review of Mrs. Humphry Ward's *Robert Elsmere*, crediting the author (who had depicted the founding of a new church based on the humanity of Christ) with "an exceedingly matured conception" at a time when it was "difficult to attach the idea of conception at all to most . . . other novels."[22] But even in those essays, James had to qualify his praise; the piece on Miss Woolson refers to the "essentially conservative" spirit of women and their overemphasis on the "tender sentiment,"[23] and that on Mrs. Ward alludes rather slyly to masculine resistance against female writers who "made the English novel speak their language."[24] Furthermore, as Leon Edel has noted, James's complimentary remarks may have resulted from his friendship with the two women—especially with Miss

Woolson, who cherished a secret passion for him.[25] Yet one also observes the critic's new willingness to isolate the more hopeful "cases" from the common run of ladies' novels.

A second factor affecting his view of popular fiction was his fear concerning the decline of the English language, especially in the United States. In "An Animated Conversation," Darcy speaks of his desire for a new American idiom, although he ruefully agrees with a British character who pronounces this to be "in the crude, the vulgar stage."[26] But as the years progressed, James became less tolerant of such vulgarity, the most famous expression of his concern being "The Question of Our Speech" (1905), in which he exhorted the graduating class at Bryn Mawr to promote cultivated language. This concern, like his antipathy toward women's novels, had a twofold effect on his criticism. First, it led him to be suspicious of novels of dialect; reviewing several of these in 1898, he wondered gloomily why "the great successes" in American fiction were "not the studies of the human plant under cultivation." But it also led him to be friendly toward authors whose style was more refined, including writers so diverse as William Dean Howells, whose expression he regarded as "highly developed,"[27] and Gustave Flaubert, whom he came to admire for his attacks on Philistinism and his efforts to achieve stylistic perfection.

Another of James's concerns was that the quantitative increase in novels—to some extent in Britain but more especially in the United States—might result in their qualitative decline. During the 1860s, one recalls, there was little native fiction for the critic to review; but by the end of the century, the American novel had become a popular literary form. James viewed this circumstance with a mixture of happiness and alarm. On the one hand, he rejoiced at the success of prose fiction: its popularity, he wrote in "The Future of the Novel," was "the most surprising example to be named of swift and extravagant growth, a development beyond the measure of every early appearance." Yet on the other, he used an ominous metaphor to describe this condition: "The flood at present swells and swells, threatening the whole field of letters, as would often seem, with submersion."[28] And in 1901 James referred to the reading public, voracious in its demand for best-sellers, as "an escaped elephant" breaking into the critic's "little garden, so neat on its traditional lines."[29] Beleaguered as he felt, however, James did his best to deal with this new monster. Whereas the early reviewer, in search of the ideal novel, dealt harshly with popular fiction, the later, more flexible critic looked for redeeming cases, educating the public through selection rather than through wholesale condemnation.

His most sustained effort at this was his series of American letters published in 1898 by the British magazine *Literature*. Here, to be sure, one finds a number of comments reminiscent of his earlier criticism. He still disliked novels which failed to delineate character—books such as Winston Churchill's *The Celebrity*, an attack on a society novelist so vaguely portrayed that the satire is ineffective,[30] and Gertrude Atherton's *American Wives and English Husbands*, whose heroine prates constantly of her "individuality" but displays none. (James opined that he could have handled this subject better, and one can hardly doubt it.)[31] Then, too, the critic still deplored the false optimism in such fiction as Robert Chambers's *Lorraine* and George Eggleston's *Southern Soldier Stories*, which treated war in the manner of an "operetta" or a "dreadful 'boys' story,'" putting "a premium upon almost every unreality."[32] (Even the realist Howells, he observed, sometimes "muffle[d] and soften[ed]" the "edges" of his fiction—as in *The Story of a Play*, the tale of a dramatist who quite improbably succeeds despite a temperamental actor and his own jealous wife.)[33] Finally, James still deplored the vulgarity of such novels as Paul Ford's *The Honourable Peter Stirling*, a heavy-handed satire concerning a New York political boss. (Commenting on the novel's popularity, the critic remarked, "Something of the fascination of the abyss solicits the mind in fixing this fact.")[34]

But elsewhere, James made an obvious effort to be more positive in his criticism. His first letter, in fact, is entitled "The Question of the Opportunities." Yes, he admitted, he was concerned about the fate of the novel in "the great common-schooled and newspapered democracy," as "literature for the million, or rather for the fast-arriving billion" would assuredly not be "literature as we have hitherto known it at its best." He observed, however, that American diversity might prove to be an advantage: "we may get individual publics positively more sifted and evolved than anywhere else, shoals of fish rising to more delicate bait." And he stated that the new conditions also gave the critic "a delicious rest from the oppressive *a priori*."[35]

Furthermore, his comments on individual authors reveal his efforts to separate the artists from the mere "producers." His remarks on Walt Whitman, prompted by the publication of some of the poet's letters, are a good index of his more

liberal attitude; whereas in the sixties he had berated
Whitman for his vulgarity, he now praised his "overflow in
the deadly dry setting," his "audible New Jersey voice,
charged thick with . . . impressions," and (in *The Wound
Dresser*) his "native feeling, pity and horror and helpless-
ness, . . . like the wail of a mother for her mangled young."[36]
Then, too, as one might infer from his comments on the
"individual publics," James welcomed the local-color
realists: "Fiction as yet in the United States," he wrote,
"strikes me . . . as most curious when most confined and most
local." And with considerable foresight, he singled out the
authors whose work was to remain well-known: Hamlin
Garland ("a case of saturation so precious as to have almost
the value of genius"),[37] Bret Harte (who may have gone too
far in dealing with "the Wild West alone," but whose devotion
to this subject was "one of the most touching things in all
American literary annals"),[38] and Mary E. Wilkins Freeman
("On the day Miss Mary Wilkins should 'sail' [for England]
I would positively have detectives versed in the practice
of extradition posted at Liverpool").[39] His interest in local
color even led him to admire such non-belletristic books as
The Workers, Walter Wyckoff's study of American day
laborers; though "as little as possible a novel," it held
the critic "under a spell."[40] James, of course, was writing
as an expatriate who found his native land to be almost as
exotic as a foreign country. Hence, he no longer thought
American fiction to be lacking in picturesqueness, and
referred favorably to such relatively unexplored subjects
as the life of the American businessman, an "obscure, but
not less often an epic, hero" whose "picture was still to be
painted."[41] One naturally thinks of James's own Adam
Verver.

Such, then, was the literary situation among the "Anglo-
Saxons"; "cases" were not abundant, and the critic thus
praised those that he could identify. He also wrote of French
and Italian literature as an antidote for Anglo-Saxon
prudishness and lack of artistry—a practice which led him
once again to find new values in the "case." As he explained
in a preface to an American edition of Maupassant's works,
he faced many "embarrassments" when dealing with that
author; but, he said, the "only excuse the critic has for
braving the embarrassments I have mentioned is that he
wishes to perform a work of recommendation, and indeed
there is no profit in talking, in English, of M. de Maupassant
unless it be in the sense of recommending him."[42]

Interestingly enough, however, the France of the later

nineteenth century hardly offered a more fertile field for cases than did the United States or England. At first, James hoped that it might; he wrote in 1888 that although the French had "almost nothing to show us in the way of the operation of character," and although they portrayed man as "the simple sport of fate" and of his own sensual desires, "their affirmation of all this is still, on the whole, the most complete affirmation that the novel at present offers us. They have on their side the accident, if accident it be, that they never cease to be artists. They will keep this advantage till the optimists of the hour, the writers for whom the moral stuff of life is also real and visible . . . begin to seem to them formidable competitors."[43] Yet as time went on, there were fewer French novelists whom James could cite as salutary examples. Maupassant died in 1893 and Daudet in 1897, leaving only Zola to carry on the tradition of Flaubert and Pierre Loti to practice a more picturesque kind of realism. The decadents and symbolists, of course, were mainly poets, and their aesthetic was of little interest to James: "we need scarcely open a parenthesis for the so-called *décadents*," he wrote in 1889; "they have produced no talent that seems particularly alive—to do so would indeed be a disloyalty to their name."[44] As for the *Revue des Deux Mondes*, the source of so much of James's inspiration during the 1870s, it had become a bastion of outworn conservatism, devoted more and more to social and political criticism and to laments on the state of French literature.

Not surprisingly, then, James admitted to a larger regret as he commemorated Daudet's death in 1897: "Distinguished as are two or three of the talents of the new generation . . . it sufficiently comes home to us that the muster of high accomplishment is now comparatively thin."[45] And his 1899 essay on "The Present Literary Situation in France," which begins with the observation that for fifty years there had been no crisis there "at which the things of the mind were so little the fashion," contains almost a dirge: "The great historians are dead, then—the last of them went with Renan; the great critics are dead—the last of them went with Taine; the great dramatists are dead—the last of them went with Dumas; and, of the novelists of the striking group originally fathered by the Second Empire, Emile Zola is the only one still happily erect." Indeed, the novel was in such a state of decline that James wondered whether there were not "some strange and fatal disparity between French talent and French life," and whether the French were not paying the penalty for their concentration on the "eternal triangle" at the expense of the "more various portrayal of character."[46]

Apart from Zola, who is mentioned as being "so little a genius of the highest distinction and so little a negligible quantity,"[47] the essay refers significantly to only two novelists. The first, Paul Bourget, had been a personal friend and would-be disciple of James's since the mid-1880s; indeed, his *Cruelle Enigme* (1884), a rather tedious analytical novel about a young man fatally corrupted by a weak, sensual woman, had been dedicated to James. But as I. D. McFarlane and Leon Edel have noted, the critic soon lost interest in Bourget's works, first because many of them were thesis novels in support of his reactionary opinions, and also because Bourget, though professing to reveal the essence of his characters, merely carried the techniques of the naturalists into the realm of psychology.[48] In his essay, to be sure, James complimented his friend, but his metaphors suggest an underlying dissatisfaction with such writing: "The [consciousness] forms for him . . . a large glass cage equipped with wheels, stoves and other conveniences, in which he moves over his field very much as a great American railway-director moves over his favorite line in his 'luxuriously-appointed' private car." Although James went on to regret his inability to "accompany him on one or two of his journeys,"[49] one infers that he was none too eager to do so.

The second novelist mentioned in the essay was Anatole France, whom James pronounced "a regular happy case" and "the great luxury of the time." Oddly enough, however, he refused to discuss his works in any more detail than he had Bourget's, excusing himself by saying that he could not "throw off a rough estimate of '*L'Orme du Mail*' and '*Le Mannequin d'Osier.*'"[50] The probable reason for James's modesty was that France's works, although they commanded his respect, were not useful to him as literary examples. The writer's earlier books, including *Le Crime de Sylvestre Bonnard* (1881), *Thaïs* (1890), and *L'Etui de nacre* (1892), were essentially philosophical works showing the influence of Renan—an author whom James admired too, of course, but more for his sensibility than for his system of thought. And as Lewis Shanks has noted, the works cited by James in this essay—*L'Orme du mail* (1897), *Le Mannequin d'osier* (1897), and *L'Anneau d'améthyste* (1899)—were not novels at all, but episodes and conversations which chronicled the political events of the day.[51] As such, they shed little light on the art of fiction.

Thus, once again, James was left with a paucity of "cases," and once again, he renewed his efforts to find them. This explains why, in 1903, he paid homage to Zola, the lone survivor among the naturalists, and why, throughout the

1890s and 1900s, he kept returning to the French novelists of his own youth—to Balzac, Sand, and Flaubert. Indeed, his essay on "The Present Literary Situation" includes an apology for his "own house . . . his own youth and the irrecoverable freshness of its first curiosities and its first responses."[52] One is reminded again of James's nostalgia, his sense of the past; but what is most significant is that this same sense led him to re-evaluate the "classic" French novelists, and in the process, to broaden his literary perspective.

Contemporary France, however, offered certain advantages that the critic thought lacking in the United States and Britain. One of these was a relatively sophisticated class of readers who could appreciate such writers as Anatole France. "The author of 'L'Anneau d'Amethyste,'" James observed, "makes others like to think . . . of his public. Who makes anyone like to think of ours?"[53] That the French were so advanced in their taste was the result, in James's opinion, of another happy circumstance—the quality of French criticism. Noting the reactionary views of such critics as Ferdinand Brunetière and Jules Lemaître (both of the *Revue des Deux Mondes*), he argued that the nation's literary standards had suffered some decline even in this respect; but he went on to praise Eugène de Voguë, a "man of genius" who had worked to introduce the French to foreign literature,[54] and Emile Faguet, who had written a study of Flaubert for Hachette's critical series, "Les Grands Ecrivains Français." This undertaking, James added, was notable for its contrast with the "English Men of Letters" series: "The authors of the English studies appear to labor, in general, under a terror of critical responsibility; the authors of the French, on the contrary, to hunger and thirst for it."[55]

Because James believed that American and British readers needed the guidance of serious critics, he attached an ever-greater importance to his own role. As early as 1880, he nearly abandoned the casual review for the lengthy essay; and in an 1891 article entitled "The Science of Criticism," he explained his unwillingness to be a mere reviewer. Whereas the French, he said, wisely refused to notice books that did not "belong to literature," the Americans fed "the huge, open mouth" of the periodicals, which he also likened to regular trains that could not run unless all their seats were occupied, if only by stuffed mannekins. And with unwonted bitterness, he pointed out the "signs of this catastrophe": "the failure of distinction, the failure of style, the failure of knowledge, the failure of thought." Literature could be saved from such a disaster, he added, only if the critic took himself seriously—only if he were like a "knight who has knelt through his long vigil and who has the piety of his office." This essay, then, suggests still another reason for the more positive tone of James's later criticism; except in a few journalistic pieces (as, for example, his "American Letters" and "London Notes"), he seldom wrote of authors whom he did not at least respect. And when dealing with writers of sufficient stature, he was increasingly willing to follow his own advice by "taking them as they [came]" instead of allowing his prejudices to obscure their "portraits."[56]

Finally, as a number of scholars have remarked, James's new tolerance as a critic was in large measure the result of his later experiences as an author. To begin with, there was the rejection of his work by the public and by other critics, resulting first in the relative failure of *The Princess Casamassima* (1885) and *The Bostonians* (1885), then in the *Guy Domville* débâcle of 1895 which ended his career as a dramatist. Thus, quite naturally, James tended to put himself on the side of the artists as against the mass of readers, especially in his essays on such controversial authors as Flaubert and Zola. Then, too, during his "middle" and "treacherous" years (to use Leon Edel's terms describing James's life in the late 1880s and 1890s), he was beset by anxieties about his own work and therefore admired any author who was able to "produce." As he wrote in his 1889 preface to the stories of Maupassant, that writer's "feat of keeping his talent fresh" was a gift creating "surprises in the mere exercise of its natural health. The dogmatist is never safe with it."[57] One also finds such comments in James's essays on Balzac, Sand, and Zola, which express admiration for the authors' fecundity and for the sheer massiveness of their works. And ultimately, as James entered his "major phase," he gained enough confidence in his own point of view to allow other artists their unique perspective. One recalls the famous metaphor in his Preface to *The Portrait of a Lady:* "The house of fiction has . . . not one window, but a million—a number of possible windows not to be reckoned, rather; every one of which has been pierced, or is still pierceable, in its vast front, by the need of the individual vision and by the pressure of the individual will."[58] As Maurice Géracht has stated, this metaphor suggests James's final conception of his role as a critic.[59] No longer was he so concerned with finding models to imitate; rather, he tried to consider each author individually, a task made easier by his own independence.

After 1884, then, a number of factors caused James to adopt a more liberal perspective: his sense that his youthful days were over, his new life in Europe, his turning from theory to the specific case, his discovery that cases were hard to find, his decision to abandon reviewing, and his own experience as a writer. In one respect, however, this liberalism was the outgrowth of his earlier critical views. Returning to James's essays on the romancers, and especially on Sand, one recalls his defense of the artist's imagination and his rejection of the naturalists' view of the author as a passive taker of notes. And from this idea, one moves easily to James's belief in the "case," which depended on his preoccupation with the artist's unique vision. Initially, of course, it was the writer of "strong stories" whom James credited with imaginative power; but subsequently, he came to believe that "Every artist who really touches us becomes in this way an individual instrument, the fiddler, the improviser of an original tune."[60] And as we shall see, James eventually used even the naturalists' own works as evidence against their aesthetic theories. First, however, we shall turn to his later essays on the romancers, who reinforced his belief in the creative imagination.

Chapter XII

Revaluations: The Romancers

For James the quintessential romancer was still George Sand, to whom he devoted three of his later essays. One of these, written in 1897, is a commentary on Sand's letters to Alfred de Musset; the other two, which first appeared in 1902 and 1914, are reviews of Madame Wladimir Karénine's biography of the author; and all three of the essays are included in James's collection of his later criticism, *Notes on Novelists* (1914). That James continued to write of Sand may seem surprising, for his early criticism suggests that she was indeed a vexing case—an author whose fiction had little intrinsic value, although it permitted the free exercise of the artist's imagination. But it is clear that James never lost his fascination with the French romancer and that he found her example more worthy of extended discussion as he himself entered his "major phase."

One reason for his writing about her was simple nostalgia; he referred rather wistfully to the "queer, vanished world" in which she had lived[1] and maintained that "no plot of her most bustling fiction" was as interesting as her life.[2] Quite naturally, then, James's later studies of Sand are more biographical than critical. At the same time, however, he admitted that he still read her fiction because he enjoyed it more than many contemporary novels: "The small fry of the hour submit to further shrinkage," he wrote, "and we revert with a sigh of relief to the free genius and large life of one of the greatest of all masters of expression."[3] From this and other comments, one infers that James found Sand's romances to be far better than the ladies' novels of his own day. Indeed, he recommended Sand as a model for liberated women, citing her as one who emulated extraordinary men, not average ones,[4] and who dealt with life "exactly as if she had been a man."[5] True, he continued to express his concern about her indelicacy ("The lovers are naked in the marketplace and perform for the benefit of humanity," he wrote of her and de Musset),[6] but he must have seen her art and life as salutary in an age when fiction was often too genteel.

Moreover, as suggested in the previous chapter, James came to regard Sand's artistic fecundity as a miracle in itself; his essays refer repeatedly to her powers of expression, her ability to work even under the most adverse conditions,[7] and her "immunity from restrictive instincts."[8] Some of these remarks may have been prompted by James's concern about his own productivity; when he writes of de Musset's "poor gift of occasional song" as against Sand's "unequalled . . . command of the last word," for example, one senses his personal sympathy for the hapless poet. More important, however, was James's abiding interest in the creative process, which he continued to regard as far more than a matter of simple note-taking. Sand, he said, was "an eminent special case" because she transmuted her "private ecstasies and pains" into "promising literary material"—the most salient example of her art being *Elle et lui*, "the picture, postponed and retouched" of her affair with de Musset. So compelling did James find this transmutation that he could almost forgive Sand for requesting the posthumous publication of her letters to the poet, "the crude primary stuff from which the moral detachment of the book was distilled."[9] This, of course, echoes James's earlier comments on Sand's artistic use of her personal impressions; as we have seen, her prefaces, showing how she drew on her experiences without reporting them in detail, may well have been the inspiration for James's own.

But these later essays are more emphatic than the earlier ones on the subject of Sand's style, which James believed to be a means of transforming crude experience into art; he referred to this as a voice lifting Sand above all "posthumous *laideurs*" and as a "citadel" where, "in spite of all rash *sorties*, she continue[d] to hold out."[10] Again, he quoted Balzac's assessment: "[Sand] holds that, without knowing the French language, she has style. And it's true."[11] In the light of James's increasing concern for style, these comments seem especially significant; like his earlier remarks on Renan, they suggest that he regarded stylistic beauty both as a means of overcoming vulgarity and as a way of dealing with it. Furthermore, it was through style that the eloquence and passion of the romance could be incorporated into the realistic novel—a point of crucial importance to James, who attempted, both in theory and in practice, to combine the two genres.

In themselves, however, Sand's romances were of but limited value to the critic. The French author's inflated and even declamatory style bears little resemblance to James's more subtle, sinuous prose, although both may be described as highly personal and distinctive "voices." Indeed, it was Sand's inimitability that aroused James's interest; and when he wrote of her style, he used the term to refer to her unique personality and "lifestyle" as well as to her literary art.[12] Then, too, he maintained that Sand's career and character were "the real thing," while her works were of less importance because of their "want of plastic intensity" and their lack of concrete detail: "A picture is never the stream of the artist's inspiration," he wrote; "it is the deposit of the stream. For the picture, in George Sand, we must look elsewhere, look at her life and nature."[13] Using another metaphor, James also complained of the lack of verisimilitude in Sand's romances: "to embark on one of her confessed fictions is to have . . . a little too much the feeling of going up in a balloon. We are borne by a fresh, cool current, and the car delightfully dangles; but as we peep over the sides we see things—as we usually know them—at a dreadful drop beneath."[14] This is the same image used by James in his Preface to *The American*, where he described the romancer as one who cuts the cable to which the "balloon of experience" is tied. But in that essay on his own earlier work, he apologized for his youthful naiveté ("I must decidedly have supposed . . . that I was acutely observing—and with a blest absence of wonder at its being so easy") and defended the romance mainly on the grounds of its realistic portrayal of Newman ("clinging to my hero as to a tall, protective, good-natured elder brother in a rough place, I leave the record to stand or fall by his more or less convincing image").[15] Obviously James found no such brothers or sisters in the characters of Sand.

The clearest statement of his attitude toward romantic

stories of figures larger than life is to be found in his 1901 essay on Edmond Rostand, the French dramatist best known for his *Cyrano de Bergerac*. This author, said James, was a true romantic—a descendant of Victor Hugo, not an "anxious, skeptical" artist like Stevenson. As such, he was a singular case, and the critic urged him to continue to set his unique example: "We wouldn't stop him for the world; we would rather lash him on. For so are exhibitions achieved, so are temperaments affirmed, so are examples multiplied, and so are little sermons preached." But James's "little sermon" on the romantic mode is rather equivocal; while praising Rostand for laying the "gold-leaf" on thick, he added that he identified the "romantic deflection" from realism by "recognising on his own part an anxiety . . . as to where it will come out if left only to itself." And again turning to metaphor, he said that the dramatist walked an "acrobatic tight-rope" when he dealt with such figures as Cyrano, the man with the monstrous nose who sacrifices everything for love and friendship, or "L'Aiglon," the son of Napoleon who dreams of nothing except his father's glory. These overdrawn characters, James hinted, ran the risk of appearing more ridiĉulous than sublime. Furthermore, he contrasted Rostand's precarious situation with that of Paul Hervieu, the author of a rather ponderous thesis play, *La Course du flambeau*, demonstrating how a woman will sacrifice her mother to save her daughter. Hervieu, the critic observed, had only a limited dramatic sense; but because he clung to the "line of life"—to psychological realism—he had an advantage over Rostand: "Now it may lucklessly happen that there be *not* as good fish in the romantic sea—as good . . . as those in respect to which [Rostand's] bamboozlement has hitherto so triumphed. . . . It is dreadful to think of, but he will then not have, as the saying is, a loaf on the shelf. There is no question, for M. Paul Hervieu, of exactly bamboozling us; but even if there were it would practically make no difference. *His* loaf on the shelf is large and certain."[16]

All these metaphors suggest that in James's view, the realist was secure while the romancer was not. The former, if accused of a lack of imagination, could always say that he had "represented life"; but the latter, whose only resources were his inspiration and his literary style, had no defense against the charge that his works were frivolous or hackneyed. Indeed, James believed that the only author who could safely write pure romance was one who had no equal: William Shakespeare. In a 1907 preface to *The Tempest*, he argued that the "story" in the play was "a thing of naught," and that Shakespeare had relied heavily on conventional plot devices, "old wives' tales." But this hardly mattered, he said, because the real subject of the drama was Shakespeare's style:

> The Tempest . . . superlatively speaks of that endowment for Expression, expression as a primary force, a consuming, an independent passion, which was the greatest ever laid upon man. It is for Shakespeare's power of constitutive speech quite as if he had swum into our ken with it from another planet, gathering it up there, in its wealth, as . . . something that was to make of our poor world a great flat table for receiving the glitter and clink of outpoured treasure. The idea and the motive are more often than not so smothered in it that they scarce know themselves, and the resources of such a style, the provision of images, emblems, energies of every sort, . . . affects us as the storehouse of a king before a famine or a siege. . . . It renders the poverties and obscurities of our world . . . in the dazzling terms of a richer and better.

Hence, for James, Shakespeare was the supreme exemplar of purely creative genius, the "divine musician who, alone in his room, preludes or improvises at close of day."[17] Other authors, in contrast, as inhabitants of "our poor world," had to deal more directly with its "poverties and obscurities." But James did not believe that they had to abandon the romance, or that he himself had to make a clear-cut choice between romance and realism. "I simply want everything," he confessed in his essay on Rostand; "I want the line of life, and I want the bamboozlement too."[18] And although this demand might seem paradoxical, he had already identified a number of works in which the balloon of romance was anchored to the solid ground of realism.

On the simplest level, such an effect could be achieved through the technique that he himself had used in *The American:* the reversal of romantic conventions, especially that of the happy ending. For example, Daudet's *Port Tarascon,* which James translated into English in 1891, appears at first to be a fairy-tale, the account of a braggart from the Midi who leads his town in a wildly improbable utopian scheme. But the dream fails; the protagonist dies in disgrace, a disillusioned man; and the once-sanguine Southerners adopt the attitudes of the cynical North. In James's view such fiction had more value than the works of Sand precisely because it showed the divergence between the real and the ideal; his preface refers to Tartarin, in "his good intentions and his perpetual mistakes," as a symbol of "human-kind,"[19] and his memorial essay on Daudet praises the author for his "vision of the brighter and weaker things, weaker natures, about us."[20]

A similar case was that of George Du Maurier, whom James knew first as the illustrator of *Punch* and of his own *Washington Square*[21] and whom he had honored in an 1883 essay as an artist distinguished by "the union of a great sense of beauty with a great sense of reality."[22] These same qualities were also evident in three semi-autobiographical romances that Du Maurier published in the 1890s: *Peter Ibbetson* (1891), the story of an Anglo-French writer who, though in prison, has such vivid dreams that he is able for a time to transcend reality; *Trilby* (1894), the popular tale of a French girl who becomes the greatest singer in the world when hypnotized by a magician; and *The Martian* (1896), whose hero is guided by a good fairy, a Martian woman. All these romances deal with the supernatural and with the protagonist's temporary retreat into an ideal world; yet Du Maurier's characters inevitably die, finally aware of the limitations of their dreams. Thus, James, who himself had urged his friend to write *Trilby*,[23] praised Du Maurier for his "fine tragic perceptions"[24] and for his treatment of "the fantastic ... not cold and curious, but warmed by an intensely human application."[25] Daudet and Du Maurier, then, stood in direct opposition to those romancers who lacked this sense of man's unfulfilled desires—particularly to Prosper Mérimée, whose supernatural tales James had once enjoyed but whom he now condemned for his detachment and "dryness."[26]

The romancer could go one step further in emulating the novelist if he abandoned the supernatural and the fantastic, focussing instead on extraordinary characters in picturesque settings—in other words, on the more exotic aspects of reality. One such author was Pierre Loti, whom James first met at Daudet's home in 1884.[27] Loti (whose real name was Julien Viaud) based much of his fiction on his own colorful life in the French Navy, and thus had affinities with Robert Louis Stevenson[28] as well as with Flaubert and his school. It was as a French "painter," however, that James first identified him; and much of his 1888 essay on the author is devoted, predictably enough, to the complaint that he resembled his countrymen in being "monstrously thin on the spiritual side." But Loti, James conceded, had "a charm *quand même*"; he was "so good" that he could be "bad with impunity." In the first place, he was remarkable for his careful descriptions of the picturesque, to which the critic devoted several pages of lengthy quotation. This, of course, distinguished him from

"Madame George Sand," who "had an admirable faculty of looking within and a comparatively small one of looking without." Yet like Sand, Loti had a taste for romantic passion carried almost to the point of implausibility. Some of his romances—notably *Rarahu* and *Aziyadé*, both based on his liaisons with primitive women—were indeed too passionate for James's taste; he admitted that he found a "rare pleasure" in them but complained that they were "not *interesting*" in the sense that Matthew Arnold had used the term. *Pêcheur d'islande*, however, James's favorite among Loti's works, attracted his attention precisely because it was "the history of a passion . . . simplified, in its strength, to a sort of community with the wind and waves." Like so many of the novels James preferred, it centers mainly on the heroine, who worships the fisherman from afar, marries him after many months of heartbreak, and then succumbs to despair after he is lost at sea. To the critic, Loti's figures had an almost archetypal value; the author, he said, "has placed his two lovers in the mere immensity of sea and sky . . . and their isolation gives Yann and Gaud a kind of heroic greatness."[29] The figures in James's own novels are of course placed in a social rather than a natural setting; yet one is reminded of his theory of the "center" and also of his defense of passionate living, which, as Larzer Ziff has noted, set the novels of his major phase apart from most American fiction.[30] Significantly, his 1898 preface to Loti's *Impressions* is still more positive in tone than his essay of ten years earlier. While noting Loti's lack of reticence and his occasional neglect of form, he pronounced the author's fiction to be "one of the joys of the time," praising his love for his characters and the sea and "his sensibility, so unquenched and on the whole so little vulgarised." Like the romancer, Loti consoled his readers for "the humdrum nature of their fate"; but like the realist, he based his work upon observation: "his perception is a sensitive plate on which aspects are forever at play."[31]

James found the same values—the portrayal of passion and the delineation of the picturesque—in the works of Matilde Serao, an Italian author who was widely read in France[32] but less so in the United States and Britain.[33] James himself seems to have been unusually well-acquainted with her fiction; although his essay on the subject did not appear until 1901, he stated that he had read almost all her "striking romantic work" dating from 1885, when he had first been impressed by "the rare energy" of *La conquista di Roma*. Serao, in his opinion, was a "signal 'case'" and yet a perplexing one, because her treatment of *passione* was even more florid than Loti's. For her depiction of Italian life James had nothing but admiration; he especially liked *Il paese di cuccagna* (1890–91), a series of sketches depicting various Neapolitan figures consumed by their interest in the state lottery. But he had reservations about such books as *Fantasia* (1883), the story of a neurotic woman who steals her friend's husband, driving her to commit suicide. On the one hand, James cited this kind of romance for its absence of Anglo-Saxon prudishness, devoting the first part of his essay to a protest against the "rigor of convention" imposed on English and American writers by women less "emancipated" than Serao. On the other, he concluded his article with a warning against her limitations: Serao, he argued quite justly, weakened her fiction not by failing to point a moral but by showing passion "unaccompanied with any reflection of our usual manners—with affection, with duration, with circumstances or consequences." Hence, he confessed, he had a sneaking desire to lay "a clinging hand on dear old Jane Austen."[34] He thus expressed his unwillingness to substitute "passion" for character and social texture, despite his interest in Serao's effort to combine the romance of Sand with the realism of Zola.

One finds similar criticism in James's 1904 study of Gabriele D'Annunzio, another Italian author who had received attention in Britain, where his work was heavily reviewed in the periodicals,[35] and in France, where two of his romances had been serialized in the *Revue des Deux Mondes*.[36] A more serious artist than Serao, D'Annunzio was hailed by the critic as a genuine "case," "one of the full-blown products that are the joy of the analyst." The first of his "unmistakable signs," James continued, was his "rare notation of states of excited sensibility." And indeed, all of D'Annunzio's heroes are moved by extraordinary passion which they struggle desperately to control: in *Il piacere* (1889), a young artist is destroyed by his sexual desires; in *L'innocente* (1892), a husband is driven to murder his wife's illegitimate child; in *Il trionfo della morte* (1894), a man, disgusted by his own lust, finally kills both his mistress and himself; and in *Il fuoco* (1900) and *Le vergini della rocce* (1896), the heroes manage with difficulty to overcome their libidos for the sake of their art. James, of course, was well aware of D'Annunzio's excesses, but he praised him for carefully depicting the conflict between his heroes' sexual and aesthetic passions and for "showing the consciousness as a full, mixed cup."[37]

D'Annunzio's second virtue was his "splendid visual sense" and his ability to render the Italian setting, which gave even his more improbable fiction a realistic texture. As James wrote of *Le vergini*, "the romance is . . . of the happiest kind, the kind that consists in the imaginative development of observable things, things present, significant, related to us, and not in a weak false fumble for the remote and disconnected." Finally, James admired the author's "ample and exquisite style," which, like his own, was "thick-sown" with "illustrative images and figures." He even translated some of these for the benefit of his readers: "his will, useless as a sword of base temper hung at the side of a drunkard or a dullard" . . . "Clear meteors, at intervals, streaked the motionless air, running over it as lightly and silently as drops of water on a diamond plate." And he stressed the fact that such metaphors were not merely decorative: "It is brought home to us afresh that there is no complete creation without style any more than there is complete music without sound; also that when language becomes as closely applied and impressed a thing as, for the most part, in the volumes before us, the fact of artistic creation is, so to speak, registered."[38] Here, surely, is a key to James's own emphasis on style in his later fiction; it was at once the expression of the artist's personality (a quality he had first sought in romance) and a way of rendering "observable things" (the essential task of the novelist).

Yet he was disturbed by the lack of substance in D'Annunzio's work and by his treatment of aesthetic and sexual passion to the exclusion of "moral beauty." James therefore repeated the point that he had made in his essay on Serao: "Shut out from the rest of life," he wrote, " . . . [passion] has no more dignity than . . . the boots and shoes that we see, in the corridors of promiscuous hotels, standing, often in double pairs, at the doors of rooms."[39] Once again, we return to James's old demand for "character" and for moral seriousness, although, as Paul Maixner has noted, the mature critic differed from the young reviewer in regarding moral and aesthetic values as inseparable.[40]

These European authors—Loti, Serao, and D'Annunzio—thus had a real but limited value for James. They were significant cases because they integrated the romance and the novel, portraying passion but carefully recording their characters' mental states, writing in a personal style but using this to render the visible world. Yet in another respect, their art was incomplete, for they represented their characters as living in a vacuum, devoid of all feelings but passion and out of touch with the world around them. Hence, James reserved his highest praise not for the French and Italians but for Robert Louis Stevenson and Nathaniel Hawthorne, writers who could find romance in the lives of figures dwelling in a less rarefied atmosphere.

Stevenson was James's close friend from 1884, the date of "A Humble Remonstrance," until his death ten years later.[41] Not surprisingly, then, the first part of James's major essay on the author (1888) and most of his review of Stevenson's letters (1900) are personal rather than critical in emphasis. James was particularly impressed that his friend could "wave so gallantly the flag of the imaginary" despite being an invalid and that he could write from vicarious experience alone. Thus, like Sand, Stevenson proved that not all art need be based on observation, the theories of the naturalists notwithstanding. Further evidence of the writer's imagination lay in the variety of his work: "Each of his books is an independent effort—a window opened to a different view." And most significantly, Stevenson was "a writer with a style." "Character, character is what he has!" James averred in 1888;[42] and in 1900, he stated that the author had "become, by a process not purely mystic and not wholly untraceable ... a Figure."[43] It is easy to perceive James's love not merely for art but for the artist, the possessor of creative instinct.

Nonetheless, he was equally aware of the value of Stevenson's work. To a greater extent than the French and Italians, who relied heavily on the exotic and the picturesque, the British author related romance to the commonplace, thus showing how it might be incorporated into the novel. It was this that attracted James's interest; he praised *The New Arabian Nights*, for example, as being "the result of a very happy idea, that of placing a series of adventures which are pure adventures in the setting of contemporary English life, and relating them in the placidly ingenious [sic] tone of Scheherezade." His criticism of *Kidnapped* is in the same vein: "There could be no better instance of the author's talent for seeing the actual in the marvelous, and reducing the extravagant to plausible detail, than the description of Alan Breck's defense in the cabin of the ship, and the really magnificent chapters of 'The Flight in the Heather.'"[44] And in his essay of 1900, James cited Stevenson's unfinished romance, *Weir of Hermiston*, for having been written "in defiance of climate and nature"—that is, for depicting Scotland rather than the more exotic Samoa.[45]

The realistic texture of Stevenson's work was equally apparent in his tales of the supernatural; even when he wrote pure romance, he took care to make it plausible. "Thrawn Janet," for example, is a tale of a woman supposed to be possessed by the devil; but we see her only through the eyes of her employer, a minister, and one of his parishioners, who narrates the story. This use of the "reflector" was of obvious interest to James, who used the same device in his own ghostly tales. Similarly, he appreciated the subtlety of *Dr. Jekyll and Mr. Hyde*, which he liked not so much for "the profundity of the idea" as for "the art of presentation— the extremely successful form": "The way the two men [Mr. Utterson and the butler], at the door of the laboratory, discuss the identity of the mysterious personage inside . . . has those touches of which irresistible shudders are made." He only regretted that Stevenson had used the rather obvious device of the powders to explain Jekyll's transformation, an "uncanny process" which would have been "more conceivable . . . if the author had not made it so definite."[46] As Janet Adam Smith has noted,[47] both of these comments anticipate James's *Turn of the Screw*, in which he used a reflector to make the reader *"think* the evil" and avoided "weak specifications."[48]

Even more important was Stevenson's depiction of character, which set him apart from the Continental writers who dealt with passion alone. James's comments on *Kidnapped*, his favorite among the author's novels, are especially revealing: "[Stevenson] makes us say, Let the tradition [of Alexandre Dumas] live, by all means, since it was delightful; but at the same time he is the cause of our perceiving that a tradition is kept alive only by something being added to it. In this particular case . . . Mr. Stevenson has added psychology." And he went on to applaud the portrayal of Alan Breck, the Jacobite hero representing "the love of glory, carried out with extreme psychological truth," and of David Balfour, the Lowland boy possessing "those qualities which combine to excite our respect and our objurgation in the Scottish character."[49] He also admired the characterization of the lovers in *Weir of Hermiston*, who in their sensibilities, less violent than those of D'Annunzio's figures, remind one of his own characters.[50] And most significantly, he wrote of *Treasure Island* not only as a "record of queer chances" but as "a study of young feelings,"[51] thus departing from his earlier view (expressed in "The Art of Fiction") that the book had no psychological element to which he could "say Yes or No." Stevenson's example, then, was of crucial importance to James, for it showed him that romance and the "deeper psychology" could be combined. Indeed, his acquaintance with Stevenson may have led to his later, more sympathetic appraisal of Hawthorne.

As Peter Buitenhuis has noted, James's two later essays on Hawthorne—the first a preface in an anthology edited by Charles Dudley Warner (1897), and the second a letter written to Robert Rantoul for the observance of the author's centenary (1904)—are far more positive in tone than his study of 1879.[52] Unlike the earlier work, James's preface deals not with Hawthorne's life (which, he said, offered "little opportunity to the biographer") but with his work, which was distinguished by his "feeling for the latent romance of New England." This element, James continued, was "far from obvious," but it was discernible in "the spiritual contortions" and "the darkened outlook" of the Puritans and their descendants.[53] Moreover, James's comments on Hawthorne's fiction show his new interest in "latent" rather than overt romance. Initially, he had declared his preference for the somewhat melodramatic figures of Dimmesdale and Chillingworth, contrasting them with the "dim and chastened image" of Hester Prynne;[54] here, however, he stated that the portraits of the men were surpassed by "the image of the branded mother and the beautiful child."[55] Similarly, he no longer blamed Hawthorne for showing, in *The House of the Seven Gables*, a mistrust of picturesque detail and of "old lines of descent";[56] instead, he praised his subtlety in depicting "the mortal shrinkage of a family once uplifted, the last spasm of their starved gentility and flicker of their slow extinction." And in criticizing *The Blithedale Romance*, James ceased to dwell so exclusively on the dark heroine, Zenobia, but cited the book as "a picture of manners," the portrayal of a whole "company" bound together by its delusions. "All this," he added, "as we read it to-day, has a soft, shy glamour, a touch of the poetry of far-off things. Nothing of the author's is a happier expression of what I have called his sense of the romance of New England." Finally, he no longer took Hawthorne to task for his failure to appreciate Europe, but wrote sympathetically of "the strife between his sense of beauty and his sense of banishment." Thus, one does not receive the impression, as one occasionally does when reading James's earlier study, that Hawthorne was George Sand *manqué;* rather, one senses the critic's admiration for the author who could find "a mystery and a glamour where there were otherwise none very ready to [his] hand."[57]

This point is even more evident in James's letter of 1904,

which contrasts Hawthorne with conventional writers who take "the mechanical, at best the pedantic view of the list of romantic properties": "What was admirable and instinctive in Hawthorne was that he saw the quaintness or the weirdness, the interest *behind* the interest, of things, as continuous with the very life we are leading, or that we were leading . . . saw it as something deeply within us, not as something infinitely disconnected from us; saw it in short in the very application of the spectator's, the poet's mood, in the kind of reflection the things we know best and see oftenest may make in our minds." And he went on to describe Hawthorne's works as "singularly fruitful examples of the real as distinguished from the artificial romantic note."[58]

That James was keenly aware of Hawthorne's example may also be inferred from his essays on two later American authors. The first, Henry Harland, was an expatriate who had become the editor of the *Yellow Book* in London. Reviewing his *Comedies and Errors* in 1898, James expressed admiration for such stories as "The Friend of Man," a simple sketch of a philanthropist so caught up in his theories that he is completely insensitive to persons. There are "two quite distinct effects" produced by the short story, said James: "that of the detached incident, single and sharp, as clear as a pistol shot," and "that of the impression, comparatively generalised . . . of a complexity or a continuity." And he complimented Harland on having chosen the "risks" of the latter form: "The 'story' is nothing, the subject everything, and the manner in which the whole thing becomes expressive strikes me as an excellent specimen of what can be done on the minor scale when art comes in." But James was somewhat less impressed by the tales in which Harland was "lost in the vision, all whimsical and picturesque, of palace secrets, rulers and pretenders and ministers of bewilderingly light comedy, in undiscoverable Balkan states." He still found these romantic properties to be "charming," but added that when Harland "really stops and begins to dig . . . the critic will more attentively look out for him."[59]

The second writer was Mary E. Wilkins Freeman, who was best known for her local color tales of New England life but who also wrote *Silence and Other Stories* (1898), a volume of tales set in Colonial times, many of them depicting the supernatural. Commenting on the book in one of his "American Letters," James noted its inferiority to her other works: "The natural note is the touching, the stirring one; and thus it befalls that she really plays the trick, the trick the romancer tries for, much more effectually with the common objects about her than with the objects preserved, and sufficiently faded and dusty, in the cracked glass case of the rococo."[60] James's remark on Freeman's Colonial tales may also suggest something of his view of Hawthorne. Previously, he had criticized the author for not having been more of a romancer and for not having devoted more attention to the picturesque; but as time went on, he may have wished that Hawthorne had been more of a realist, that he had relied more on the "deeper psychology" and less on stock romantic properties. Indeed, there is a comment in his 1897 essay which suggests, however obliquely, that Hawthorne did not delve quite deeply enough into his characters: "On the surface—the surface of the soul and the edge of the tragedy—he preferred to remain. He lingered, to weave his web, in the thin exterior air."[61] James, of course, did sound the depths of character, having come to regard it as the supreme "adventure."

In his later career, then, James had comparatively little use for the romance as a genre but wished to incorporate some of its elements into the novel. Furthermore, his prefaces to his own works confirm the tendencies seen in his essays on other authors. He did acknowledge the romance as a separate form, one dealing with "experience liberated and disengaged"; that is, he no longer argued, as he had in "The Art of Fiction," that all authors necessarily dealt with "character." And he confessed that he was still "beset and beguiled" by his "love of 'a story as a story,'" calling this the "spolied child of art." Yet as he had devoted more space to Sand's creative power than to her melodramatic plots, so he found a "beguiling charm" not merely in his own stories but in the way he had written them, emphasizing how he had created his plots and characters from mere "germs" of observation and how he had found "romance" in his aesthetic labor. He also stressed that his characters, especially those endowed with passionate natures, might lend romance to the commonplace. Writing of *The Portrait of a Lady*, for example, he said that Isabel's "adventures" were "mild," but that "her sense of them" made them exciting: "isn't the beauty and the difficulty just in showing their mystic conversion by that sense, conversion into the stuff of drama or, even more delightful word still, of 'story'?" And in discussing his "ghostly tales," he called attention to their realistic texture and to their psychological interest: "The moving accident, the rare conjunction . . . doesn't make the story . . . ; the human emotion and the human attraction, the clustering human conditions we expect presented, only make it."[62] His essays on Stevenson and Hawthorne come easily to mind.

Not only does this criticism illuminate James's fiction, but it also helps to establish his place in literary history. Edwin Cady, in *The Light of Common Day*, has made a compelling case for classifying him as a realist—as an author for whom "the old world of spirit simply disappeared" and who therefore espoused humanism, a concern for "personhood alone." And to an extent James's critical essays confirm this judgment. His belief that pure romance was "irresponsible" surely stemmed from his rejection of ideality; his taste for the inverted romances of Daudet and Du Maurier show his awareness of the disappointments awaiting those who dreamt of transcendence (the theme, as Cady has noted, of *The Portrait of a Lady* and "The Beast in the Jungle"); and his praise of Hawthorne and Stevenson's psychological themes are evidence of his concern that fiction be grounded in human reality.[63]

Yet there are some aspects of James's writing which lead one to question his commitment to realism. As Cady suggests, novelists like Howells dealt with experience which was "common or shared, not highly personal or esoteric";[64] but James is well-known for his predilection to shun the banal as fictional material, to place his characters in extreme situations, and to depict motives of unusual intensity (though not, as a rule, the *passione* of Serao and D'Annunzio). One must also contend with James's persistent taste for "story"—a taste which is manifested not only in his supernatural tales but also in his major novels, in which, as John O'Neill has observed, the author "frequently manipulates character so as to give it a pathos, heroism, and a dignity unattainable were it left to the resources of its own internal development and forced to adhere to probability."[65] Then, too, there is the seeming anomaly of James's later style, which is far removed from conventional prose and is surely more than a device for evoking a "Common Vision."[66] His art is less puzzling, however, if one notes that he was not simply a realist and that the theory of fiction set forth in his essays is imaginative and expressive as well as mimetic and humanistic. He thus attempted to reconcile romance and realism, following the examples of Hawthorne, Stevenson, and other writers whose works defied easy categorization.

Nonetheless, it is true that he regarded himself primarily as a novelist and that he continued to view pure romancers as being in a dangerous position—in a balloon, on a tightrope, or lost at sea without provisions. We must therefore turn to his essays on Balzac and his descendants, the authors who remained on solid ground.

Chapter XIII
Revaluations: The Realists

WE HAVE seen that in his middle and later years, James found new values in the romance, which he had earlier considered to be trivial or superficial; but it is equally true that he reshaped his attitudes toward the realistic novel, which he had previously dismissed as unclean or uninteresting. Indeed, if one returns to his essays of the late 1880s, one finds that it was the realists even more than the romancers who were responsible for his increased flexibility and his determination to lay aside his *a priori* theories.

It has already been shown that James's 1885 essay on George Eliot marks an important change in his critical stance, in that it deemphasizes "philosophy" and dwells instead on the value of the artist's personal impressions. What is equally significant, however, is that it contains at least an implied defense of realism. As he reviewed John Cross's biography of his late wife, James observed that "its most interesting passage," the one he "should have been most sorry to lose," was a short entry in Eliot's journal of 1859: "We have just finished reading aloud Père Goriot, a hateful book." Eliot's reaction, James said, "illuminates the author's general attitude with regard to the novel, which, for her, was not primarily a picture of life, capable of deriving a high value from its form, but a moralized fable, the last word of a philosophy endeavoring to teach by example." And he went on to note Eliot's weakness in dealing with characters and situations in her own fiction: "They are deeply studied and elaborately justified, but they are not *seen* in the irresponsible plastic way."[1]

These comments are worthy of discussion, for they suggest both James's view of the novel and the direction that his criticism would take in years to come. One notices first his defense of Balzac against Eliot—a significant departure from his essays of the seventies, in which he had praised the latter for her profound sense of "life" and criticized the former for his superficiality. To be sure, he had always admired Balzac's gift for painting "pictures," as he had always disliked Eliot's excessive intellectuality; but the change in emphasis suggests that James was becoming more empirical not only in his critical approach but also in his literary taste, placing greater value on the author's ability to deal with the phenomenal world instead of adhering to preconceived views of "life" and "character." This is one reason why he ultimately came to regard Balzac as "the father of us all."

Another point of importance is James's use of the word "irresponsible" to describe the "plastic sense," a gift he in turn attributed to the French novelists. This, of course, represents a change from his earlier conception of "irresponsibility," which he had associated primarily with the works of Scott and Sand—that is, with fiction that was not only non-didactic but also romantic, affording the reader and author an escape from everyday life. Now, however, he suggested that a writer could exercise his imaginative freedom not by resorting to fantasy but by observing the world unencumbered by preconceived ideas. Such an attitude naturally opened the way to James's new appreciation of the realists, particularly of those who did not adhere too closely to deterministic theories. (Writing of Eliot's friend George Henry Lewes, and of his questionable influence on her fiction, he noted that "*scientific* observation" was "but another form" of "reflection"—the same reflection having impaired the author's work.)[2]

For further evidence of James's new sympathy for realism during the 1880s, we can return to his essay on Maupassant. His verdict on that novelist, one recalls, was rather ambiguous; at some points he wrote as a partisan "Anglo-Saxon," while at others he tried to be a judge dealing fairly with a "case," however embarrassing it might be. Yet two themes appear consistently throughout the essay. The first is that Maupassant is a brilliant if limited writer because of the power of his sensory impressions: "there is scarcely a page in all his twenty volumes that does not testify to their vivacity." The second is that Maupassant's would-be critics must separate his naturalistic theories from his artistic practice. As an example, James noted that *Pierre et Jean* (his favorite among the writer's works) was "a faultless production" because of its powerful treatment of jealousy and its depiction of the *petit bourgeoisie*. But he was much less enthusiastic about "Le Roman," an essay used by Maupassant as the preface to his novel. True, he joined in the French author's plea for artistic freedom, using it as the basis for his own defense of the "case"; yet in other respects, he said, the preface proved his personal dictum that the "doctrine is apt to be so much less inspired than the work," and the work "often so much more intelligent than the doctrine." In particular he disagreed with Maupassant's theory that psychology should be "hidden" in art as it is in life—an idea undermined by *Pierre et Jean* itself—and also with his belief in artistic impersonality: "M. de Maupassant is remarkably objective and impersonal, but he would go too far if he were to entertain the belief that he has kept himself out of his books. They speak of him eloquently, even if it only be to tell us how easy . . . he has found this impersonality.[3]

Here, of course, is a clear indication of the difference between the critic's view of art and that of the naturalists: whereas James held to a theory that was largely expressive and creative, the French had adopted one that was objective and scientific. This difference can also be seen in his argument against Maupassant's formula for "becoming original." In his essay Maupassant had repeated Flaubert's advice to aspiring authors: "to sit down in front of a blazing fire, or a tree in a plain, or any object [they] encounter. . . and remain there until . . . the object, whatever it be, become different for [them] from all other objects of the same class." But such advice, James said, was simply naive: "The best originality is the most unconscious, and the best way to describe a tree is the way in which it has struck us."[4] Again, the distinction between James's impressionism and the naturalists' emphasis on objectivity is quite apparent. More significant, however, was his willingness to lay aside Maupassant's theories, or rather to use the author's own works as evidence against them. Nowhere did he argue that Maupassant's fiction was unoriginal; on the contrary, he found the artist's personality reflected, for better or for worse, on every page of his writing.

This was an important development in James's critical viewpoint, because it enabled him to see the realists as writers whose works transcended their theories and as artists who were as creative, each in his own way, as George Sand was in hers.

James's recognition of Maupassant's originality can also be observed in his comments on the author's style. Indeed, so far as style was concerned he endorsed Maupassant's theory as well as his practice, quoting with approval his remarks (again derived from Flaubert) on the importance of the "mot juste" and on the difficulty of "drawing new sounds from the old familiar pipe" of the French language. Maupassant, added James, had been faithful to the "religion of his mother tongue," writing in a style "in which every phrase is a closed sequence, every epithet a paying piece, and the ground is completely cleared of the vague, the ready-made and the second-best."[5] As Maupassant rendered physical detail far more effectively than did Sand, so too did James use different terms when writing of the two authors; but once again, one sees his concern for style both as an expression of the artist's originality and as evidence of his aesthetic faith. One notices, too, that he found something inspiring—perhaps even romantic—in Maupassant's dedication to his lonely calling; in fact, he seems to have acquired a new sympathy for the realist, who struggled to forge a perfect style, as against the romancer, to whom eloquence came naturally. This impression is borne out by James's subsequent reappraisals of Maupassant's master, Gustave Flaubert.

The first of these, published in 1893, is more a portrait of the artist than a critique of his work—an emphasis dictated both by its being a review of Flaubert's correspondence and by James's belief that a writer's character determined the nature of his art. Furthermore, because James still thought of Flaubert as a cynical aesthete, the portrait is in many respects far from flattering; it depicts him as the artist "absolutely dishumanized," lacking in "elasticity," "good-humor," and a balanced view of human nature. "He should at least have listened at the chamber of the soul," concluded James. "This would have floated him on a deeper tide; above all it would have calmed his nerves."[6]

Yet these comments on "poor Flaubert" are less significant than James's respect for the artist, whom he also referred to as "an extraordinary, a magnificent 'case'" that only another writer could properly appreciate. Paradoxically, in James's view, Flaubert's worst vice was also his greatest virtue; if he was a narrow aesthete, he was also one who sacrificed himself for his art, going to any lengths to achieve "beauty of style" despite "the mortal indifference to it of empires and republics." And if Flaubert's existence was sterile, it was also, strangely enough, both rewarding and adventurous: "his life was that of a pearl-diver, breathless in the thick element while he groped for the priceless word, and condemned to plunge again and again." This same image of hard-won treasure appears elsewhere in the essay: "all that his reputation asks of you is an occasional tap of the knuckle at those firm thin plates of gold which constitute the leaves of his books."[7] Here, as in so many of James's later studies, the critic's images may be more important than his prose statements; as Maupassant, for all his faults, was ultimately a "lion in the path" of the would-be commentator, so Flaubert, whose faults resembled those of his disciple, was a seeker of treasure—one who not only provided an "adventure" for the critic but who himself had had experiences that a mere reader could hardly fathom. Thus, despite its echoes of his earlier strictures on Flaubert, this essay shows that James's attitude had changed considerably since 1884, when he had written that the French author and his friends, in worrying incessantly about the "torment of style," had had "the look of galley-slaves tied to a ball and chain."[8]

Some of the causes of James's shift in viewpoint have already been suggested, but they may be worth summarizing here. First, as David Cook has noted, the later James, who felt himself to be misunderstood by hostile readers and critics, probably identified his own situation with that of the "martyred" Flaubert and hence depicted the Frenchman as an author for the "initiated."[9] Moreover, as we saw in James's essay on Maupassant, his dismissal of the naturalists' scientific theories enabled him to regard these authors with a new sympathy. "'Impersonal' as he wished his work to be," he wrote of Flaubert, "it was his strange fortune to be the most expressive, the most vociferous, the most spontaneous of men."[10] Then, too, James distinguished Flaubert from his followers because of his single-minded devotion to his art. The Goncourts, for example, shared many of the master's strengths and weaknesses, yet their notorious journal, unlike Flaubert's letters, was so gossipy and sensational that it defaced their image as artists.[11] As for Zola, we shall see that in many respects the critic believed him to be a greater novelist than Flaubert; but it was the latter, with his passionate concern for stylistic beauty and for the *mot juste*, whom James perceived as his ally in the fight against vulgarity.

All of Flaubert's attributes—his lonely dedication to his art, his creative genius, and his hatred of the vulgar—led James toward the conclusion that the French author was not so much a committed realist as a would-be romantic. Indeed, the critic portrayed him as an artist struggling heroically to create formal beauty from unpromising material:

> Four times, with his *orgueil*, his love of magnificence, he condemned himself incongruously to the modern and familiar, groaning at every step over the horrible difficulty of reconciling "style" in such cases with truth and dialogue with surface. He wanted to do the battle of Thermopylae, and he found himself doing *Bouvard et Pécuchet*. One of the sides by which he interests us, one of the sides that will always endear him to the student, is his extraordinary ingenuity in lifting without falsifying, finding a middle way into grandeur and edging off from the literal without forsaking truth.

This is an important passage, for it suggests James's belief that Flaubert had a literary affinity with such authors as Stevenson and Hawthorne. The latter, as we have seen, reconciled romance and realism by lending substance to the unusual; Flaubert did the same by rendering beauty to the commonplace. In James's view, his effort fell short of success only because he had neglected moral questions and the deeper psychology: "No one will care for him at all who does not care for his metaphors, and those moreover who care most for these will be discreet enough to admit that even a style rich in similes is limited when it renders only the visible. The invisible Flaubert scarcely touches; . . . he had no faith in the power of the moral to offer a surface."[12] Such a comment brings to mind the criticism that James was later to make of Serao and D'Annunzio, authors who rendered the surface of life without treating its substance. Nonetheless, as Philip Grover has remarked, James himself emulated Flaubert in forging a language which was beautiful in itself and yet capable of presenting the banal and the trivial.[13]

Further evidence of James's regard for Flaubert may be found in the second of his later essays on the author, a preface to an English translation of *Madame Bovary* published in 1902. Here, he repeated almost all of his earlier strictures, even going so far as to say that the novelist was "more interesting . . . as a failure however qualified than as a success however explained." Yet taken as a whole, this essay is still more positive than James's study of 1893, ending not with a lament that the author ignored the soul but rather with the remark that more and more "perceptive private readers" had recognized *Madame Bovary* as a "classic." Concluded James: "Such is my reason, definitely, for speaking of Flaubert as the novelist's novelist. Are we not moreover—and let it pass this time as a happy hope!—pretty well all novelists now?"[14] One notices, then, a further shift in the critic's position: although previously he had dealt with Flaubert as a writer of interest mainly to other professional novelists, he now treated him as one whose classic work might be, and indeed ought to be, acknowledged by a growing number of readers.

This latter observation was prompted in part by an event that James had recorded in his "London Notes." In 1897 his friend Paul Bourget had lectured at Oxford on the subject of Flaubert and his works, James himself having been in the audience.[15] Writing of this occasion, the critic rejoiced "that the author of 'Madame Bovary' could receive in England a public baptism of such peculiar solemnity," adding: "No novelist . . . worth his salt could fail of a consciousness, under the impression, of his becoming rather more of a novelist than before."[16] Obviously James hoped that Flaubert might exert a beneficial influence on a reading public dominated by women and largely unconscious of literary form,[17] and praised the "novelist's novelist," who now was gaining some of the honor that he deserved, for having been among the first to defy popular taste.

But it was not external factors alone that accounted for James's altered perspective; it was also his recognition that *Madame Bovary* was indeed a masterpiece, a success making up for the failure of the author's other efforts.[18] In arriving at this appreciation of the novel, he was aided by the French critic Emile Faguet, whose study of Flaubert he called a "model" of its kind.[19] Like James in his essay of 1893, Faguet stressed the idea that Flaubert was a romantic who became a realist only because his conscience required him to do so: "Il était romantique en son fond même. . . . On peut dire de Flaubert que l'imagination était sa muse et la réalité sa conscience." And Faguet went on to say that it was the author's frustrated romantic tendency which enabled him to portray his heroine so vividly: "Le fond de l'âme de Madame Bovary, c'est le tour d'esprit romanesque."[20] Quite naturally, then, James, who had already noted Flaubert's taste for romance, elaborated on the critic's comments in his enthusiastic discussion of the novel: "[Flaubert's] separate idiosyncrasies, his irritated sensibility to the life around him, with the power to catch it in the fact and hold it hard, and his hunger for style and history and poetry, for the rich and the rare, great reverberations, great adumbrations, are here represented together as they are not in his later writings."[21] Thus, James no longer regarded *Madame Bovary* as an unpleasant and didactic book but instead saw it as evidence of its author's imaginative power.

Yet he disagreed with Faguet on two important points. The French critic, carried away by his admiration for Flaubert, pronounced *Madame Bovary* to be "le plus complet portrait de femme . . . dans toute la littérature, y compris Shakespeare, y compris Balzac."[22] James, in contrast, protested that this was not the case: "Our complaint is that Emma Bovary, in spite of the nature of her consciousness and in spite of her reflecting so much that of her creator, is really too small an affair."[23] This comment echoes James's old arguments against the realists' characters, serving as a reminder that even the later critic preferred superior subjects to more common ones.[24] Related to this preference was his belief that Emma, a limited figure, could not serve as a symbol of her sex or of humanity at large. In his study Faguet had argued that Flaubert's heroine did play such a role, being "assez générale pour être un sujet de méditation pour tous et pour toutes, assez particulière pour donner continuellement la sensation d'un être complètement et minitieusement vivant."[25] But James wrote of "the poverty of her consciousness for the typical function," arguing: "she is conditioned to such an excess of the specific, and the specific in her case leaves out so many even of the commoner elements of conceivable life in a woman when we are invited to see that life as pathetic, as dramatic agitation, that we challenge both the author's and the critic's scale of importances."[26] Here again, one observes James's bias in favor of heroines such as his own, figures who might lend to the novel some of the "poetry" of romance and who might symbolize the potential for "consciousness" inherent in all women.

To James, then, Flaubert was an author who did not quite succeed in uniting the romance and the novel; as his adherence to the "visible" limited his style, so his inability to create figures larger than life limited his characterizations. But he almost succeeded through the greatness of his art, his ability to confer on "sufficiently vulgar elements of exhibition a final unsurpassable form." As James wrote of *Madame Bovary*, "Where else shall we find in anything proportionately so small such an air of dignity of size? Flaubert *made* things big—it was his way, his ambition and his necessity." Moreover, it was through this effort that he overshadowed George Sand, whom James described as being "loose and liquid and iridescent" but capable of inspiring "compositions quite without virtue—the virtue, I mean, of sticking together."[27] Thus, although Flaubert did not create heroic figures, he became, in James's eyes, something of a hero himself.

One may still ask, however, why the critic persisted in regarding Flaubert's failure as more noteworthy than his success. The answer is that there were other realists who made that author's achievements appear limited, in much the same way that Hawthorne and Stevenson, as romancers, prevailed over Sand, Serao, and D'Annunzio. The former authors were superior to the latter because they stressed the psychological elements in romance; similarly, Henrik Ibsen surpassed Flaubert because he dramatized the romance inherent in psychological realism.

Ibsen's importance to James has sometimes been doubted, in part because James's own dramas, as Viris Cromer has observed, bear more resemblance to late Victorian social comedy than to the unconventional works of the Norwegian playwright.[28] Then, too, James's critical essays might lead one to believe that his tastes in drama were essentially conservative. He never devoted a full-length study to Ibsen (perhaps, according to Leon Edel, because he was reluctant to discuss an author whom he had read only in translation);[29] yet he did write a lengthy tribute to Alexandre Dumas, whose well-made plays were in many respects the antithesis of Ibsen's works.[30] Nonetheless, the dramatist's example was more important to him than these facts might indicate. Despite his own authorship of well-made plays, James seems to have had little respect for the form in which he worked;[31] and a reading of his essay on Dumas shows that he considered the French playwright "sentimentally" rather than "scientifically," as a character in his own right rather than as a creator of characters. The figures in Dumas' thesis plays, he wrote, lacked "a charm of mystery and poetry and oddity, a glory of unexpectedness."[32] These were precisely the qualities that he had found, though with some difficulty, in the characters of Ibsen.

James first became familiar with Ibsen's plays in 1891, having been urged to read them by his friend Edmund Gosse. To Gosse, Ibsen was admirable because he resisted the demand that modern writing be "light, amusing, romantic, and unreal." "There is no doubt." he stated in an article praising the dramatist, "that he takes his literary analysis and his moral curiosity very 'hard.'"[33] James respected his friend's desire for serious art yet looked with suspicion on authors who took life too hard—a failing, he complained to Gosse, which caused Ibsen's plays to be "of a grey mediocrity...

moral tales in dialogue without the objectivity, the visibility of the drama."[34] Upon seeing Elizabeth Robins play Hedda Gabler, however, he reversed his judgment and wrote a review of the drama which placed him on the side of the Ibsenites as against the conservative Victorians.[35] More readily than had Gosse, he conceded that he found it difficult to reconcile himself to "the absence of humor, the absence of free imagination, and the absence of style" in Ibsen's plays; in direct contrast to Hawthorne, he wrote, the dramatist never treated his material in a picturesque fashion, even when he might have had the incentive to do so. Yet elsewhere in the review, he described Ibsen in terms echoing his praise of Hawthorne, giving him credit for having "a mind saturated with the vision of human infirmities; saturated, above all, with a sense of the infinite, for all its mortal savor, of *character*, finding that an endless romance and a perpetual challenge." Like the other realists, Ibsen had chosen, in *Hedda Gabler*, to deal with an unpromising subject—"an exasperated woman"—but like the romancers, he had succeeded in giving her an aura of mystery: "She is various and sinuous and graceful, complicated and natural; she suffers, she struggles, she is human, and by that fact exposed to a dozen interpretations, to the importunity of our suspense." It seems clear, then, that James found more "poetry" in Hedda than in Madame Bovary, who was surely another "exasperated woman" but who had been reduced in stature as the result of Flaubert's analytical, undramatic technique. Furthermore, he admired the intensity achieved by Ibsen through his focus on the heroine, her passions, and their effect on those around her: "Wrought with admirable closeness is the whole tissue of relations between [sic] the five people whom the author sets in motion and on whose behalf he asks of us so few concessions. . . . The spectator's situation is different enough when what is given him is the mere dead rattle of the surface of life, into which *he* has to inject the element of thought, the 'human interest.'"[36] This comment in particular shows the distinction James made between Ibsen and those realists who remained outside "the chamber of the soul."

His later reviews express his interest not only in the psychology of Ibsen's characters, but also in their symbolic function. Initially, as he discussed *Hedda Gabler*, he wondered whether the playwright did not lose sight of the "type-quality" of his figures, giving "his spectators free play to say that even caught in the fact his individuals are mad."[37] But according to Leon Edel, a letter from one of Ibsen's translators,

William Archer, may have changed James's mind on this point. Calling Ibsen "the greatest *poet* who has as yet enslaved himself to the conditions of realistic, or perhaps I should rather say everyday, drama," Archer wrote: "Remember, it is not as a realist, but rather as a symbolist, that I chiefly admire Ibsen."[38] Thereafter, James saw Ibsen's characters as being larger than life and as having the "type-quality" that Madame Bovary lacked. In 1893, writing of *The Master Builder*, he observed that its heroine is not merely a less blasée version of Hedda but a symbol of the protagonist's youth and fate: "Hilde Wangel, a young woman whom the author may well be trusted to have made more mystifying than her curiously charmless name would suggest, is only the indirect form, the animated clock-face, as it were, of Halvard Solness's destiny; but the action, in spite of obscurities and ironies, takes its course by steps none the less irresistible. The mingled reality and symbolism of it all gives us an Ibsen within an Ibsen."[39] And in 1897, writing of *John Gabriel Borkman*, James noted that its characters—a defeated man with delusions of grandeur, his emotionally sterile wife, his jealous sister-in-law, and his son, through whom the others attempt to redeem their wasted lives—are

> highly animated abstractions, with the extraordinary, the brilliant property of becoming, when represented, at once more abstract and more living. . . . There is no small-talk, there are scarcely any manners. . . . The background, at any rate, is the sunset over the ice. Well in the very front of the scene lunges, with extraordinary length of arm, the Ego against the Ego, and rocks, in a rigor of passion, the soul against the soul—a spectacle, a movement, as definite as the relief of silhouettes in black paper or of Eskimo dogs on the snow.[40]

Brief though they are, these passages suggest the reason for James's fascination with Ibsen. As John O'Neill has noted in *Workable Design*, the author's novels, notwithstanding their depiction of "small-talk" and "manners," deal essentially with the polar conflicts between figures who symbolize divergent human passions. In *The Spoils of Poynton*, for example, the source of the drama is the struggle between Fleda Vetch, who embodies selflessness, and Mrs. Gereth, who represents possessiveness; in *The Wings of the Dove*, it is the opposition of Milly, who personifies transcendent love, to Kate, who symbolizes the desire for social and sexual power.[41] And as Michael Egan has suggested, both of these novels may have been inspired by Ibsen, notable as he was for his "intense investigations of character, of states of mind and soul."[42]

But there was another author whose works James had

known for several decades, and who was equally famous for his use of symbolic drama: Honoré de Balzac, the great writer of "realistic romances." In 1875 the critic had described his fiction in precisely these terms; yet because of his concern for moral seriousness, he believed him to be superficial in comparison to Turgenev and Eliot. Subsequently, however, he could hardly have forgotten Balzac, although he did not again deal with him at length until the turn of the century. One thinks, for example, of *The Princess Casamassima* (1885), his most Balzacian novel, and of his essay on Eliot (1885), with its reference to the French author as a painter of pictures rather than a writer of moralized fables. And James's essays on Flaubert, whom he had first identified as Balzac's pupil, inevitably remind one of the older novelist if only through the principle of contrast: whereas Flaubert, in James's view, had written but one great novel, Balzac had written many; whereas Flaubert had created a single memorable character, Balzac, like Shakespeare, had depicted a gallery of colorful figures. As for Ibsen, his plays may well have renewed James's interest in the "vision of human infirmities" that Balzac also shared; yet the dramatist, restricted by a genre demanding "selection," had to neglect the depiction of manners and the delineation of his characters' "histories"[43]—two salient aspects of Balzac's fiction and indeed of James's own. The critic's awareness of Balzac during the 1890s is, of course, a subject for speculation, but it is clear that the author's importance to him increased as he himself entered his "major phase." In 1899 he referred to Balzac as one of the novelists of his youth who towered above his successors;[44] in 1902 he eagerly accepted Edmund Gosse's invitation to write a preface to a translation of *Les Deux Jeunes Mariées*—a piece that turned out to be a major essay on the author; and in 1905, while on a lecture tour of the United States, he spoke to a fashionable Philadelphia audience on "The Lesson of Balzac."[45]

James's preface of 1902 is a fascinating piece of criticism, for even more than in his eassays on Flaubert, his metaphors predominate over his prose statements. Initially he confesses that he is akin to "the Prodigal Son" coming back "to the parental threshold and hearthstone, if not, more fortunately, to the parental presence." The reason for his long neglect of his literary father is implied by images suggesting that Balzac is too great to be easily analyzed: he is likened to "Gulliver among the pigmies," to a monument so massive that one can hardly walk around it, to a "mysterious and various stranger" who "makes us fold up our yard-measure and put away our note-book," and to "an army gathered to besiege a cottage equally with a city, and living voraciously, in either case, on all the country about."[46] Immediately, then, one notices the difference in tone between this essay and James's study of 1875; whereas the young critic had written rather self-confidently of Balzac, praising his "power" but lamenting his lack of "charm," the later James was much more conscious of the novelist's greatness and hence less self-assured in evaluating his work.

Perhaps because of his own difficulty in dealing with his subject, James wrote with feeling about Balzac's attempt to create art out of the "multitudinousness" of life. Here again he turned to metaphor, likening Balzac to a "rare animal" trapped in the cage of "the dreadfully definite French world that . . . roofed itself so impenetrably over him." Elaborating on this image, he added that the novelist was not merely "caged" but held in "the convolutions of the serpent he had with a magnificent courage invited to wind itself round him." Clearly these passages evoke Balzac's effort to treat the whole of French life, an attempt so overwhelming that it caused his premature death at age fifty. Moreover, in James's view, his desire for completeness took an aesthetic toll, for the unity of his work suffered whenever the artist handed over his data "to his twin brother the impassioned economist and surveyor." As an example, the critic cited *Le Curé de village*, the study of a woman who shields her lover after he has committed a murder and who consequently suffers terrible remorse. Her "drama" interested James to "the highest degree"; but when Balzac transferred his attention "from the centre of his subject to its circumference"—that is, when he dealt with matters of irrigation, land management, and other projects to which Madame Graslin lends her support in expiation of her sin— the critic found that he was no longer under the novelist's "spell."[47] This comment, of course, reminds one of James's early preference for unity and for psychological focus, yet one also notices his new tolerance of Balzac's heroines. In 1875 he used Madame Graslin's story as an example of how "purity in Balzac's hands is apt to play us the strangest tricks";[48] but in 1902 he only wished that Balzac had dealt with the adulteress more intensively.

Furthermore, though he wrote at length of the novelist's "catastrophe," James also discussed the ways in which he broke out of the cage of ponderous realism. Balzac's strength, he wrote, was his ability "to bring the fantastic into the circle and fit it somehow to his conditions"—that is, to incorporate romance into the novel. As an illustration, he described an episode in *Les Illusions perdues*, a scene in which the Parisian Madame Bargeton "chucks" the provincial Lucien de Rubempré because her fashionable friend, Madame d'Espard, is shocked by his cheap clothing. This scene, said James,

> is either a magnificent lurid document or the baseless fabric of a vision. The great wonder is that, as I rejoice to put it, we can never really discover which, and that we feel, as we read, that we can't, and that we suffer at the hands of no other author this particular helplessness of immersion. . . . He warms his facts into life. . . . If the great ladies in question *didn't* behave, wouldn't, couldn't have behaved, like a pair of frightened snobs, why, so much the worse, we say to ourselves, for the great ladies in question. We *know* them to be so—they owe their being to our so seeing them.[49]

As Peter Brooks has noted, the early James had cited this same incident to exemplify Balzac's lack of taste and his overdramatization of his characters; yet the later James obviously came to enjoy the author's melodrama, or in Brooks's words, the "intense, excessive representations of life" which reveal the conflicts behind the facade of everyday manners.[50] That James admired this intensity as a means of transcending realism is confirmed by his description of Louise de Chaulieu, the anti-heroine of Balzac's epistolary novel *Les Deux Jeunes Mariées*. In her letters to her friend, who has settled for happy domesticity, the passionate Louise seems incredibly hot-headed and egotistical; however, observed the critic, "we swallow her bragging, against our better reason, or at any rate our startled sense, under coercion of the total intensity." Balzac, then, more than any other novelist, conveyed the adventure inherent in "character" by allowing his most passionate figures to express themselves through language and through symbolic gestures. This, concluded James, was the result not merely of the novelist's art but of his "hunger . . . to take on, in all freedom, another nature"; indeed, he possessed "the very spirit and secret of transmigration."[51]

James's lecture of 1905, "The Lesson of Balzac," is even more laudatory than his preface, the critic having adopted his subject's extravagance as the most fitting mode of doing him honor. Here James represents himself not merely as a prodigal son but as one "who is conscious of so large a debt to repay that it has had positively to be discharged in instalments"; Balzac becomes not just the author's father, but "the father of us all" and the only one who can enable the family to "pull itself together"; he is no longer in a cage, but riding "astride of his imagination"; and the monument in the critic's path has been transformed into "a towering idol" in "the sacred grove," gilded thick "with so much gold—plated and burnished and bright." Obviously some of this rhetoric was for dramatic effect, the result of James's desire to impress his audience. Then, too, he presented Balzac as a "father" and "idol" partly because he furnished a lesson to "our huge Anglo-Saxon array of producers and readers" that other novelists could not. George Sand, for one, was "eloquent," but her work had "about as few pegs for analysis to hang upon as if it were a large, polished, gilded Easter egg"; she and George Meredith, said James, wrote mainly from a lyrical impulse, presenting "not the *image* of life . . . so much as life itself." The romancers thus encouraged "sentimental judgment"—the kind of adulation given to the Brontë sisters by a public that confused life with art. As for Jane Austen, another sentimental favorite, the critic wrote that she "leaves us hardly more conscious of her process, or of the experience in her that fed it, than the brown thrush who tells his story from the garden bough." But Balzac, in contrast to the romancers, created believable characters, and in contrast to Austen, got deep into their "consciousness," their "very skin and bones": "There is no such thing in the world as an adventure pure and simple; there is only mine and yours, and his and hers—it being the greatest adventure of all, I verily think, just to *be* you or I, just to be he or she. To Balzac's imagination that was indeed in itself an immense adventure— and nothing appealed to him more than to show *how* we all are, and how we are placed and built-in for being so."[52]

James proceeded with his "lesson" by discussing Balzac's techniques, the ways in which he rendered his characters and their adventures. That he dealt with the author's methods was in itself a tribute to him, for despite his interest in literary form, he seldom treated matters of "execution" unless he was convinced of the writer's "dignity" and of his "saturation with his idea." (There is almost no technical discussion, for example, in James's essays on Sand or in his later reviews of minor novelists.) One thing he admired in Balzac's fiction was its dense texture; his descriptions of the "outward and inward" aspects of his characters gave them both solidity and "intensity," as in the scene showing Madame d'Espard's reaction to Lucien's green coat, white trousers, and cheap vest. Also contributing to this effect was his narrative technique—not his philosophical digressions, which James disliked, but his rendering of his characters' consciousness, allowing the reader to see their situation "from their point of vision." In this respect, James added, Balzac's technique was the opposite of Thackeray's; whereas the "English writer wants to make sure, first of all, of your moral judgment[,] the French is willing, while it waits a little, to risk, for the sake of his subject, your spiritual salvation." Early in his career, one recalls, James had objected to narratorial intrusions that robbed characters of their "liberty"; but here he showed a new enthusiasm for "intensity" as opposed to moral seriousness, contrasting Becky Sharpe, whom Thackeray had merely "exposed," with Balzac's Madame Marneffe, whom her creator "loved" and could therefore bring to life.[53]

James also commended Balzac for balancing "the art of complete representation," the delineation of his characters' backgrounds, against the demands of "composition," which entailed "foreshortening."[54] As readers of James's Prefaces are aware, this was one of his major preoccupations: if a novelist were not "complete," his figures might seem factitious, yet if he were too thorough, he might lose sight of his subject.[55] To be sure, James had accused Balzac of falling into the latter error; but in *Père Goriot,* he said, the artist had united all elements of his "picture"—character, action, setting, and social conditions—to create a coherent whole. Finally, he praised Balzac for representing "the lapse of time" in his novels without resorting to "a blank space" or a "row of stars" and without overusing dialogue, which "has its function perverted, and therewith its life destroyed, when forced, all clumsily, into the constructive office."[56] What James meant by this was that Balzac focussed on his characters' perception of time, reporting on their sense of the way things happened instead of using their conversations to inform the reader of prior events. As the critic wrote in one of his "London Notes," many modern writers failed to convey the sense of the "dark backward and abysm" that the French author created so well.[57]

Thus, Balzac was the novelist whom James ultimately regarded as his master; by his own account, he "learned from him more of the lessons of the engaging mystery of fiction than from any one else."[58] Unlike Flaubert, Balzac depicted a multitude of figures whose gestures and speech made them seem larger than life, and unlike Ibsen, he dealt with his characters' histories, showing that the story of how they came to be as they were was as exciting as the drama of their passions. Not surprisingly, then, James forgave him for the occasional lack of composition in his works and for the coarseness that had offended some critics, including himself. Indeed, his last essay on the novelist, written in 1913, defends him against a critique similar to his own study of 1875. Like the younger James, Emile Faguet had written of Balzac in a laudatory yet somewhat snobbish manner, depicting him as a creator of powerful characters yet chastizing him for his lack of "philosophy" and for the vulgarity which spoiled most of his work.[59] Reviewing Faguet's book, James conceded Balzac's inability to depict the "cultivated consciousness" but added that the author's "vulgarity—since we are not afraid of the word"—was "a force that simply got nearer than any other could have done to the whole detail, the whole intimate and evidenced story, of submission and perversion, and as such it could but prove itself immensely human."[60]

James's acknowledgment of Balzac may have led to his revaluation of Emile Zola, who derived his inspiration from his "literary great-grandfather's heroic example."[61] As there was a long interval between James's early and late studies of Balzac, so too was there a gap between his 1880 review of *Nana* and his 1903 essay on the naturalist; and again, he became more tolerant in the course of the intervening years. For one thing, he acquired a measure of personal sympathy for Zola after another meeting with him in 1893. "Nothing, literally nothing," he told Robert Louis Stevenson, "has ever happened to him but to write the Rougon-Macquart."[62] As we shall see, this observation renewed his sense of Zola's weakness, but it also increased his respect for the artist as a lonely and prodigious worker, a descendant of Balzac and a colleague of Flaubert. Furthermore, Zola's participation in the Dreyfus affair, in which he emerged as a "hero," made him a more human figure in James's eyes,[63] while he also gained in importance as an artist because of the general dearth of literary talent in the 1890s. Hence, the critic's gloomy survey of "The Present Literary Situation in France" refers to him as a "patriarch," a "large enough figure to make us lose time in walking around him for the most convenient view,"[64] and his memorial essay identifies him as one of the few modern "cases" worth studying.[65] Finally, one must recall James's lessening concern for "philosophy" and his growing interest in Balzacian "representation"—an interest which caused him to re-examine novels portraying "an immense deal of life," though not the "cultivated consciousness."[66]

But as James made clear in his study of 1903, Zola's art was hampered by his scientific theories; whereas Balzac was "overtaken by life," the younger author seldom quit "his magnificent treadmill of the pigeonholed and documented." This meant that he had to sacrifice the "shades" of individual characters in order to deal with the passions common to all men, and hence that he oversimplified his fiction: "He was *obliged* to be gross."[67] Two years later, in "The Lesson of Balzac," James repeated the point, again contrasting Zola's "mechanical" art with Balzac's treatment of the "individual case . . . that permits of supreme fineness."[68] The elder novelist, then, was superior to Zola because he adhered to no theories that made him lose sight of human idiosyncrasies. And although Balzac was hardly notable for his taste or for his intellectual modesty, his literary great-grandson had still less "discretion"; even as he paid tribute to Zola, James ruefully recalled his saying that he had never been to Rome and then announcing that he would make that city the subject of a future novel. To the critic this incident proved a melancholy dictum: that when an artist lacks "Taste," his "imagination itself inevitably breaks down as a consequence." Both of Zola's failings—his tastelessness and his reduction of his characters to mere automatons—were evident in his thesis novels, which were even more dogmatic than Balzac's philosophical fiction. *Vérité*, the last of his works, was also one of the worst; inspired by the Dreyfus affair, it portrays a schoolmaster who invariably champions "Truth," defending a Jewish colleague falsely accused of murder, establishing public schools in opposition to religious ones, making his Catholic wife see the error of her ways, and in the end presiding over a nearly utopian society after defeating a series of cardboard villains. Quite justly, James observed that the novel was a failure: "We really rub our eyes," he said, " . . . to see so great an intellectual adventure as Les Rougon-Macquart terminate in unmistakable desert sand."[69]

Yet even in this observation, his respect for Zola is evident, and it is equally clear that he had passed far beyond the point of attacking the naturalist merely for his "uncleanness." Moreover, he acknowledged that Zola's fiction, like that of Maupassant and Flaubert, was sometimes better than the theory underlying it. His description of *L'Assommoir*, for example, reminds one of his praise of Balzac's novels: "Gervaise . . . is a lame washerwoman, loose and gluttonous, without will, without any principle of cohesion, the sport of every wind that assaults her exposed life, and who, rolling from one gross mistake to another, finds her end in misery, drink, and despair. But her career . . . has fairly the largeness that . . . we feel as epic, and the intensity of her creator's vision of it and of the dense sordid life hanging about it is to my sense one of the great things the modern novel has been able to do." Because Gervaise seemed the most human of Zola's characters, *L'Assommoir* was always the critic's favorite among his works; yet here again, one sees the difference between this essay and James's earlier reviews. Previously his distaste for the novel had almost overshadowed his respect for its power; but now he expressed unqualified admiration for Zola's art, even admitting that "the thing would have suffered from timidity. The qualification of the painter was precisely his strength of stomach." Furthermore, he took a new interest in Zola's social novels, again because of his liking for their intensity: "To make his characters swarm, and to make the great central thing they swarm about 'as large as life,' portentously, heroically big . . . that was the secret he triumphantly mastered." In particular he praised *Germinal*, Zola's depiction of coal mining, and *La Débâcle*, his chronicle of the French defeat at Sedan during the Franco-Prussian War: "The long, complex, horrific, pathetic battle . . . was 'done' . . . in a way to shut our mouths."[70] Obviously, then, he applauded Zola's vividness, his ability to make his figures assume heroic dimensions, and his "intensity"—a key word in this essay, as it is in the critic's studies of Balzac. And although it has been observed that Zola's fiction was fundamentally different from James's,[71] one also recalls the latter's desire to give "intensity" to his own fiction, especially in his rendering of such figures as the "compromised and compromising father" of Kate Croy (*The Wings of the Dove*).[72] It would seem, then, that James was posing more than a rhetorical question when he wrote of Zola's fiction: "How in the world is it made, this deplorable, democratic, malodorous Common, so strange and so interesting?" At his worst, Zola was merely "mechanical"; but at his best, he joined Balzac in making the commonplace "receive into its loins the stuff of the epic and still, in spite of this association with poetry, never depart from its nature."[73]

It is clear, then, that the later James acquired a new taste for realism, particularly when it included an element of romance. In Flaubert's fiction, this was created primarily by a style which lent beauty to the commonplace; in the works of Balzac and Zola, it was achieved through characters and events so colorful that they assumed symbolic or "epic" proportions. Moreover, James accepted the premise underlying all realistic fiction—that it is the task of the novelist to deal with the life around him, not with fantasy, mythology, or philosophy. In this respect, of course, the critic was very much a member of the post-Emersonian generation. Yet one cannot describe James as a "realist" without qualifying the term. Unlike William Dean Howells and many of his other contemporaries, he never saw the depiction of ordinary life as an end in itself; rather, he looked for "intensity," for realistic detail that had a degree of symbolic resonance. And despite his acceptance of Balzac and Zola, he still believed the "cultivated consciousness" to be the most rewarding of literary subjects. Indeed, there was a certain ambivalence in his outlook apparent whenever he wrote of an author and his *donnée;* although he praised George Gissing for his "contact with the lower, with the lowest middle-class,"[74] he continued to value Ivan Turgenev precisely because he did not deal with "vulgar things," having chosen instead to portray a gallery of "nobly disinterested" heroines.[75] He also persisted in regarding character as the "center" of the novel and hence in criticizing most fiction for its lack of structure. Apart from his own Prefaces, the best exposition of his theory of the "center" is found in "The Novel in *The Ring and the Book*," an address he delivered in 1912 to the Royal Society of Literature. In the course of this speech he explained how he would rewrite Browning's poem, converting it from a series of dramatic monologues to a novel whose central consciousness would be that of Canon Caponsacchi: "To lift our subject out of the sphere of anecdote and place it in the sphere of drama, liberally considered, to give it dignity by extracting its finest importance, causing its parts to flower together into some splendid special sense, we supply it with a large reflector, which we find only . . . in that mind and soul concerned in the business that have at once the highest sensibility and the highest capacity, or that are . . . most admirably agitated."[76] Quite naturally, then, James perceived a lack of unity in the fiction of Balzac and Zola despite his admiration for its "epic" qualities, and even late in his career, continued to cite Turgenev as the great master of literary form.[77]

The disparity between James's position and that of the orthodox realists is most clearly seen in his last major essay, "The Younger Generation" (1914). This title refers to Arnold Bennett, H. G. Wells, and their contemporaries—novelists characterized by their "saturation" with their material and their "appetite for a closer notation" of its details. In James's view, "saturation" was indeed a "value," but his own conception of the novel still differed markedly from that of the authors about whom he wrote. As he himself noted, Bennett and Wells were explicitly anti-romantic;[78] unlike

Flaubert, they attached little value to stylistic beauty, and unlike Balzac or even Zola, they made little attempt to show the "adventure" inherent in ordinary life, focusing instead on its mundane aspects. Moreover, their desire to write social novels precluded their rendering the complexities of character; Wells in particular challenged the prevalence of the "character-interest" in fiction to the exclusion of "issues of custom and political and social change."[79] Thus, according to James's standards, their novels seemed amorphous and devoid of a proper center. The chief metaphor he used to describe their art—or rather, their artlessness—was that of the squeezing of an orange, an image suggesting both the richness of "life" and the crudity with which they treated it. And sometimes he resorted to more negative images, as when he referred to Bennett's *Clayhanger*, the annals of a provincial printer, as a heap of "stones and bricks and rubble and cement," and as when he wrote of Wells: "The more he knows and knows, . . . the greater is our impression of his holding it good enough for us, such as we are, that he shall but turn out his mind and its contents upon us by any free familiar gesture and as from a high window forever open."[80] Overtly, James admired Bennett's diligence and Wells's intellectual curiosity, but his fundamental distaste for these authors was so great that even his compliments on their work assumed a double meaning. (One thinks, for example, of a letter he wrote to Wells after reading *The New Machiavelli:* "Your big feeling for life, your capacity for chewing up the thickness of the world in such enormous mouthfuls, while you fairly slobber, so to speak, with the multitudinous taste—this constitutes for me a rare and wonderful exhibition.")[81]

There were some members of the "younger generation" whom James treated more favorably, but in many cases his motives seem to have been personal rather than literary. He could hardly avoid being kind to his protegé Hugh Walpole, whose society novel, *The Duchess of Wrexe*, included numerous quotations from the Master's fiction and had a superficially Jamesian theme—the idea that everybody must face the "Tiger" within himself. In return for this tribute James commented favorably on Walpole's youth but avoided any discussion of his fiction. More serious was his praise of his friend Edith Wharton, who stood apart from her contemporaries because of her sense of "artistic economy" and her concern for style and metaphor. Furthermore, he admired the incisive satire in *The Custom of the Country*, her chronicle of a vulgar, social-climbing woman who preys first on an

American gentleman and then on a French nobleman and his family.[82] But as Millicent Bell has noted, James's commendation of the novel may have been somewhat less than sincere; privately, he accused Mrs. Wharton of having neglected a "magnificent subject" which ought to have been her "main theme." He probably wished that she had dwelt more on the psychology of her heroine and on the nuances of her relationship to the French family[83]—in other words, that she had treated Undine Spragg as Balzac had treated Madame Marneffe, making her an object of fascination rather than of simple irony. The only young novelist whose characters did hold such an interest for James was Compton Mackenzie, a writer of *bildungsromanen* as opposed to mere chronicles. Because of its portrayal of "boyish consciousness," the critic gave special notice to his *Sinister Street* (Volume I),[84] the account of a lad who becomes increasingly sensitive to the rituals of the Catholic Church, to the poetry of Keats and Swinburne, and to the fact of his own illegitimacy. The novel was loosely structured, James wrote, and its episodes were strung together like beads on a cord; yet some of these—for example, the scene of young Michael's meeting with a depraved monk—showed Mackenzie's flair for the "literary gesture," a gift James obviously appreciated.[85] Here again, one observes the critic's taste for vivid portraiture, which could redeem the "new" novel from dullness and triviality.

Notwithstanding its lukewarm praise of the younger generation, James's essay is best remembered—and most frequently criticized—for its pejorative references to two of his most famous contemporaries, D. H. Lawrence and Joseph Conrad. The former was briefly mentioned as a novelist hanging "in the dusty rear" of the others, one whose *Sons and Lovers* might be dealt with if the critic wished to be "very friendly" to him;[86] the latter, though scarcely "young," was subjected to a lengthier treatment which he rightly perceived to be condescending.[87] If one recalls James's dislike of "physiological" detail, one can understand his lack of enthusiasm for Lawrence; after all, he had struggled valiantly to overcome his antagonism toward the naturalists and may well have been unwilling, in his later years, to take on a still more difficult "case." His reaction to Conrad's *Chance*, however, is more puzzling and requires further explanation. Unlike most of the "new" fiction, *Chance* was not a social chronicle but a carefully structured novel concerning the oddities of human character. Its heroine, Flora, brings out the romantic impulse in a series of Conradian idealists: her father, DeBarral, an ex-convict who is jealously possessive of her; her husband, Captain Anthony, who takes her and her father aboard his ship despite the older man's hatred and her own apparent indifference; and a sailor, Powell, who befriends her and Anthony, saving the latter's life when DeBarral tries to poison him. But the real protagonist is Marlow, the principal narrator, who reconstructs the complex plot and speculates on the mysteries of women, the mad generosity of men, and the fate that brings them together. One might think that James would have approved of Conrad's psychological themes and of his use of a "reflector"; and indeed, he did praise him for standing alone as "a votary of the way to do a thing that shall make it undergo most doing." Yet he went on to criticize the vagueness of the novel, the "baffled relation between the subject-matter and its emergence," and the needless complexity of Conrad's narrative technique:

> It literally strikes us that his volume sets in motion more than anything else a drama in which his own system and his combined eccentricities of recital represent the protagonist in face of powers leagued against it, and of which the *dénouement* gives us the system fighting in triumph, though with its back desperately to the wall, and laying the powers piled up at its feet. This frankly has been *our* spectacle, our suspense and our thrill; with the one flaw on the roundness of it all the fact that the predicament was not imposed rather than invoked, was not the effect of a challenge from without, but that of a mystic impulse from within.[88]

One may ask, then, whether James was not perverse in his judgments, criticizing Wells and Bennett for their lack of artistry while condemning Conrad for his excessive fascination with technique. But a reading of *Chance* may lead one to conclude that it was Conrad who was perverse, both in his choice of banal subject-matter and in his use of Marlow to invest it with a spurious profundity.[89] For example, after Fyne, an unimaginative civil servant, becomes Flora's temporary guardian, Marlow insists that "The possibilities of dull men are exciting"; and when Flora falls prey to a scheming governess and her "nephew," he philosophizes at length on the girl's awakening to evil:

> her unconsciousness was to be broken into with profane violence, with desecrating circumstances like a temple violated by a mad, vengeful impiety. . . . And if you ask me how, wherefore, for what reason? I will answer you: Why, by chance! By the merest chance as things do happen, lucky and unlucky, terrible or tender, important or unimportant; and even things which are neither, things so completely neutral

in character that you would wonder why they do happen at all if you didn't know that they, too, carry in their insignificance the seeds of further incalculable chances.[90]

To an extent, as Ian Watt has observed, Conrad's technique here is quite Jamesian;[91] he uses Marlow to reveal the romance in the commonplace and to elaborate on the psychological significance of melodrama. But precisely because Conrad did adhere to James's formulae, the critic was probably distressed at his carrying them to an extreme verging on parody. Further, James may well have been vexed at the popularity of *Chance*, which far exceeded that of his own fiction.[92] In his essay he gave credit to the reading public for its appreciation of Conrad's technical subtleties; but his concluding remark—"Great then would seem to be after all the common reader!"[93]—suggests a certain degree of irony, an implied doubt as to whether the novel had succeeded because of its author's artistry or because of his exploitation of popular themes.

There were thus limits to James's flexibility; he disliked both Conrad's neglect of substance and the realists' neglect of form, and his re-reading of nineteenth-century authors, the inhabitants of his "own house," did little to make him more charitable toward his younger contemporaries. Yet it did have a profound influence on his own work, as the briefest examination of his Prefaces will show. There one confirms his acceptance of the lesson of Balzac, that "the art of interesting us in things . . . can *only* be the art of representing them." And whereas the younger James feared that the values of romance might have to be sacrificed to those of "representation," the later James, through his knowledge of the realists and their works, came to believe that the novel might be given a symbolic, poetic, or epic dimension. When he writes, for example, of how style and composition can confer an interest on "vulgar" material, one discerns the influence of Flaubert, and when he states that the "fictive hero" should be a "typical" yet "eminent instance . . . of our own conscious kind," one thinks of his reviews of Ibsen. Moreover, despite his concern for the protagonist as "center," James also wanted his figures to be "connected . . . with the general human exposure"; like Balzac and Zola, he too wished to be an historian, showing how his characters came to be as they were. And throughout the Prefaces, one perceives his concern for "intensity," which counterbalanced his preoccupation with the "cultivated consciousness." True, he observed that "there are degrees of merit in subjects"; yet he also wrote, "The thing of profit is to *have* your experience—to recognise it and understand it, and for this almost any will do; there being no absolute ideal about it beyond getting from it all it has to give."[94] It was this attitude, derived from his reading of Balzac and his followers, which in turn enabled him to adapt the lessons of their art to the demands of his own.

Chapter XIV
Henry James in Perspective

BECAUSE of their number and complexity, James's critical essays cannot easily be summarized—a fact significant in itself, as it dispels some myths concerning the author and his place in literary history. For one thing, it is clear that he was hardly an isolated figure who derived his inspiration solely from his own sensibility. It is true, of course, that his familiarity with nineteenth-century fiction was far greater than his knowledge of literature in general, and also that he maintained his independence rather than joining any school of writers, French, British, or American. Yet his essays and reviews attest to his close reading of a large variety of novels, both major and minor, and of a smaller but substantial body of poetry and non-fictional prose. In this book it has been impossible to trace all the influences on James's art, but these are obviously more complex than most source studies would suggest. Like some of the authors about whom he wrote, he himself presents a case of "saturation"—one that should keep scholars occupied for decades to come.

His essays also refute the idea that he was "a rigid lawgiver" who evolved a set of narrow technical principles. Despite his abiding interest in the art of fiction his discussion of technique was always related to his concern for "life." His conception of character as center, for example, derived not merely from an aesthetic ideal but from a humanistic philosophy, his response to the materialism of the naturalists. Furthermore, especially in his later writings, James was willing to bend his principles to accommodate individual cases. Indeed, some of his critiques are almost maddeningly equivocal; he often assumes a position, modifies it, then elaborates on it, using a metaphor which alters the entire essay. Interpreting James's criticism is thus as difficult as interpreting his fiction; no amount of summary will do justice to the original, and one must constantly guard against being less flexible—one is tempted to say, less protean—than James himself.

Nonetheless, a reading of his criticism does reveal some important patterns, if not a simple "figure in the carpet." To a large extent James was a conservative, a product of the nineteenth century rather than a prophet of the twentieth. His distaste for vulgarity pervades his essays no less than his fiction; it was the impulse behind his initial undertaking of his "arduous" critical mission, the cause of his rejection of the unclean French and the uncultivated Americans, and the reason for the fastidiousness that marked his later essays, his flexibility notwithstanding. There is thus an obvious connection between his review of *Drum Taps*, written in 1865, and his essay on "The Younger Generation," written forty-nine years later; whatever their merits, neither Whitman nor Wells appealed to the "cultivated consciousness." Moreover, on a less superficial level, James always retained what Oscar Cargill has called "his faith in human will and in character,"[1] the only faith available to him in the post-Romantic age. When this was threatened by the naturalists, he turned to those authors who presented a more hopeful view of humanity—particularly to Eliot, Turgenev, and Hawthorne, but also to a number of lesser novelists. And even his ultimate acceptance of Zola depended on the latter's ability to make his figures seem heroic, if not in consciousness, then at least in the epic quality of their lives. Hence, as a "philosopher," James adhered to the idealism of the mid-nineteenth century; and as a man of sensibility, he was more conservative still. To appreciate the strength of his nostalgia, one has only to recall his taste for the poems of Tennyson, the memoirs of Renan, and the romances of Sand. These authors encouraged him to develop a highly poetic and personal style which became a defense against the ugliness of modern life and a means of asserting his creative power in an age when many novelists regarded themselves as mere "note-takers."

But it is equally important to see James as a writer who tried to come to terms with his own era and with the authors who depicted it. As early as 1865, he acknowledged the distinction between "philosophy" and the novel, implying that no matter how great an author's ideas might be, they were of little value unless he dramatized them in his characters. This was a crucial insight on James's part, for it enabled him to reject some of the worst fiction of the century—the Sunday-school novels and the more didactic works of the naturalists—and ultimately, to accept the best—the classic fiction of authors so diverse as Hawthorne and Flaubert. Furthermore, James's essays reveal his broadening conception of what constituted "life" in the novel. His earliest reviews are almost tedious in their focus on a single stock figure: the heroine of sensibility, who appeared, nearly without fail, in the fiction of Eliot, Trollope, Droz, Cherbuliez, and Turgenev. Gradually, however, James perceived the interest inherent in other types of figures, even to the point of seeing Balzac's Valérie Marneffe and Zola's Gervaise Coupeau as characters whose "history" was worth recording. Finally and most importantly, one must recall the new tolerance displayed by the critic after 1884, his willingness to consider "cases" without resorting too often to the "oppressive *a priori.*" This tolerance extended to many writers, but especially to those who related romance to the commonplace—notably Stevenson and Hawthorne—and to those who stressed the symbolic aspects of realism—notably Ibsen, Balzac, and Zola. Of all his critiques, his essays on these authors are the most significant, for they represent his attempt to reconcile his own idealism with his impulse to deal with "life."

This same attempt, moreover, was the motive force behind his own fiction. It has long been recognized that James's romances (*The American* and *The Turn of the Screw,* for example) are notable for their psychological and human interest, and it has become increasingly apparent to many scholars that his novels share a number of characteristics with romance. Despite being grounded in human reality, they deal with the extraordinary, not the commonplace; and as John O'Neill has demonstrated in *Workable Design,* such characters as Isabel Archer, Milly Theale, and Fleda Vetch (or Gilbert Osmond, Kate Croy, and Mrs. Gereth) are not so much representations of "real people" as symbols of divergent human impulses. And as Peter Brooks has remarked in his excellent study of James and Balzac, the tension between these groups of figures enabled the American author, like his French predecessor, to create drama "from the banal stuff of reality."[2] James's criticism is thus an important key to his fiction, in that it reveals the central influence of Balzac, from whom he acquired his taste for "intensity," and of Hawthorne, who taught him that "the quaintness or the weirdness, the interest *behind* the interest, of things" is "continuous with the very life we are leading."

The adequacy of James's "romantic vision of the real"[3] is, of course, an open question. Undoubtedly, he had some blind spots, never giving proper recognition to Mark Twain, H. G. Wells, and D. H. Lawrence; and undoubtedly, there are values in their art which are not to be found in his. Furthermore, to a critic of Maxwell Geismar's persuasion, James will always appear to have lived in a world of his own, removed from the "mainstream" of literature. Indeed, toward the end of his life, James himself questioned the assumptions on which his career had been founded. We return to the passage which opened this study, his description of the *Nation* and of the ideals of those who wrote for it:

> The whole scene and the whole time flushed to my actual view with a felicity and a unity that make them rather a page of romance than a picture of that degree of the real, that potentially so terrible truth of the life of man, which has now learnt to paint itself with so different a brush. They *were*, they flourished, they temporarily triumphed, that scene, that time, those conditions. . . . I measure the spread as that of half a century— only with the air turning more and more to the golden as space recedes, turning to the clearness of all the sovereign exemptions, the serenity of all the fond assurances, that were to keep on and on, seeing themselves not only so little menaced but so admirably crowned. This we now perceive to have been so much their mistake that . . . it can only rest with us to write down the fifty years I speak of, in the very largest letters, as the Age of the Mistake.[4]

Significantly, James was writing at the beginning of World War I, in many respects the line of demarcation between the nineteenth and the twentieth centuries. For fifty years he had tried to balance his idealism against the demands of his age; but in 1915 he feared that he had lived in a world of illusion. Thus, on the eve of the modern era, he anticipated the views of his worst detractors.

But James's self-doubt illuminates his central strength as a critic—that despite his idiosyncrasies, he was less a confirmed "Jacobite" than some of his interpreters were to be. In his criticism as in his fiction, he was never quite predictable; and hence, his own "case" remains compelling in its interest.

Notes

Notes to Preface

1. *Lamp*, 28 (February 1904), 49–50.
2. "The Aesthetic Idealism of Henry James," in *The Question of Henry James*, ed. F. W. Dupee (New York: Henry Holt, 1945), p. 75.
3. *The Great Tradition* (New York: Macmillan, 1933), p. 106.
4. *The American Novel, 1789–1939* (New York: Macmillan, 1940), p. 188.
5. *A Literary History of England* (New York: Appleton-Century-Crofts, 1948), p. 1551.
6. *Literary History of the United States*, ed. Robert E. Spiller et al. (3rd ed. rev.; Toronto and London: Collier-Macmillan, 1963), p. 1047.
7. "Henry James," *Atlantic*, 95 (April 1905), 513.
8. Cady, *The Light of Common Day* (Bloomington: Indiana University Press, 1971), pp. 7, 10–11; Quinn, *American Fiction* (New York: Appleton, 1936), p. 239.
9. *Literature of the American People* (New York: Appleton-Century-Crofts, 1951), p. 688.
10. *Main Currents in American Thought* (New York: Harcourt, Brace, 1930), III, 240.
11. *The Foreground of American Fiction* (New York: American Book, 1934), p. 368.
12. *The Complex Fate* (London: Chatto and Windus, 1952), pp. 2–3.
13. *The American Henry James* (New Brunswick: Rutgers University Press, 1962).
14. *The Great Tradition* (London: Chatto and Windus, 1948), p. 15.
15. *Henry James: A Critical Study* (New York: Dodd, 1916), p. 137. Ford conceded that superficially, James disliked Flaubert and Baudelaire.
16. *Henry James and the French Novel: A Study in Inspiration* (New York: Barnes and Noble, 1973).
17. *Henry James and the Naturalist Movement* (East Lansing: Michigan State University Press, 1971), p. 27.
18. *Henry James: The Ibsen Years* (New York: Barnes and Noble, 1972).
19. *The Novels of Henry James* (New York: Macmillan, 1961).
20. *A Bibliography of Henry James* (2nd ed. rev.; London: Rupert Hart-Davis, 1961). Four major anthologies of James's reviews have also been

197

published in this century. These are *Views and Reviews*, ed. Le Roy Phillips (Boston: Ball Publishing, 1908); *Notes and Reviews*, ed. Pierre de Chaignon La Rose (Cambridge, Mass.: Dunster House, 1921); *Literary Reviews and Essays on American, English, and French Authors*, ed. Albert Mordell (New York: Vista House, 1957); and *Selected Literary Criticism*, ed. Morris Shapira (New York: Horizon Press, 1964). James Miller has excerpted passages from the author's reviews in his *Theory of Fiction: Henry James* (Lincoln: University of Nebraska Press, 1972).

21. Cornelia P. Kelley has discussed the author's reviews prior to 1881 in *The Early Development of Henry James* (Urbana: University of Illinois Press, 1930). But because she examines his fiction as well as his criticism, she cannot treat the latter in sufficient detail; and because she adheres rigorously to a chronological scheme, one often loses sight of the pattern of James's work. Maurice Géracht's dissertation, "Windows on the House of Fiction" (University of Wisconsin, 1970), deals with James's "Art of Fiction" and his commentaries on six authors (Balzac, Trollope, Sand, Eliot, Zola, and Turgenev); it stresses his "judgment of the works on [each] author's own terms" (p. 43) without giving attention to the development of his particular point of view. Mary D. Farnham's "Henry James on Three Victorian Novelists" (University of North Carolina Diss., 1970) discusses the author's critiques of Eliot, Trollope, and Stevenson without placing these in any larger context.

22. Morris Roberts's early study, *Henry James's Criticism* (Cambridge: Harvard University Press, 1929), attacks the young James for his parochialism, emphasizing the relative merits of his Prefaces. Two dissertations have elaborated the obvious truth that the early critic was no abstract theorist: Elizabeth Coleman's "Henry James's Criticism: A Reëvaluation" (Columbia, 1965); and Walther G. Prausnitz's more comprehensive study, "The Craftsmanship of Henry James" (Chicago, 1956).

23. *The Method of Henry James* (Philadelphia: Alfred Saifer, 1954), p. 155. Originally published in 1918.

24. *Image and Idea* (Norfolk: New Directions, 1949), pp. 1-4.

25. *Henry James and the Jacobites* (Boston: Houghton Mifflin, 1963), pp. 7, 13, 25, 416.

26. *The Battle and the Books: Some Aspects of Henry James* (Athens: Ohio University Press, 1964), pp. 9, 21.

27. Cargill, *The Novels of Henry James*, p. 375.

Notes to Chapter I

1. Henry James, "The Founding of the 'Nation,'" *Nation*, 101 (July 8, 1915), 44.
2. *Main Currents in American Thought*, III, 239.
3. Frank Luther Mott, *A History of American Magazines* (Cambridge: Harvard University Press, 1938), II, 243.
4. Charles Eliot Norton, ed., *The Letters of James Russell Lowell* (New York: Harper's, 1894), I, 334-335.
5. Sara Norton and Mark DeWolfe Howe, eds., *The Letters of Charles Eliot Norton* (London: Constable, 1913), I, 266, 281.
6. The term is Willard Throp's in *Literary History of the United States*, p. 809.
7. "An American Art-Scholar: Charles Eliot Norton," *Notes on Novelists* (New York: Scribner's, 1914), pp. 413-415.
8. Mott, II, 495-496.

9. *Literary Friends and Acquaintance* (New York: Harper's, 1902), p. 115.

10. Ibid., p. 12; Mott, III, 331, 335; *Letters of Norton*, II, 439.

11. Rollo Ogden, ed., *The Life and Letters of E. L. Godkin* (New York and London: Macmillan, 1906), I, 238.

12. Henry Holt, "A Young Man's Oracle," *Nation*, 101 (July 8, 1915), 45.

13. "Critics and Criticism," *Nation*, 1 (July 6, 1865), 11.

14. "The Paradise of Mediocrities," *Nation*, 1 (July 13, 1865), 44.

15. Parrington, III, 155.

16. James, "The Founding of the 'Nation,'" p. 45.

17. Review of *Essays in Criticism, North American Review*, 101 (July 1865), 209-210, 211.

18. Ibid., pp. 206, 210.

19. Cf. [Anonymous], "Essays in Criticism," *Atlantic*, 16 (August 1865), 255-256; [E. W. Gurney], "Matthew Arnold's Essays," *Nation*, 1 (July 6, 1865), 24-25.

20. "A French Critic," *Nation*, 1 (October 12, 1865), 469.

21. *Nouvelles études sur la littérature contemporaine*, 2nd. ed. (Paris: Michel Lévy Frères, 1876), pp. 336, 365, 383. Translation: "A modest woman who lets slip vulgar words, a pure woman who calls *Faublas* 'a pretty novel,' a sensitive woman who demands that heads roll—these are the disparities one faces when one studies Madame Roland. . . . We have put so much physiology into our psychology that we are in danger of confusing love with appetites or pleasures. . . . One feels the need to assure oneself that even in the midst of these saturnalia, human virtue is not left without some witness; and then, strangely, it is women who attract one's notice and console one: . . . it is, finally, Madame Roland, with her great heart and her sublime illusions."

22. Henry James, *Autobiography*, ed. F. W. Dupee (New York: Criterion Books, 1956), p. 23. This usage of the term was also current in the 1860s: "One principal object of THE NATION is to promote and develop a higher criticism" (Bristed, "Critics and Criticism," p. 10). For a discussion of James's early fiction as "higher criticism," see James Kraft, *The Early Tales of Henry James* (Carbondale: Southern Illinois University Press, 1969), pp. 4, 7.

23. "Mr. Walt Whitman," *Nation*, 1 (November 16, 1865), 626.

24. *Marian Rooke; or The Quest for Fortune* (New York: Sheldon and Co., 1865), p. 296.

25. "Marian Rooke," *Nation*, 2 (February 22, 1866), 247.

26. *Letters of J. R. Lowell*, II, 4.

27. For an account of Taylor and Mrs. Stoddard's standings among the New England writers, see Howells, *Literary Friends and Acquaintance*, pp. 3-5, 87.

28. Leon Edel, ed., "Autobiography in Fiction: An Unpublished Review by Henry James," *Harvard Library Bulletin*, 11 (September 1957), 252-255.

29. James Kraft, ed., "An Unpublished Review of Henry James," *Studies in Bibliography*, 20 (1967), 271.

30. Everett Carter, *Howells and the Age of Realism* (Philadelphia: Lippincott, 1954), p. 35. Cf. also Richard Harter Fogle, "Organic Form in American Criticism," *The Development of American Literary Criticism*, ed. Floyd Stovall (Chapel Hill: University of North Carolina Press, 1955), p. 76, re: the opposition of the *North American Review* to the Transcendentalists; and Arthur Sedgwick, "The 'Nation's' Critics," *Nation*, 101 (July 8, 1915), p. 54: "[The] object [of the *Nation*] was to be the cultivation of reasonableness. The onset [sic] sounded by it was that of the critical, the scientific, the sound, the cosmopolitan, the rational."

31. *Turn West, Turn East* (Boston: Houghton Mifflin, 1951), p. 51.

32. Review of *Essays in Criticism*, pp. 208, 213.

33. F. O. Matthiessen, *The James Family* (New York: Knopf, 1947), pp. 70, 79.

34. Review of *Essays on Fiction, North American Review*, 99 (October 1864), 580, 581, 586, 583.

35. Review of *The Life and Death of Jason, North American Review*, 105 (October 1867), 692.

36. Review of *The Earthly Paradise, North American Review*, 107 (July 1868), 359, 360.

37. Cf. Roger B. Salomon, "Realism as Disinheritance: Twain, Howells, and James," *American Quarterly*, 16 (Winter 1964), 531-544.

Notes to Chapter II

1. "Our Mutual Friend," *Nation*, 1 (December 21, 1865), 787.

2. Mott, *A History of American Magazines*, III, 223.

3. Review of Senior's *Essays on Fiction*, p. 580.

4. Review of *Wilhelm Meister, North American Review*, 101 (July 1865), 284-285.

5. *The Early Development of Henry James*, p. 55.

6. Review of *Wilhelm Meister*, pp. 283-284.

7. "Our Mutual Friend," p. 787; "Miss Mackenzie," *Nation*, 1 (July 13, 1865), 51.

8. William K. Wimsatt and Cleanth Brooks, *Literary Criticism: A Short History* (New York: Vintage Books, 1957), p. 264.

9. Henry James, *A Small Boy and Others* (New York: Scribner's, 1913), pp. 113-114, 117; Leon Edel, *Henry James: The Untried Years* (Philadelphia: Lippincott, 1953), pp. 98-99.

10. "Our Mutual Friend," p. 787.

11. Loc. cit.

12. Henry James, Sr. "The Social Significance of Our Institutions," cited in F. O. Matthiessen, *The James Family*, p. 61.

13. Cf. Quentin Anderson, *The American Henry James*.

14. Cf. again James's comments in "Our Mutual Friend," p. 787.

15. "Miss Braddon," *Nation*, 1 (November 9, 1865), 593-594.

16. *Aurora Floyd: A Domestic Story* (Philadelphia: T. B. Peterson, n. d.), pp. 167, 196, 234.

17. "Miss Braddon," p. 594.

18. "An Unpublished Review of Henry James," p. 272.

19. *Two Men* (New York: Bunce and Huntington, 1865), p. 103.

20. "An Unpublished Review of Henry James," p. 271.

21. Review of *Emily Chester, North American Review*, 100 (January 1865), 284, 282, 281.

22. "A Noble Life," *Nation*, 2 (March 1, 1866), 276.

23. Review of *The Gayworthys: A Story of Threads and Thrums, North American Review*, 101 (October 1865), 620.

24. "Winifred Bertram," *Nation*, 2 (February 1, 1866), 148.

25. Review of *The Gayworthys*, p. 621.

26. "Waiting for the Verdict," *Nation*, 5 (November 21, 1867), 410-411.

27. "Dallas Galbraith," *Nation*, 7 (October 22, 1868), 330-331.

28. Review of *Moods, North American Review*, 101 (July 1865), 277.

29. "Waiting for the Verdict," p. 411.

30. "Our Mutual Friend," p. 787.

31. "Dallas Galbraith," p. 331.

32. C. Hartley Grattan, *The Three Jameses* (London: Longmans, Green, 1932), p. 71.

33. Cf. Beach, *The Method of Henry James*, p. lxxxvi; Carter, *Howells and the Age of Realism*, pp. 253-254; and John P. O'Neill, *Workable Design: Action and Situation in the Fiction of Henry James* (Port Washington, N. Y.: Kennikat Press, 1973).

34. "Autobiography in Fiction," p. 256.

35. *John Godfrey's Fortunes: A Story of American Life* (New York: G. P. Putnam; Hurd and Houghton, 1865), p. 429.

36. James, *Autobiography*, pp. 250-251.

37. Review of Prescott's *Azarian*, *North American Review*, 100 (January 1865), 271; cf. "Autobiography in Fiction," p. 254.

38. "Miss Mackenzie," pp. 51-52.

39. "Can You Forgive Her?," *Nation*, 1 (September 28, 1865), 410.

40. "The Belton Estate," *Nation*, 2 (January 4, 1866), 22.

41. "Felix Holt, the Radical," *Nation*, 3 (August 16, 1866), 127-128.

42. "The Novels of George Eliot," *Atlantic Monthly*, 18 (October 1866), 480, 481, 487, 486, 491.

43. Anonymous review of *The Small House at Allington*, *Atlantic*, 14 (August 1864), 255. Cf. [A. V. Dicey], "Anthony Trollope," *Nation*, 18 (March 12, 1874), 174-175; [Thomas Sergeant Perry], "Recent Literature," *Atlantic*, 33 (May 1874), 618.

44. "Felix Holt, the Radical," *North American Review*, 103 (October 1866), 557-563; [A. G. Sedgwick], "Recent Literature," *Atlantic*, 31 (April 1873), 490-503; [A. V. Dicey], "Middlemarch," *Nation*, 16 (January 23, 1873), 60-62 and (January 30, 1873), 76-77.

45. *The Art of the Novel*, ed. Richard P. Blackmur (New York: Scribner's, 1934), p. 67.

46. Op. cit., especially pp. 11 and 146.

47. "The Noble School of Fiction," *Nation*, 1 (July 6, 1865), 22.

48. "The Novels of George Eliot," p. 492.

49. Ibid., pp. 485, 487, 489-490.

50. "Can You Forgive Her?," p. 410.

51. "Linda Tressel," *Nation*, 6 (June 18, 1868), 494-495.

52. *Wives and Daughters* (New York: Harper and Brothers, 1866), pp. 90, 93.

53. "Wives and Daughters," *Nation*, 2 (February 22, 1866), 247.

54. "Felix Holt," p. 128.

55. Mott, II, 508.

56. Unsigned review of *Griffith Gaunt*, *Atlantic*, 18 (December 1866), 768-769.

57. (Minneapolis: University of Minnesota Press, 1957), pp. 36-37.

58. Review of *Wilhelm Meister*, pp. 284, 292.

59. Preface to *The Tragic Muse*, *The Art of the Novel*, p. 84.

60. Review of *Lindisfarn Chase*, *North American Review*, 100 (January 1865), 278.

61. "The Noble School of Fiction," p. 22.

62. "Can You Forgive Her?," p. 410.

63. "Miss Mackenzie," p. 52.

64. "Felix Holt," p. 127.

65. Review of *Emily Chester*, p. 281.

66. "An Unpublished Review of Henry James," pp. 271-272; "The Schönberg-Cotta Family," *Nation*, 1 (September 14, 1865), 345; Review of *Azarian*, p. 269.

67. *Azarian: An Episode* (Boston: Ticknor and Fields, 1864), pp. 67-68.

68. Review of *Azarian*, p. 269.

69. Kelley, pp. 280-281.

70. Review of *Azarian*, pp. 272-273.

71. "Can You Forgive Her?," p. 409; "The Belton Estate," pp. 21-22.

72. "Felix Holt," p. 127.

73. "The Novels of George Eliot," p. 485.

74. Ibid., p. 490.

75. Cf. Preface to *The Aspern Papers (The Turn of the Screw):* "Make [the reader] think the evil, make him think it for himself, and you are released from weak specifications" (*The Art of the Novel*, p. 176).

76. Edward L. Burlingame, "New American Novels," *North American Review*, 125 (September 1877), 310, 314-315; [Thomas Sergeant Perry], "James's 'American,'" *Nation*, 24 (May 31, 1877), 325-326; [W. C. Brownell], "James's 'Portrait of a Lady,'" *Nation*, 34 (February 2, 1882), 102-103.

77. "Autobiography in Fiction," pp. 255-256.

78. Cf. James's later objections to making Lambert Strether "at once hero and historian" (Preface to *The Ambassadors, The Art of the Novel*, p. 320). His reasoning, however, differed from that in his early criticism; he attacked first-person narrative as such because of its *"fluidity"* and because the third-person narrator could make "certain precious discriminations" that the protagonist could not (Ibid., p. 321). This shift probably reflects the later James's confidence in representing extraordinary characters; whereas at first he was concerned about the author's inferiority to his imagined heroes, he subsequently assumed his own superiority to them.

79. "An Unpublished Review of Henry James," p. 272.

80. "Dallas Galbraith," p. 331.

81. "Wives and Daughters," p. 247.

82. Once again, James's criticism reflected his own literary practice. In this connection, an 1868 letter from William James to his brother is of particular interest: "You seem to acknowledge that you can't exhaust any character's feelings or thoughts by an articulate displaying of them. . . . You expressly restrict yourself, accordingly, to showing a few external acts and speeches, and by the magic of your art making the reader *feel* back of these the existence of a body of being of which these are casual features. You wish to suggest a mysterious fulness which you do not lead the reader through" [Ralph Burton Perry, ed., *The Thought and Character of William James* (Boston: Little, Brown, and Co., 1935), I, 271; also cited in Kraft, *The Early Tales of Henry James*, pp. 18-19].

83. "The Novels of George Eliot," p. 487.

84. Review of *The Spanish Gypsy, North American Review*, 107 (October 1868), 624.

85. "Chastelard," *Nation*, 2 (January 18, 1866), 83.

86. Review of *The Spanish Gypsy*, p. 633.

87. Charles T. Samuels has commented on this same dichotomy—that between the "dispassionate observer" and the "moral celebrant"—in James's fiction. He contends that it damages even his later work [*The Ambiguity of Henry James* (Urbana: University of Illinois Press, 1971), p. 216].

88. In *The Turn of the Screw*, for example, the governess is supposed to convey the emotions of bewilderment and horror, but also to keep "crystalline her record of so many intense anomalies and obscurities" (Preface to *The Aspern Papers, The Art of the Novel*, p. 173).

89. "George Sand's Mademoiselle Merquem," *Nation*, 7 (July 16, 1868), 53.

90. Review of *The Spanish Gypsy*, p. 626.

91. *The Art of the Novel*, p. 33.

92. Review of *The Life and Death of Jason*, p. 690.

93. Review of *The Earthly Paradise*, p. 360.

94. Cf. Kraft, *The Early Tales of Henry James*, pp. 19-21.

95. "Victor Hugo's Last Novel," *Nation*, 2 (April 12, 1866), 466-468.

96. "Hereward," *Nation*, 2 (January 25, 1866), 115–116.
97. Review of *Essays on Fiction*, pp. 584–587.
98. "George Sand's Mademoiselle Merquem," pp. 52–53.
99. "George Sand," *Galaxy*, 24 (July 1877), 58.
100. "A Noble Life," p. 276.
101. "The Belton Estate," p. 22.
102. "The Schönberg-Cotta Family," p. 345.
103. "Miss Mackenzie," p. 51.
104. Review of *Lindisfarn Chase*, p. 278.
105. "Miss Braddon," p. 593.
106. Richard Chase, *The American Novel and Its Tradition* (Garden City: Doubleday, 1957), p. 135.
107. "Wives and Daughters," p. 247.
108. "Linda Tressel," p. 495.
109. "Sainte-Beuve's Portraits," *Nation*, 6 (June 4, 1868), 454–455. Note that James's treatment of the "empiric" Sainte-Beuve is more favorable here than in his essay on Schérer.
110. Preface to *The American, The Art of the Novel*, pp. 31–32. Cf. Brooks, *The Melodramatic Imagination: Balzac, Henry James, Melodrama, and the Mode of Excess* (New Haven and London: Yale Univ. Press, 1976), pp. 154–155.
111. "The Novels of George Eliot," pp. 480, 482–485, 486, 488–489.

Notes to Chapter III

1. *The Selected Letters of Henry James*, ed. Leon Edel (New York: Farrar Straus, 1955), pp. 22–23.
2. Leon Edel, *Henry James: The Untried Years*, p. 279; and *Henry James: The Conquest of London*, pp. 62, 201, 271.
3. *Selected Letters*, p. 23.
4. Review of *Italian Journeys*, *North American Review*, 106 (January 1868), 336–338.
5. *Italian Journeys* (New York: Hurd and Houghton, 1867), pp. 18, 138, 46, 58.
6. Review of *Italian Journeys*, p. 339.
7. "Hawthorne's French and Italian Journals," *Nation*, 14 (March 14, 1872), 172–173.
8. Review of *Winter Sunshine*, *Nation*, 22 (January 27, 1876), p. 66; "Nadal's Impressions of England," *Nation*, 21 (October 7, 1875), 232–233; Review of *Days Near Rome*, *Nation*, 20 (April 1, 1875), 229.
9. Review of *Tableaux de siège*, *Nation*, 14 (January 25, 1872, 61 (James's translation). Cf. Gautier, *Tableaux de siège* (Paris: Bibliothèque-Charpentier, 1895), pp. 156–157.
10. Gautier, pp. 369, 370, 366. Translation: a city "too refined, too elegant . . . to stoop to vulgar pleasures. . . . The serious! that nice invention of modern cant to disparage likable talents, . . . that dreary refuge where fools silently ruminate on their absence of ideas."
11. Review of *Tableaux de siège*, p. 62.
12. "Gautier's Winter in Russia," *Nation*, 19 (November 12, 1874), 321.
13. Review of Ernest Feydeau's *Théophile Gautier, souvenirs intimes* and Gautier's *Histoire du romantisme*, *North American Review*, 119 (October 1874), 418.
14. Ibid., p. 416; Review of Gautier's *Constantinople*, *Nation*, 21 (July 15, 1875), 45.

15. "Théâtre de Théophile Gautier," *North American Review*, 116 (April 1873), 321, 314, 324, 329. Cf. "Théophile Gautier," *French Poets and Novelists* (London: Macmillan, 1878), pp. 57, 46, 61, 70.

16. Powers, *Henry James and the Naturalist Movement*, p. 17.

17. "Taine's Italy," *Nation*, 6 (May 7. 1868), 374-375.

18. "Taine's Notes on England," *Nation*, 14 (January 25, 1872), 59-60.

19. "Taine's English Literature," *Atlantic Monthly*, 29 (April 1872), 469-470.

20. *Notes on Paris: The Life and Opinions of M. Frédéric-Thomas Graindorge*, trans. John Austin Stevens (New York: Henry Holt, 1875), p. 59.

21. "Taine's Italy," p. 374.

22. "Taine's Notes on Paris," *Nation*, 20 (May 6, 1875), 319.

23. See Robert Blake, *Disraeli* (London: Eyre and Spottiswoode, 1966), pp. 517-519. The novel, inspired by the Marquis of Bute's conversion to Catholicism, includes fictional representations of Cardinal Manning, Bishop Wilberforce, and others.

24. Review of *Lothair*, *Atlantic*, 26 (August 1870), 251. The author of *Hedged In* was Mrs. Elizabeth Stuart (Phelps) Ward; of *Margaret Howth*, Mrs. Rebecca Harding Davis.

25. "Disraeli's Lothair," *Edinburgh Review*, 132 (July 1870, 279; "Lothair," *Blackwood's Magazine*, 107 (June 1870), 773.

26. Review of *Lothair*, pp. 250, 251.

27. Edel, *Henry James: The Untried Years*, p. 193; James, *Autobiography*, p. 281. For information on these writers as a group, see René Dumesnil, *Le Réalisme, Histoire de la littérature française*, ed. J. Calvet (Paris: J. de Gizard, 1936), IX, 50-53; and George Pallisier, "Le Roman," in *Histoire de la langue et de la littérature française*, ed. L. Petit de Julleville (Paris: Armand Colin, 1899), VIII, 179-182. Essentially, these writers, many of whom were members of the French Academy, stood in opposition to Flaubert and his school.

28. "Camors," *Nation*, 7 (July 30, 1868), 92. Cf. Feuillet, *Monsieur de Camors*, *Revue des Deux Mondes*, 69 (May 15, 1867), 287-290.

29. Ibid., pp. 92-93.

30. *Affaire Clémençeau* (Paris: Michel Lévy, 1869), pp. 145, 321, 105. Translation: "For me, it was not a young girl, it was not a child, it was not a woman, it was the Woman: Symbol, Poem, Abstraction, eternal Enigma."

31. "The Last French Novel," *Nation*, 3 (October 11, 1866), 287.

32. "A Source for *Roderick Hudson*," *Modern Language Notes*, 63 (May 1948), 303-310.

33. "Recent Literature" [Review of *Around a Spring*], *Atlantic*, 28 (August 1871), 249.

34. Ibid., pp. 249, 250.

35. Ibid., p. 249.

36. Viola Dunbar, "A Note on the Genesis of *Daisy Miller*," *Philological Quarterly*, 27 (April 1948), 184-186; Edward Stone, "A Further Note on *Daisy Miller* and Cherbuliez," *Philological Quarterly*, 29 (April 1950), 213-216.

37. Review of *Meta Holdenis*, *North American Review*, 117 (October 1873), 461-464.

38. Ibid., pp. 462, 465-468.

39. See also Joseph Tribble, "Cherbuliez's *Le Roman d'une Honnête Femme*: Another Source of James's *The Portrait of a Lady*," *American Literature*, 40 (November 1968), 279-293.

40. Oscar Cargill, for example, laments that James imitated Cherbuliez and Feuillet when he wrote *The Europeans* and *Confidence (The Novels of Henry James*, pp. 65, 73). Motley F. Deakin has written an excellent

article on the tradition behind *Daisy Miller* ["Daisy Miller, Tradition, and the European Heroine," *Comparative Literature Studies,* 6 (March 1969), 45-59] but does not discuss James's other works.

41. *Henry James: The Major Phase* (New York: Oxford University Press, 1963), p. 51.

42. One critic noted that *Autour d'une source* "was highly praised and widely read" ["Recent Literature," *Atlantic,* 30 (October 1872), 495]—an impression one receives after reading other reviews of his works. Cherbuliez, a more prolific novelist, seems to have been even more popular; see Edward Stone, "A Further Note on *Daisy Miller* and Cherbuliez," p. 215.

43. [Anonymous], "Gustave Droz," *Nation,* 12 (February 23, 1871), 129-130; [A. G. Sedgwick], "Three Novels," *Nation,* 25 (August 23, 1877), 122-124; Thomas S. Perry, "Victor Cherbuliez," *Atlantic,* 37 (March 1876), 279-287.

44. Review of *Around a Spring,* p. 248.

45. "New Novels," *Nation,* 21 (September 23, 1875), 202.

46. Review of *Miss Rovel, Nation,* 20 (June 3, 1875), 381.

47. "Dumas and Goethe," *Nation,* 17 (October 30, 1873), 293-294.

48. "Recent Novels" [Note on *Un Mariage dans le monde*], *Nation,* 22 (January 13, 1876), 34; cf. Review of *Les Amours de Philippe, Nation,* 25 (November 15, 1877), 306.

49. Dumesnil, p. 43.

50. Review of "Jean de Thommeray" and "Le Colonel Evrard," *Nation,* 18 (February 5, 1874), 95.

Notes to Chapter IV

1. Leon Edel, *Henry James: The Conquest of London,* pp. 214-226.

2. *The Letters of Henry James,* ed. Percy Lubbock (New York: Scribner's, 1920), I, 51.

3. This essay was first published during James's stay in Paris (1876) but was written before his departure (Edel, *Henry James: The Conquest of London,* p. 235).

4. Cf. Emile Zola's contemptuous reference to Cherbuliez: "toutes ses héroines sont des anges qui passent par l'enfer ou le purgatoire, dont la vertu se dégage quand même au dénouement." (Translation: "all his heroines are angels who go through hell or purgatory, but whose virtue is rescued all the same in the denouement.") He adds that the author always chose exotic settings, in effect creating a kind of never-never land ["Les Romanciers contemporains," *Les Romanciers naturalistes* (Paris: Bibliothèque-Charpentier, 1914), p. 348].

5. "The Minor French Novelists," *Galaxy,* 21 (February 1876), 227; "Charles de Bernard and Gustave Flaubert," *French Poets and Novelists,* pp. 261-262.

6. Ibid., p. 226; "Charles de Bernard and Gustave Flaubert," p. 258. Contrast Lyall Powers's account of this essay in his *Henry James and the Naturalist Movement:* that James called *Madame Bovary* "the last word in realism" (p. 32).

7. "Three French Books," *Galaxy,* 20 (August 1875), 278.

8. Review of *Une Page d'amour, Nation,* 26 (May 30, 1878), 362.

9. Review of *La Fille Elisa, Nation,* 24 (May 10, 1877), 280.

10. *Nana* (Paris: Charpentier, 1880), p. 504. Translation: "the fly taking wing from the ordure of the slums, bringing the ferment of social decay, had poisoned these men, simply by lighting on them."

11. "Nana," *Parisian*, No. 48 (February 26, 1880), p. 9; reprinted in James, *The Future of the Novel*, ed. Leon Edel (New York: Vintage Books, 1956), pp. 92, 95, 96. Cf. Powers, op. cit., p. 38. But Powers's general comment —that James's review "apparently exhibits a somewhat ambivalent attitude" toward the novel—is seriously misleading.

12. "The Minor French Novelists," pp. 219-222, 223-224; "Charles de Bernard and Gustave Flaubert," pp. 237-251.

13. Ibid., pp. 228-229; "Charles de Bernard and Gustave Flaubert," pp. 263, 265.

14. Ibid., p. 229; "Charles de Bernard and Gustave Flaubert," p. 267.

15. Review of *Une Page d'amour*, p. 362.

16. "Nana," *The Future of the Novel*, pp. 90, 91, 93.

17. "The Minor French Novelists," p. 221; "Charles de Bernard and Gustave Flaubert," pp. 242-243.

18. "The Minor French Novelists," pp. 230-232.

19. Edmond and Jules de Goncourt, *Soeur Philomène* (Paris: Alphonse Lemerre, 1890), p. 231. Translation: "Into the bottom of the glass he poured the absinthe, from which arose immediately the scent of intoxicating herbs. From above, and drop by drop, he let the water fall upon it, which disturbed it and moved in little clouds the pearly whiteness of an opal. . . . The corpse was transfigured into a fading image. Memory did nothing more than float through him under a pink shroud."

20. "The Minor French Novelists," p. 232.

21. "Flaubert's Temptation of Saint Anthony," *Nation*, 18 (June 4, 1874), 365-366.

22. "Charles Baudelaire," *Nation*, 22 (April 27, 1876), 280.

23. Anonymous note, *Nation*, 13 (August 10, 1871), 95.

24. "Recent Literature," *Atlantic*, 34 (August 1874), 242-243; Elie Reclus, "Edmond and Jules Goncourt," *Atlantic*, 41 (February 1878), 180-188; James Gargano, "Henry James on Baudelaire," *Modern Language Notes*, 75 (November 1960), 559-561.

25. "Zola's Last Novel," *Atlantic*, 45 (May 1880), 695-696.

26. *North American Review*, 131 (July 1880), 79.

27. "Gustave Flaubert," *Revue des Deux Mondes*, 39, 3rd. ser. (June 15, 1880), 848; "Revue Littéraire: Le Roman Expérimental," *Revue des Deux Mondes*, 37, 3rd. ser. (February 15, 1880), 946; "Le Faux Naturalisme," *Revue des Deux Mondes*, 49, 3rd ser. (February 15, 1882), 935; "Le Roman Réaliste Contemporain," *Revue des Deux Mondes*, 8, 3rd. ser. (April 1, 1875), 713.

28. "L'Esthétique Naturaliste," *Revue des Deux Mondes*, 35, 3rd. ser. (September 15, 1879), 428. Translation: "If human dramas take place, above all, in the consciousness, if it is there that true literary interest lies, these dramas are particularly engaging . . . when the consciousness is the most complex and the most developed."

29. "La Littérature et les Malheurs de la France," *Revue des Deux Mondes*, 11, 3rd. ser. (October 15, 1875), 909, 913, 919. James wrote a favorable notice of this essay in the *Nation*, 21 (December 30, 1875), 419.

30. "Nana," p. 9; *The Future of the Novel*, p. 94.

31. "The Minor French Novelists," p. 227; "Charles de Bernard and Gustave Flaubert," p. 261.

32. *The Melodramatic Imagination*, p. 198.

33. "The Minor French Novelists," pp. 227, 228, 225-226; "Charles de Bernard and Gustave Flaubert," pp. 260-261, 263, 257. Contrast Lyall Powers's assertion that James was "receptive to the kind of literature that was encouraged by *scientisme*"—the belief that through observing "the external features of man" one could "reach the essential man" (op. cit., pp. 9, 7).

34. p. 233.
35. Ibid., pp. 223, 225; "Charles de Bernard and Gustave Flaubert," pp. 250, 256. Cf. Powers, p. 33. But I would still argue that Powers distorts his account by ignoring the degree of James's fondness for Bernard and the reluctance of his admiration for Flaubert.
36. Review of *Une Page d'amour*, pp. 362, 361.
37. Review of *Nana*, p. 9; *The Future of the Novel*, pp. 91, 89.

Notes to Chapter V

1. p. 224.
2. "Honoré de Balzac," *Galaxy*, 20 (December 1875), 818, 820; *French Poets and Novelists*, pp. 96-97, 102-104.
3. Ibid., pp. 821, 822; *French Poets and Novelists*, pp. 105, 109-110.
4. Ibid., pp. 824, 814; *French Poets and Novelists*, pp. 115, 95.
5. "Balzac," *Nouveaux essais de critique et d'histoire*, 5th ed. (Paris: Hachette, 1892), p. 125. The essay was originally published in the *Journal des Débats*, 1858. Translation: "[The force] draws us out of ourselves; we escape from the triviality where we are dragged along by the smallness of our faculties and the timidity of our instincts."
6. "Honoré de Balzac," pp. 825, 817, 826; *French Poets and Novelists*, pp. 117, 94, 122.
7. Ibid., pp. 826-827, 825, 831; *French Poets and Novelists*, pp. 122-123, 117, 136, 135, 134. Compare Taine's comments on the parallels between Balzac and Shakespeare ("Balzac," pp. 125, 139-140).
8. Ibid., p. 827; *French Poets and Novelists*, p. 124. He also said that Balzac was superior to Dickens in the physical evocation of his figures.
9. p. 11.
10. "Honoré de Balzac," p. 828; *French Poets and Novelists*, pp. 125-126.
11. *The Melodramatic Imagination*, p. 5.
12. "Honoré de Balzac," pp. 835, 836; *French Poets and Novelists*, pp. 147, 150.
13. "Balzac," p. 54. Translation: "he understood that money is the mainspring of modern life."
14. "Honoré de Balzac," pp. 814, 816; *French Poets and Novelists*, pp. 86, 91. This is also the main theme of James's later review, "The Letters of Honoré de Balzac," *Galaxy*, 23 (February 1877), 183-195 (reprinted as "Balzac's Letters," *French Poets and Novelists*, pp. 151-189).
15. Ibid., pp. 816, 834; *French Poets and Novelists*, pp. 92, 144-145.
16. Ibid., pp. 823, 824, 825, 822, 833, 834; *French Poets and Novelists*, pp. 113, 114-115, 116-117, 107-108, 141, 144, 142-143. It is interesting that Taine also had objected to Balzac's portraits of virtuous women: "Le naturel des femmes se compose de finesse nerveuse, d'imagination délicate et agile, de réserve innée et acquise. C'est dire que presque toujours il échappe à Balzac" ("Balzac," pp. 102-103). (Translation: "Feminine nature is composed of nervous fineness, of delicate and agile imagination, of innate and acquired reserve. This is to say that it almost always escapes Balzac.") In this early essay, Taine assumed a more idealistic position than he was to take in *Notes sur Paris*.
17. "Honoré de Balzac," pp. 833-834; *French Poets and Novelists*, pp. 142-143.
16. See Maurita Willett, "Henry James's Indebtedness to Balzac," *Revue de Littérature Comparée*, 41 (April-June 1967), 204-227.
19. "Three French Books," p. 278.

20. The first of these, published in the *Atlantic*, was a review of Ernest Daudet's *Mon Frère et moi: souvenirs d'enfance et de jeunesse;* the second, a more general essay, was published in *Century Magazine* and reprinted in James's *Partial Portraits* (1888).

21. "Alphonse Daudet," *Atlantic*, 49 (June 1882), 847–849, 851. Hereafter cited as "Daudet" (1882).

22. "Alphonse Daudet," *Century Magazine*, 26 (August 1883), 501, 500 (*Partial Portraits*, pp. 208, 202); cf. *Une Compagne, 1880–1881* (Paris: Charpentier, 1913), pp. 384, 394.

23. *Numa Roumestan* (Paris: G. Charpentier, 1881), pp. 8–9. Translation: "This sky so clear, this sunshine of vaporized silver, these Latin intonations preserved in the Provencal idiom, here and there . . . static poses which the vibration of the air rendered antique, almost sculptural, the stamp of the place, these heads struck like medals with their short aquiline noses . . . everything completed the illusion of a Roman carnival, even the lowing of steers echoing through the tunnels, from which the lions and elephants of combat once came forth."

24. "Alphonse Daudet," p. 503; *Partial Portraits*, p. 214.

25. *Les Rois en exil* (Paris: E. Dentu, 1879), pp. 30–31. Translation: "In the midst of the transformations of the Latin quarter, of these large gaps where the originality, the memories of old Paris vanish in the dust of demolitions, Monsieur-le-Prince Street retains the aspect of a students' street. The booksellers' displays, the delicatessens, the cook-shops, the peddlers, the 'purchase and sale of gold and silver' are there in succession up to the hill of Sainte-Geneviève, and the students stride up and down the street at all hours of the day—no longer the students of Gavarni with long hair escaping from a woolen beret, but future lawyers, . . . with huge leather portfolios under their arms, and already the cunning and cold look of men of business; or else future doctors, a little freer in their bearing." For a parallel passage, see *The Ambassadors, The Novels and Tales of Henry James* (New York: Scribner's, 1907–17), XXI, 79–80.

26. "Alphonse Daudet," pp. 499–500, 508; *Partial Portraits*, pp. 201–202, 234–235.

27. "Three French Books," p. 278.

28. "Alphonse Daudet," pp. 505, 499, 506, 508, 507, 504; *Partial Portraits*, pp. 224, 199–200, 226, 234–235, 230, 218.

29. "Daudet" (1882), p. 851. In his novels, James used the adjective "little" to describe such figures as Ned Rosier and Hyacinth Robinson, characters who are deceived by aesthetic appearances. And he depicted Adam Verver as "a great . . . little man," an oxymoron which, as in the case of Daudet, suggests both naive aestheticism and poetic insight.

30. Ibid., pp. 498, 506, 499, 509, 503; *Partial Portraits*, pp. 197, 226, 199, 237, 217.

31. See F. O. Matthiessen and Kenneth B. Murdock, *The Notebooks of Henry James* (New York: Oxford University Press, 1961), pp. 47–48.

32. "The Letters of Honoré de Balzac," pp. 194–195; "Balzac's Letters," p. 187.

33. "Daudet" (1882), pp. 849–850.

Notes to Chapter VI

1. "Taine's Notes on England," p. 60.
2. Review of *Middlemarch, Galaxy*, 15 (March 1873), 428, 425.
3. Cargill, *The Novels of Henry James*, p. 81.

4. *Letters of Charles Eliot Norton*, I, 468, 475-476.
5. *Selected Letters of Henry James*, p. 46.
6. Review of *Middlemarch*, p. 425.
7. Ibid., p. 427.
8. Ibid., pp. 427-428.
9. Ibid., pp. 425, 428, 426.
10. "Recent Novels," p. 34.
11. Review of *Middlemarch*, pp. 426, 428.
12. [A. G. Sedgwick], "Recent Literature," *Atlantic*, 31 (April 1873), 490-494; [Albert V. Dicey], "Middlemarch," *Nation*, 16 (January 23, 1873), 60-62 and (January 30, 1873), 76-77; "George Eliot's Middlemarch," *North American Review*, 116 (April 1873), 432-440. But like James, all these critics praised Eliot's characterization.
13. Cited by Leon Edel in *Henry James: The Conquest of London*, p. 225.
14. *The Letters of Henry James*, ed. Percy Lubbock, I, 51.
15. "Daniel Deronda: A Conversation," *Atlantic*, 38 (December 1876), 684, 693, 685-686, 692; *Partial Portraits*, pp. 65, 92, 70, 88.
16. Ibid., pp. 684, 685, 688, 693, 692; *Partial Portraits*, pp. 67, 69, 71, 77, 88.
17. Ibid., pp. 685, 686, 689; *Partial Portraits*, pp. 69, 72, 80.
18. Ibid., pp. 692, 693; *Partial Portraits*, pp. 89, 91.
19. "Felix Holt, the Radical," p. 128.
20. "Daniel Deronda," p. 690.
21. "James's Roderick Hudson," *North American Review*, 122 (April 1876), 420-425; cf. [G. P. Lathrop], "Recent Literature," *Atlantic*, 37 (February 1876), 237-238.
22. "Daniel Deronda," pp. 693-694; *Partial Portraits*, p. 92.
23. *The Early Development of Henry James*, pp. 231-232.
24. "Far from the Madding Crowd," *Nation*, 19 (December 24, 1874), 423-424.
25. "Anthony Trollope," *Century Magazine*, 26 (July 1883), 387, 391, 385, 395; *Partial Portraits*, pp. 104, 120, 98-99, 133.
26. Ibid., pp. 392, 386, 387; *Partial Portraits*, pp. 122, 124, 102, 104.
27. Ibid., pp. 394-395, 398; *Partial Portraits*, pp. 131-132, 108, 127.
28. Ibid., pp. 389, 388, 390, 394, 395, 393; *Partial Portraits*, pp. 113-114, 110, 129, 132, 126, 115.
29. Ibid., p. 387; *Partial Portraits*, p. 105.
30. See note 21 above; and [Constance F. Woolson], "The Contributors' Club," *Atlantic*, 43 (February 1879), 279; [Horace Scudder], "The Portrait of a Lady and Dr. Breen's Practice," *Atlantic*, 49 (January 1882), 126-130; [W. C. Brownell], "James's Portrait of a Lady," *Nation*, 34 (February 2, 1882), 102-103.
31. "Anthony Trollope," p. 390; *Partial Portraits*, pp. 116-117.
32. Edel, *Henry James: The Conquest of London*, p. 220.
33. "Ivan Turgénieff," *Atlantic*, 53 (January 1884), 45, 54, 46, 43; *Partial Portraits*, pp. 300, 322, 302, 294.
34. *The Clement Vision* (Port Washington, NY and London: Kennikat Press, 1975), p. 6.
35. See Royal Gettman, *Turgenev in England and America, University of Illinois Studies in English*, 27, no. 2 (Urbana: University of Illinois Press, 1941), pp. 42-43; and Peterson, *The Clement Vision*, pp. 7-21.
36. Review of *Frühlingsfluthen* and *Ein König Lear des Dorfes*, *North American Review*, 118 (April 1874), 326, 334, 331; "Ivan Turgénieff," *French Poets and Novelists*, pp. 270, 282, 277.
37. See *On the Eve*, trans. C. E. Turner (London: Hodder and Stoughton, 1871), pp. 233-234.

38. Review of *Frühlingsfluthen*, pp. 337, 336; *French Poets and Novelists*, pp. 287, 288, 286.

39. Review of *Frühlingsfluthen*, pp. 332, 339-340; *French Poets and Novelists*, pp. 279, 291-294.

40. Daniel Lerner has noted the resemblance in plot between *A Nest of Noblemen* and *The American* ["The Influence of Turgenev on Henry James," *Slavonic and East European Review*, 20 (1941), 43]. But Mme. de Cintré is a more conventional figure than either Lisa or Milly.

41. *The Clement Vision*, p. 2.

42. Review of *Frühlingsfluthen*, pp. 345, 338, 334, 335; *French Poets and Novelists*, pp. 302, 289, 284.

43. *The Art of the Novel*, p. 246.

44. Review of *Frühlingsfluthen*, pp. 349, 335; *French Poets and Novelists*, pp. 306-307, 284-285. Cf. Lerner, p. 48.

45. "Ivan Turgenef's New Novel," *Nation*, 24 (April 26, 1877), 253.

46. Lerner, pp. 47-53.

47. "Ivan Turgenef's New Novel," p. 253.

48. Review of *Frühlingsfluthen*, p. 330; *French Poets and Novelists*, p. 276.

49. Ibid., p. 332; *French Poets and Novelists*, pp. 79-80.

50. "Ivan Turgénieff," p. 52; *Partial Portraits*, pp. 315-316. An example of Turgenev's flexibility was his portrayal of Zimushka and Zomushka, the old couple in *Virgin Soil*. Wrote James: "We have seen the episode ... condemned as a *hors d'oeuvre*—an excrescence; but this strikes us as an inattentive judgment. The picture of their ancient superstitions, their quaintness and mellowness and serenity, is intended as a dramatic offset to the crude and acrid unrest of the young radicals who come to see them; it has a 'value' as the painters say. It is, moreover, very charming in itself" ("Ivan Turgenef's New Novel," p. 253).

51. *The Art of the Novel*, pp. 43-44.

52. Review of *Frühlingsfluthen*, p. 330; *French Poets and Novelists*, p. 276.

53. "Ivan Turgénieff," p. 52; *Partial Portraits*, p. 315.

54. See *The Art of the Novel*, pp. 43-44.

55. Review of *Frühlingsfluthen*, pp. 341, 335; *French Poets and Novelists*, pp. 295, 285.

56. Ibid., pp. 350, 341, 351-352, 352-353, 355; *French Poets and Novelists*, pp. 309, 295-296, 311-313, 317. Cf. Howells, *Criticism and Fiction and Other Essays*, ed. Clara M. and Rudolf Kirk (New York: New York University Press, 1959), p. 62.

57. Thomas S. Perry, "Ivan Turgénieff, *Atlantic*, 33 (May 1874), 572, 569, 574; William Dean Howells, "Recent Literature," *Atlantic*, 31 (February 1873), 239 and 32 (September 1873), 369-370. See also Gettman and Peterson.

58. "Daniel Deronda," p. 687; *Partial Portraits*, p. 74. He judged her storytelling gift to be better displayed in two of her shorter pieces: "The Lifted Veil," a supernatural story involving a man with the gift of foresight; and "Brother Jacob," a humorous tale about a confectioner whose idiot brother reveals his misdeeds. These James described as "the *jeux d'esprit* of a mind that is not often—perhaps not often enough—found at play" [(Untitled note), *Nation*, 26 (April 25, 1878), 277].

59. "Anthony Trollope," pp. 387-388; cf. *Partial Portraits*, p. 107.

60. Review of *Frühlingsfluthen*, p. 326; *French Poets and Novelists*, p. 270.

Notes to Chapter VII

1. See Kelley, *The Early Development of Henry James*, pp. 245, 255.
2. Review of George B. Smith's *Poets and Novelists*, *Nation*, 21 (December 30, 1875), 423.
3. "Charles Baudelaire," p. 280; *French Poets and Novelists*, p. 76.
4. James, *Autobiography*, p. 292; Edel, *Henry James: The Untried Years*, p. 164. For discussions of James's use of Mérimée, see Philip Grover, "Mérimée's Influence on Henry James," *Modern Language Review*, 63 (October 1968), 810-817; and Buitenhuis, *The Grasping Imagination*, pp. 12-13.
5. Review of Mérimée's *Dernières nouvelles*, *Nation*, 18 (February 12, 1874), 111.
6. Grover, p. 811.
7. Review of *Dernières nouvelles*, p. 111. In two subsequent reviews, James again referred to Mérimée as a talented but limited author. See "The Letters of Prosper Mérimée," *Independent*, (April 9, 1874), pp. 9-10; and Review of *Lettres à une autre inconnue*, *Nation*, 22 (January 27, 1876), 67-68.
8. "Victor Hugo's Ninety-Three," *Nation*, 18 (April 9, 1874), 238-239.
9. Review of *Idolatry*, "Recent Literature," *Atlantic*, 34 (December 1874), 747-748. See also James's review of the author's *Garth*, which he criticized in much the same manner [*Nation*, 24 (June 21, 1877), 369].
10. Review of *Signa*, "Recent Novels," *Nation*, 21 (July 1, 1875), 11.
11. "Recent Novels," *Nation*, 22 (January 13, 1876), 34.
12. "The Minor French Novelists," p. 233.
13. "George Sand," *New York Tribune*, 3 (July 22, 1876), 1-2. Reprinted in *Parisian Sketches*, ed. Leon Edel and Ilse Dusoir Lind (New York: New York University Press, 1957), pp. 178-187.
14. *The Selected Letters of Henry James*, p. 51. In this same letter, James expressed his wish to write an article on Eliot's *Daniel Deronda*. Clearly, he found the novel easier to criticize than the romance.
15. "George Sand," *Derniers essais de critique et d'histoire* (Paris: Librairie Hachette, 1896), pp. 129, 131. The essay was originally published in the *Journal des Débats* (July 2, 1876). Translation: "no one has more continually, or with more good faith, debated serious questions; she was preoccupied with them to the point of being obsessed by them, and in following her novels, one could construe the moral and material history of the age."
16. [Untitled note], *Nation*, 23 (July 27, 1876), 61.
17. "George Sand," *Galaxy*, 24 (July 1877), 45, 59; *French Poets and Novelists*, pp. 190-191, 231. But whereas Taine had been interested in Sand's family history as a key to her way of thinking, James dwelt on the colorfulness of her ancestors (patrician and plebeian) and their numerous irregular love affairs, adding: "It was a very picturesque pedigree—quite an ideal pedigree for a romancer."
18. "George Sand," pp. 52-53, 56-57; *French Poets and Novelists*, pp. 211-213, 225-227.
19. *Lucrezia Floriani* (Paris: Michel Lévy, 1869), pp. 36, 38, 21.
20. "George Sand," pp. 57, 61; *French Poets and Novelists*, pp. 224-225, 234-235.
21. Ibid., pp. 48, 60, 61; *French Poets and Novelists*, pp. 200, 232, 235-236.
22. Ibid., pp. 54-55; *French Poets and Novelists*, pp. 218-219.
23. "George Sand's Mademoiselle Merquem," p. 52.
24. "George Sand," pp. 57-58, 53, 50; *French Poets and Novelists*, pp. 225-227, 215, 206.
25. *Oeuvres illustrées de George Sand* (Paris: J. Hetzel, 1853), V, 89.

Translation: "She was a very lovely person, extremely intelligent, who came several times *to pour out her heart at my feet*, or so she said. I saw perfectly well that she was *posing* in front of me and most of the time was not thinking of a word she was saying. She could have been that which she was not. Thus it is not she whom I have depicted in *Isidora*."

26. *Oeuvres illustrées de George Sand* (Paris: J. Hetzel, 1852), I, 37-38.

27. "George Sand," pp. 51-52; *French Poets and Novelists*, pp. 209-211.

28. Preface to *The Aspern Papers*, *The Art of the Novel*, p. 161.

29. *Henry James: The Creative Process* (New York: Yoseloff, 1958), p. 29.

30. *Mind*, 4 (January 1879), 9.

31. "Great Men, Great Thoughts, and the Environment," *Atlantic*, 46 (September 1880), 457.

32. F. O. Matthiessen, *Henry James: The Major Phase* (1944; rpt. New York: Oxford University Press, 1963), p. 60; Cargill, *The Novels of Henry James*, p. 425.

33. See Daniel G. Hoffman, *Form and Fable in American Fiction* (New York: Oxford University Press, 1961), pp. 5-7, 106.

34. *A Study of Hawthorne* (1876; rpt. New York: AMS Press, 1969), pp. 20-33, 237.

35. *Hawthorne* (London: Macmillan, 1879), p. 43.

36. "James's Hawthorne," *Atlantic*, 45 (February 1880), 284.

37. *Hawthorne*, pp. 20, 67; cf. pp. 25, 106-107.

38. Ibid., pp. 84, 29.

39. "The Correspondence of Carlyle and Emerson," *Century*, 26 (July 1883), 270.

40. *The Complete Tales of Henry James*, ed. Leon Edel (Philadelphia: Lippincott, 1962), III, 401.

41. *Hawthorne*, pp. 117-119, 169-170, 64-65, 113, 123, 129, 166.

42. Ibid., pp. 81, 117, 136, 114, 123, 170.

43. *Some Passages in the Life of Mr. Adam Blair, Minister of the Gospel at Cross-Meikle* (Edinburgh: Edinburgh University Press, 1963), pp. 69, 103, 150, 166, 190. Original date of publication: 1822.

44. *Hawthorne*, pp. 116-117.

45. Ibid., pp. 50, 65, 85-86.

46. Ibid., p. 99.

47. Ibid., pp. 57, 58, 27.

48. Ibid., pp. 59, 183.

49. "The Hawthorne Aspect," *The Question of Henry James*, ed. F. W. Dupee (New York: Henry Holt, 1945), p. 116.

50. *Hawthorne*, pp. 112-113, 136, 168.

51. *The Complex Fate*, pp. 11-76.

52. *Hawthorne*, pp. 167, 144.

53. Ibid., pp. 121-122, 136, 128.

Notes to Chapter VIII

1. *Literary Criticism in America* (New York: L. MacVeagh, The Dial Press, 1931), p. 160.

2. Mott, *A History of American Magazines*, I, 361-362.

3. See, for example, Higginson's "Americanism in Literature," *Atlantic*, 25 (January 1870), 56-63; Howells's laudatory essays on Eggleston, DeForest and Stowe ["Recent Literature," *Atlantic*, 29 (March 1872), 362-366] and his equally favorable review of Twain's sketches ["Recent Literature," *Atlantic*, 36 (December 1875), 749-750]; Gordon's "Mr. DeForest's Novels," *Atlantic*,

32 (November 1873), 611–621; and Preston's spirited defense of Helen Hunt Jackson's *Mercy Philbrick's Choice* ["Recent Literature," *Atlantic*, 39 (February 1877), 243–244], which may well have been written in response to James's negative review of the same novel (see below).

4. "Recollections of an Atlantic Editorship," *Atlantic*, 100 (November 1907), 601–602.

5. The exception is a favorable review of Howells's *A Foregone Conclusion*. This was published in the *North American Review*, an even more conservative journal than the *Nation*.

6. See Perry's negative review of Edward Eggleston's *The Circuit-Rider* ["Recent Novels," *Nation*, 19 (September 24, 1874), 207] and his condescending critique of American novels in general ["Recent Novels," *Nation*, 25 (September 20, 1877), 183]; and Lathrop's lament that Charles Coffin's *Caleb Krimble*, a Western melodrama, was subtitled *A Story of American Life*: "This it emphatically is, in the sense of most novels that of late have laid claim to the protection of the national flag" ["Recent Novels," *Nation*, 20 (February 25, 1875), 138]. It should be noted that the *Nation*, which published no fiction, seldom reviewed the better American novels, its serious criticism being devoted to such authors as Trollope and Turgenev.

7. *Hawthorne*, p. 43.

8. "Professor Masson's Essays," *Nation*, 20 (February 18, 1875), 115.

9. "Recent Novels," *Nation*, 22 (January 13, 1876), 32–33. "Charles H. Doe," incidentally, was probably not a pseudonymn; see Lyle H. Wright, *American Fiction, 1851–1875* (San Marino: Huntington Library, 1965), p. 102.

10. Review of *We and Our Neighbors*, *Nation*, 21 (July 22, 1875), 61.

11. *Literary History of the United States*, p. 883.

12. Review of *Honest John Vane*, *Nation*, 19 (December 31, 1874), 442.

13. "An American and an English Novel," *Nation*, 23 (December 21, 1876), 372–373.

14. "Henry James the American: Some Views of his Contemporaries," *Twentieth-Century Literature*, 1 (July 1955), 73.

15. Review of *Kismet*, *Nation*, 24 (June 7, 1877), 341.

16. Review of *Mirage*, *Nation*, 26 (March 7, 1878), 172.

17. Ibid., pp. 172–173; *Mirage* (Boston: Roberts Brothers, 1878), pp. 29, 28.

18. Review of *A Foregone Conclusion*, *North American Review*, 120 (January 1875), 211.

19. Ibid., p. 211; "Howells's Foregone Conclusion," *Nation*, 20 (January 7, 1875), 12.

20. "Howells's Foregone Conclusion," pp. 12–13.

21. Review of *A Foregone Conclusion*, p. 213.

22. *A Foregone Conclusion* (Boston: James R. Osgood, 1875), pp. 261, 264, 259.

23. Review of *A Foregone Conclusion*, p. 214; "Howells's Foregone Conclusion," p. 12.

24. [Untitled note], *Nation*, 26 (May 30, 1878), 357.

25. *An International Episode*, *Cornhill Magazine*, 38 (December 1878), 687. Howell Daniels has also identified "Irene Macgillicuddy" as a source of James's tale. See his "Henry James and *An International Episode*," *British Association for American Studies Bulletin*, n.s. 1 (1960), 3–35.

26. See Constance Rourke's discussion of *The American* in *American Humor* (New York: Harcourt, Brace, 1931), pp. 238–272.

Notes to Chapter IX

1. See Walter McDonald, "The Inconsistencies in Henry James's Aesthetics," *Texas Studies in Language and Literature*, 10 (Winter 1969), 594.

2. "The Literary Criticism of the Genteel Decades, 1870-1900," in *The Development of American Literary Criticism*, ed. Floyd Stovall (Chapel Hill: University of North Carolina Press, 1955), p. 134.

3. "The Art of Fiction," *Longman's Magazine*, 4 (September 1884), 512; *Partial Portraits*, p. 393.

4. *The Art of Fiction* (Boston: Cupples, Upham and Company, 1884), pp. 3, 5-6. Hereafter cited as Besant.

5. "The Art of Fiction," pp. 505-506; *Partial Portraits*, p. 382.

6. See [G. P. Lathrop], "Recent Literature," *Atlantic*, 40 (July 1877), 108; "Current Literature," *Galaxy*, 24 (July 1877), 137; [T. S. Perry], "James's American," *Nation*, 24 (May 31, 1877), 325.

7. [Horace Scudder], "The Portrait of a Lady and Dr. Breen's Practice," *Atlantic*, 49 (January 1882), 127; "James's Roderick Hudson," *North American Review*, 122 (April 1876), 420; [W. C. Brownell], "James's Portrait of a Lady," *Nation*, 34 (February 2, 1882), 102.

8. See [G. P. Lathrop], "Recent Literature," *Atlantic*, 37 (February 1876), 237; [W. D. Howells], "Recent Literature," *Atlantic*, 35 (April 1875), 495; and reviews of *The Portrait of a Lady* and *Roderick Hudson* cited in note 7.

9. *Criticism and Fiction and Other Essays*, p. 62.

10. [G. P. Lathrop], "Recent Literature," *Atlantic*, 37 (February 1876), 238; Richard Grant White, "Recent Fiction," *North American Review*, 128 (January 1879), 101; [James Russell Lowell], "James's Tales and Sketches," *Nation*, 20 (24 June 1875), 426.

11. "The Art of Fiction," p. 503.

12. *Longman's Magazine*, 5 (December 1884), 142.

13. Warner, "Modern Fiction," *Atlantic*, 51 (April 1883), 469. James referred specifically to this article.

14. "Alphonse Daudet," *Century Magazine*, 26 (August 1883), 506; *Partial Portraits*, pp. 227-228.

15. "The Art of Fiction," pp. 504-505; cf. *Partial Portraits*, pp. 378-380.

16. Besant, p. 3. Besant's "third proposition," it should be noted, modified his second one: "like other fine Arts, Fiction is so far removed from the mere mechanical arts, that no laws or rules whatever can teach it to those who have not already been endowed with the natural and necessary gifts" (ibid, pp. 3-4). This argument closely resembles James's own; but for polemical reasons, he ignored Besant's concession.

17. "The Art of Fiction," pp. 508-509; *Partial Portraits*, pp. 386-387.

18. Besant, pp. 17-18.

19. Ibid., pp. 509-510; *Partial Portraits*, pp. 388-390. In this essay, however, James referred not to Sand but to "an English novelist, a woman of genius" who had written a tale concerning "the nature and way of life of the French Protestant youth." The author has been identified by Gordon Haight, Malcolm Elwin, and Percy Lubbock as Anne Thackeray Ritchie, whose novel, *The Story of Elizabeth*, was first published in 1862-63 (*New York Times Book Review*, December 14, 1952, p. 31; *Times Literary Supplement*, July 29, 1955, p. 429; *Times Literary Supplement*, August 12, 1955, p. 461).

20. Ibid., pp. 507, 510-511; *Partial Portraits*, pp. 384, 390.

21. Besant, p. 25.

22. "The Art of Fiction," p. 511; *Partial Portraits*, p. 391.

23. "The Minor French Novelists," pp. 230-231; "Far From the Madding Crowd," pp. 423-424; "George Sand," p. 48.

24. Review of *Middlemarch*, pp. 424-428; Review of *Frühlingsfluthen* and *Ein König Lear des Dorfes*, p. 341; Review of *Around a Spring*, p. 249; Review of *Meta Holdenis*, pp. 462-464.

25. "The Art of Fiction," p. 511; *Partial Portraits*, p. 392.

26. Ibid., pp. 511-513; *Partial Portraits*, pp. 392-394.

27. "A Humble Remonstrance," pp. 143-146.

28. *The Art of the Novel*, pp. 30-32, 175.

29. "The Art of Fiction," p. 513; *Partial Portraits*, pp. 394-395.

30. Ibid., pp. 514-515; *Partial Portraits*, pp. 396-397.

31. Besant, p. 15; see also p. 24.

32. "Modern Fiction," p. 464.

33. "The Art of Fiction," pp. 515-516; *Partial Portraits*, pp. 398-399.

34. Besant, p. 34.

35. "The Art of Fiction," p. 517; *Partial Portraits*, p. 402.

36. Ibid., p. 518; *Partial Portraits*, p. 403.

37. *Chérie* (Paris: Charpentier, 1884), p. 297.

38. Besant, pp. 29-30.

39. "The Art of Fiction," pp. 510-521; *Partial Portraits*, pp. 406-408.

40. "Henry James in Reality," *Critical Inquiry*, 3 (Spring 1976), 585-590.

41. "The Art of Fiction," p. 507; *Partial Portraits*, p. 384.

42. "Sainte-Beuve," *North American Review*, 130 (January 1880), 55.

43. *Henry James and Robert Louis Stevenson: A Record of Friendship and Criticism*, ed. Janet Adam Smith (London: Rupert Hart-Davis, 1948), p.102.

Notes to Chapter X

1. "Mr. Walt Whitman," pp. 625-626; "Browning's Inn Album," *Nation*, 22 (January 20, 1876), 49-50; "Charles Baudelaire," p. 281 (*French Poets and Novelists*, p. 83).

2. "Howells's Poems," *Independent*, January 8, 1874, p. 9.

3. "Realism as Disinheritance: Twain, Howells, and James," *American Quarterly*, 16 (Winter 1964), 531-533, 540.

4. "Howells's Poems," p. 9.

5. Loc. cit.; cf. Howells, *Poems* (Boston: James R. Osgood, 1873), p. 31.

6. *Life in Letters of William Dean Howells*, ed. Mildred Howells (Garden City: Doubleday, 1928), I, 181.

7. "Matthew Arnold," *English Illustrated Magazine*, 1 (January 1884), 244, 246.

8. Review of *The Legend of Jubal and Other Poems*, *North American Review*, 119 (October 1874), 485, 489.

9. "Howells's Poems," p. 9.

10. "Mr. Tennyson's Drama," *Galaxy*, 20 (September 1875), 396-397.

11. Ibid., pp. 398, 399, 397. In a later review, James criticized the author's *Harold* on the same grounds. See "Mr. Tennyson's New Drama," *Nation*, 24 (January 18, 1877), 43-44.

12. "Alfred de Musset," *Galaxy*, 23 (June 1877), 792, 798, 800, 799, 801, 802; *French Poets and Novelists*, pp. 9, 25, 31-33, 27-28, 34, 38. Translations: "Because you know how to sing, my friend, you know how to cry." . . . "The most despairing songs are the most beautiful / And I know some immortal ones that are pure sobs."

13. "Realism as Disinheritance," pp. 542-543.
14. See Ralph Perry, *The Thought and Character of William James*, I, 366-368.
15. *Literary History of the United States*, p. 1046.
16. (Paris: Calmann Lévy, 1883), p. 148. Hereafter cited as *Souvenirs*. Translation: "[My] bent was determined. I was not a priest by profession, but I was one in spirit."
17. "The Reminiscences of Ernest Renan," *Atlantic*, 52 (August 1883), 279; cf. *Souvenirs*, pp. i-ii.
18. Loc. cit.; cf. *Souvenirs*, p. 358.
19. Ibid., pp. 279-280; cf. *Souvenirs*, pp. x-xi.
20. *Souvenirs*, p. xxii. Translation: "The real men of progress are those who have as a point of departure a profound respect for the past."
21. (Paris: Calmann Lévy, n. d.), p. 58. Hereafter cited as *Dialogues*.
22. "Parisian Topics," *New York Tribune*, 3 (June 17, 1876), 1-2; rpt. *Parisian Sketches*, p. 161. Cf. *Dialogues*, pp. 133-134.
23. *The Novels and Tales of Henry James* (New York: Scribner's, 1909), XVI, 235, 236, 250.
24. *Souvenirs*, p. 8. Translation: "The intellect burned by reason is thirsty for pure water. When reflection has led us to the last limit of doubt, what there is in the feminine consciousness of the spontaneous affirmation of the good and the beautiful enchants us and settles the question for us. The beautiful and virtuous woman is the mirage that supplies our great moral desert with lakes and willow groves."
25. *Henry James: The Major Phase*, p. 51.
26. *The Rhetoric of Fiction*, pp. 223-224.
27. *Parisian Sketches*, p. 162.
28. "Mr. Tennyson's Drama," pp. 395, 396.
29. "Armor Against Time," *Hound and Horn*, 7 (April-June 1934), 373-384.
30. "Renan's Dialogues," *Nation*, 23 (August 3, 1876), 78-79; rpt. *Collected Essays and Reviews* (London: Longmans, Green, 1920), pp. 36-39.
31. *The Thought and Character of William James*, I, 369.

Notes to Chapter XI

1. "The Life of Emerson," *Macmillan's*, 57 (December 1887), 87; "Emerson," *Partial Portraits*, p. 4.
2. "James Russell Lowell," *Atlantic*, 69 (January 1892), 42; *Essays in London and Elsewhere* (New York: Harper's, 1893), p. 60.
3. "James Russell Lowell," in *Library of the World's Best Literature*, ed. Charles Dudley Warner (New York: R. S. Peale and J. A. Hill, 1897), XVI, 9231.
4. "The Founding of the 'Nation,'" p. 44.
5. "Mr. and Mrs. James T. Fields," *Atlantic*, 116 (July 1916), 23.
6. *Henry James: The Middle Years*, p. 235.
7. Smith, *Henry James and Robert Louis Stevenson*, p. 102. For a discussion of James's belief in aesthetic freedom, see Elizabeth Coleman, "Henry James's Criticism: A Reëvaluation" (Diss. Columbia, 1965).
8. "Guy de Maupassant," *Fortnightly Review*, 49 (March 1888), 370, 365, 366; *Partial Portraits*, pp. 256-257, 246, 247.
9. *Mine Own People* (New York: Manhattan Press, n.d.), pp. 3, 7, 6.
10. "Emile Zola," *Atlantic*, 92 (August 1903), 193-194; *Notes on Novelists* (New York: Scribner's, 1914), pp. 26-27.

11. "George Eliot's Life," *Atlantic*, 55 (May 1885), 673, 677; "The Life of George Eliot," *Partial Portraits*, pp. 51, 60–61.

12. "William Dean Howells," *Harper's Weekly*, 30 (June 19, 1886), 394–395.

13. *Henry James: The Treacherous Years*, pp. 51–52.

14. *Mine Own People*, pp. 10–11, 19, 12.

15. "Guy de Maupassant," pp. 370, 385, 369, 381, 375, 379, 380, 378; *Partial Portraits*, pp. 254, 285, 278, 265–266, 274, 275, 272.

16. Ibid., pp. 385, 377, 384, 386; *Partial Portraits*, pp. 284, 269, 270, 282, 283–284, 287.

17. *New York Tribune* (August 4, 1889), II, 10: 3–4.

18. *The American 1890's* (New York: Viking, 1966), p. 41.

19. "The Future of the Novel," *The International Library of Famous Literature*, ed. Richard Garnett (London: Standard, 1899), XVI, xi–xxii.

20. "An Animated Conversation," *Scribner's*, 5 (March 1889), pp. 375, 372; *Essays in London and Elsewhere*, pp. 277–278, 270–271.

21. "The Future of the Novel," pp. xi–xxii.

22. "Mrs. Humphry Ward," *English Illustrated Magazine*, 9 (February 1892), 400; *Essays in London and Elsewhere*, p. 255.

23. "Miss Constance Fenimore Woolson," *Harper's Weekly*, 31 (February 12, 1887), 114; "Miss Woolson," *Partial Portraits*, pp. 178, 188.

24. "Mrs. Humphry Ward," p. 399; *Essays in London and Elsewhere*, p. 255.

25. *Henry James: The Middle Years*, pp. 203–204, 207.

26. "An Animated Conversation," pp. 383–384; *Essays in London and Elsewhere*, pp. 303–304.

27. "American Letter," *Literature*, 3 (July 9, 1898), 18.

28. "The Future of the Novel," pp. xi–xxii.

29. "Edmond Rostand," *Cornhill Magazine*, n.s. 11 (November 1901), 578.

30. "American Letter," *Literature*, 2 (April 30, 1898), 511.

31. "American Letter," *Literature*, 2 (April 9, 1898), 423.

32. "American Letter," *Literature*, 2 (May 28, 1898), 620; "American Letter," *Literature*, 2 (May 7, 1898), 541–542.

33. "American Letter," *Literature*, 3 (July 9, 1898), 18.

34. "American Letter," *Literature*, 2 (May 7, 1898), 542.

35. "American Letter: The Question of the Opportunites," *Literature*, 2 (March 26, 1898), 356–358.

36. "American Letter," *Literature*, 2 (April 16, 1898), 452–453; "American Letter," *Literature*, 2 (May 7, 1898), 541.

37. "American Letter," *Literature*, 2 (April 9, 1898), 422.

38. "American Letter," *Literature*, 2 (April 30, 1898), 512.

39. "American Letter," *Literature*, 2 (April 9, 1898), 422–423.

40. "American Letter," *Literature*, 2 (April 23, 1898), 484.

41. "American Letter: The Question of the Opportunities," p. 357.

42. Preface to Guy de Maupassant, *The Odd Number*, trans. Jonathan Sturges (New York: Harper's, 1889), p. xi.

43. "Pierre Loti," *Fortnightly Review*, 49 (May 1888), 663; *Essays in London and Elsewhere*, p. 183.

44. Preface to *The Odd Number*, pp. xii–xiii.

45. "Alphonse Daudet," *Literature*, 1 (December 25, 1897), 306.

46. "The Present Literary Situation in France," *North American Review*, 169 (October 1899), 487,489–490, 496, 497.

47. Ibid., p. 498.

48. I. D. McFarlane, "A Literary Friendship—Henry James and Paul Bourget," *Cambridge Journal*, 4 (December 1950), 147, 149; Leon Edel, *Henry James: The Middle Years*, p. 114.

49. "The Present Literary Situation in France," p. 499.
50. Ibid., p. 500.
51. *Anatole France* (Port Washington, N.Y.: Kennikat Press, 1919), p. 130.
52. "The Present Literary Situation in France," p. 489.
53. Ibid., p. 500; cf. "London Notes," *Harper's Weekly*, 41 (June 5, 1897), 563.
54. Ibid., pp. 491–493, 495; Dumesnil, *Le Réalisme*, p. 275.
55. Ibid., p. 491.
56. "The Science of Criticism," *New Review*, 4 (May 1891), 398–402; "Criticism," *Essays in London and Elsewhere*, pp. 263, 259–260, 261–262, 264, 266.
57. Preface to *The Odd Number*, p. xvii.
58. *The Art of the Novel*, p. 46.
59. See his "Windows on the House of Fiction" (Diss. Wisconsin, 1970).
60. "Pierre Loti," in Loti, *Impressions* (Westminster: Constable, 1898), p. 2.

Notes to Chapter XII

1. "She and He: Recent Documents," *Yellow Book*, 12 (January 1897), 27; "George Sand, 1897," *Notes on Novelists*, p. 173.
2. Review of Mme. Wladimir Karénine's *George Sand, sa vie et ses oeuvres*, *Quarterly Review*, 220 (April 1914), 337; "George Sand, 1914," *Notes on Novelists*, p. 243.
3. "She and He: Recent Documents," p. 15; "George Sand, 1897," p. 160.
4. "George Sand: The New Life," *North American Review*, 174 (April 1902), 554; "George Sand, 1899," *Notes on Novelists*, p. 213.
5. Review of *George Sand*, p. 319; "George Sand, 1914," p. 220.
6. "She and He: Recent Documents," p. 25; cf. "George Sand, 1897," p. 171.
7. Ibid., p. 19; "George Sand, 1897," p. 165.
8. Review of *George Sand*, p. 327; "George Sand, 1914," p. 230.
9. "She and He: Recent Documents," pp. 35, 16–17; "George Sand, 1897," pp. 182, 162.
10. Ibid., pp. 19, 23; "George Sand, 1897," pp. 165, 169.
11. "George Sand: The New Life," p. 552; "George Sand, 1899," p. 210.
12. See, for example, Review of *George Sand*, p. 318; "George Sand, 1914," p. 219.
13. "George Sand: The New Life," p. 540; cf. "George Sand, 1899," pp. 192–193.
14. "She and He: Recent Documents," p. 36; "George Sand, 1897," p. 184.
15. *The Art of the Novel*, pp. 33–34, 26, 39.
16. "Edmond Rostand," *Cornhill Magazine*, n. s. 11 (November 1901), 585, 581, 591, 582, 594, 595, 598.
17. "Introduction," *The Tempest, The Complete Works of William Shakespeare*, ed. Sidney Lee (Boston and New York: Jefferson Press, 1907), VIII, xxi, xviii–xix.
18. "Edmond Rostand," p. 598.
19. Preface to *Port Tarascon* (New York: Harper's, 1891), p. 5.
20. "Alphonse Daudet," *Literature*, 1 (December 25, 1897), 306–307.
21. Edel, *Henry James: The Treacherous Years*, p. 170.
22. "Du Maurier and London Society," *Century*, 26 (May 1883), 53; "George Du Maurier," *Partial Portraits*, p. 341.
23. Edel, *Henry James: The Treacherous Years*, p. 172.
24. "George Du Maurier," *Harper's New Monthly Magazine*, 95 (September 1897), 606.

25. "George Du Maurier," *Harper's Weekly*, 38 (April 14, 1894), 342.
26. "Prosper Mérimée," *Literature*, 3 (July 23, 1898), 66–68.
27. Edel, *Henry James: The Middle Years*, pp. 96–97.
28. See "The Letters of Robert Louis Stevenson," *North American Review*, 170 (January 1900), 76–77.
29. "Pierre Loti," *Fortnightly Review*, 49 (May 1888), 652, 660, 649, 656, 659, 661, 662; *Essays in London and Elsewhere*, pp. 161, 177, 156, 169, 174, 179, 181.
30. *The American 1890's*, p. 61.
31. "Pierre Loti," in Loti, *Impressions* (Westminster: Constable, 1898), pp. 7, 5, 1, 9, 11, 15.
32. Dumesnil, *Le Réalisme*, p. 276.
33. Anthony M. Gisolfi, *The Essential Matilde Serao* (New York: Las Americas, 1968), pp. 121–133.
34. "Matilde Serao," *North American Review*, 172 (March 1901), 371, 373, 367–370, 378, 380, 375; *Notes on Novelists*, pp. 300, 302–303, 294–299, 310, 313, 305–306.
35. Paul Maixner, "James on D'Annunzio—'A High Example of Exclusive Estheticism,'" *Criticism*, 13 (Summer 1971), 293.
36. *La Triomphe de la mort* appeared in 1895; *Les Vierges aux rochers*, in 1896.
37. "Gabriele D'Annunzio," *Quarterly Review*, 199 (April 1904), 383, 384, 390, 392; *Notes on Novelists*, pp. 245, 246, 254, 257.
38. Ibid., pp. 390, 408, 390–391; cf. *Notes on Novelists*, pp. 254, 278, 255.
39. Ibid., pp. 388, 418; *Notes on Novelists*, pp. 252, 292.
40. Maixner, p. 307.
41. See Edel, *Henry James: The Middle Years*, p. 125; and Smith, *Henry James and Robert Louis Stevenson*, pp. 9–47.
42. "Robert Louis Stevenson," *Century*, 35 (April 1888), 876, 874, 870, 869; cf. *Partial Portraits*, pp. 165, 158, 163, 142, 139.
43. "The Letters of Robert Louis Stevenson," p. 77; "Robert Louis Stevenson," *Notes on Novelists*, p. 24.
44. "Robert Louis Stevenson," pp. 877, 878; cf. *Partial Portraits*, pp. 166–167, 172–173.
45. "The Letters of Robert Louis Stevenson," pp. 75–76; *Notes on Novelists*, pp. 21–22.
46. "Robert Louis Stevenson," pp. 873, 878; *Partial Portraits*, pp. 155, 169–171.
47. *Henry James and Robert Louis Stevenson*, pp. 37–38.
48. *The Art of the Novel*, p. 176.
49. "Robert Louis Stevenson," pp. 877, 872, 879; *Partial Portraits*, pp. 166, 148, 173.
50. "The Letters of Robert Louis Stevenson," p. 76; *Notes on Novelists*, p. 23.
51. "Robert Louis Stevenson," p. 877; *Partial Portraits*, p. 168.
52. "Henry James on Hawthorne," *New England Quarterly*, 32 (June 1959), 207–225.
53. "Nathaniel Hawthorne," *Library of the World's Best Literature*, ed. Charles Dudley Warner (New York: International Society, 1897), XII, 7053–7054.
54. *Hawthorne*, p. 117.
55. "Nathaniel Hawthorne," p. 7056.
56. *Hawthorne*, p. 129.
57. "Nathaniel Hawthorne," pp. 7057, 7058–7059, 7060, 7054.
58. Letter to Robert S. Rantoul, in Essex Institute, *Proceedings in*

Commemoration of the One Hundredth Anniversary of the Birth of Nathaniel Hawthorne (Salem, Mass.: Essex Institute, 1904), pp. 58–59.

59. "The Story-Teller at Large: Mr. Henry Harland," *Fortnightly Review*, 69 (April 1898), 652–653, 654.

60. "American Letter," *Literature*, 2 (July 9, 1898), 19.

61. "Nathaniel Hawthorne," p. 7061.

62. *The Art of the Novel*, pp. 33, 252, 315, 3–4, 119, 56, 257.

63. *The Light of Common Day* (Bloomington: Indiana University Press, 1971), pp. 31–33, 7, 39–43. I disagree, however, with Cady's contention that James failed to take Hawthorne seriously (pp. 129–130).

64. Ibid., p. 16.

65. *Workable Design*, p. 11.

66. Cady, p. 5.

Notes to Chapter XIII

1. "George Eliot's Life," pp. 672–673; *Partial Portraits*, pp. 49–51.

2. Ibid., p. 674; *Partial Portraits*, pp. 52–53.

3. "Guy de Maupassant," pp. 367, 381, 364, 370–371, 372; *Partial Portraits*, pp. 250, 277, 244, 256–257, 259.

4. Ibid., pp. 372, 373; *Partial Portraits*, p. 260.

5. Ibid., pp. 373, 374; *Partial Portraits*, pp. 261, 262, 263.

6. "Gustave Flaubert," *Macmillan's*, 67 (March 1893), 333, 336, 343; *Essays in London and Elsewhere*, pp. 125, 131, 150.

7. Ibid., pp. 333, 339, 338, 341, 342; *Essays in London and Elsewhere*, pp. 125, 138, 136, 143, 147–148.

8. Edel, *Henry James: The Middle Years*, p. 101.

9. "James and Flaubert; the Evolution of Perception," *Comparative Literature*, 25 (Fall 1973), 297.

10. "Gustave Flaubert," pp. 333–334; *Essays in London and Elsewhere*, p. 125.

11. "The Journal of the Brothers de Goncourt," *Fortnightly Review*, 50 (October 1888), 516, 520; *Essays in London and Elsewhere*, pp. 214, 188. The journal included lengthy accounts of the writers' sexual adventures, a description of Jules's death from syphilis, and many libelous comments on the authors' acquaintances, including the great Sainte-Beuve.

12. "Gustave Flaubert," pp. 341, 342; *Essays in London and Elsewhere*, pp. 145, 147.

13. *Henry James and the French Novel: A Study in Inspiration* (New York: Barnes and Noble, 1973), p. 83.

14. "Gustave Flaubert," in *Madame Bovary*, trans. W. G. Blaydes (New York: D. Appleton, 1902), pp. v–xliii; *Notes on Novelists*, pp. 68, 107, 108.

15. Edel, *Henry James: The Treacherous Years*, pp. 182–183.

16. "London," *Harper's Weekly*, 41 (August 21, 1897), 234; "London Notes, August 1897," *Notes on Novelists*, pp. 448, 449.

17. "Gustave Flaubert," pp. v–xliii; *Notes on Novelists*, p. 91.

18. According to James, *L'Education sentimentale* was "a curiosity for a literary museum," while *Salammbô* and *La Tentation de Saint Antoine* were "monstrous monuments" to their author's desire to escape altogether into the romantic mode. Ibid., pp. v–xliii; *Notes on Novelists*, pp. 85, 100.

19. Ibid., pp. v–xliii; *Notes on Novelists*, p. 65.

20. Emile Faguet, *Flaubert* (Paris: Hachette, 1899), pp. 65, 66, 88. Translation: "He was truly a romantic at heart. . . . One can say of Flaubert that imagination was his muse and reality, his conscience. . . . The essence of Madame Bovary's soul is the romantic temperament."

21. "Gustave Flaubert," pp. v-xliii; *Notes on Novelists*, p. 76.

22. Faguet, p. 87. Translation: "the most complete portrait of a woman ... in all of literature, including Shakespeare, including Balzac."

23. "Gustave Flaubert," pp. v-xliii; *Notes on Novelists*, p. 81.

24. See, for example, the preface to *The Princess Casamassima*, *The Art of the Novel*, p. 67.

25. Faguet, p. 102. Translation: "general enough to be a subject of meditation for all men and women, particular enough to continually give the feeling of a creature completely and minutely alive."

26. "Gustave Flaubert," pp. v-xliii; *Notes on Novelists*, pp. 83-84.

27. Ibid., pp. v-xliii; *Notes on Novelists*, pp. 80, 91, 105.

28. "James and Ibsen," *Comparative Literature*, 25 (Spring 1973), 116.

29. *Henry James: The Treacherous Years*, p. 30.

30. James did believe, however, that the dramatists shared a certain moral seriousness and "concern about life." See "On the Death of Dumas the Younger," *New Review*, 14 (March 1896), 288-302; "Dumas the Younger, 1895," *Notes on Novelists*, p. 382.

31. Michael Egan, *Henry James: The Ibsen Years* (New York: Barnes and Noble, 1972), p. 27; Herbert Edwards, "Henry James and Ibsen," *American Literature*, 24 (May 1952), 214.

32. "On the Death of Dumas the Younger," pp. 288-302; "Dumas the Younger," p. 380.

33. Edmond Gosse, "Ibsen's Social Dramas," *Fortnightly Review*, n.s. 45 (January 1889), 108.

34. Egan, p. 41.

35. Edel, *Henry James: The Treacherous Years*, p. 28; Egan, pp. 39-40.

36. "On the Occasion of Hedda Gabler," *New Review*, 4 (June 1891), 519-530; Part I of "Henrik Ibsen," *Essays in London and Elsewhere*, pp. 235, 237-238, 240, 242-243.

37. Ibid., pp. 519-530; Part I of "Henrik Ibsen," p. 247.

38. *Henry James: The Treacherous Years*, p. 29.

39. "Ibsen's New Play," *Pall Mall Gazette* (February 17, 1893), 1-2; Part II of "Henrik Ibsen," *Essays in London and Elsewhere*, pp. 252, 251.

40. "London," *Harper's Weekly*, 41 (February 6, 1897), 134; "London Notes, January 1897," *Notes on Novelists*, pp. 426-427.

41. *Workable Design*, pp. 70, 126-127.

42. Egan, pp. 75, 125, 29.

43. "On the Occasion of *Hedda Gabler*," pp. 519-530; Part I of "Henrik Ibsen," p. 241.

44. "The Present Literary Situation in France," p. 489.

45. Edel, *Henry James: The Master*, pp. 130, 263.

46. "Honoré de Balzac," in *The Two Young Brides*, trans. Lady Mary Loyd (New York: D. Appleton, 1902), pp. vi, vii, xviii, xxvi, xxxviii; "Honoré de Balzac, 1902," *Notes on Novelists*, pp. 110, 111, 121, 128, 138.

47. Ibid., pp. xix, xxii, xxiv, xxv, xiv, xiii-xiv; "Honoré de Balzac, 1902," pp. 121, 124, 126, 127, 117, 116.

48. "Honoré de Balzac," *Galaxy*, 20 (December 1875), 833; *French Poets and Novelists*, p. 141.

49. "Honoré de Balzac," *The Two Young Brides*, pp. xl-xli; "Honoré de Balzac, 1902," pp. 140-141.

50. *The Melodramatic Imagination*, pp. 7-8, 3.

51. "Honoré de Balzac," pp. xli, xliii; "Honoré de Balzac, 1902," pp. 141, 142.

52. "The Lesson of Balzac," *Atlantic*, 96 (August 1905), 169-180; *Two Lectures*, pp. 70, 67, 76, 116, 56-57, 71-72, 65, 60, 106.

53. Ibid., pp. 176, 173; *Two Lectures*, pp. 95, 88, 99, 96-97.

54. Ibid., pp. 177-179; *Two Lectures*, pp. 103-109.

55. *The Art of the Novel*, pp. 86, 278, 296–300.

56. "The Lesson of Balzac," pp. 178, 179; *Two Lectures*, pp. 106–107, 109–112.

57. "London," *Harper's Weekly*, 41 (July 31, 1897), 754: "London Notes, July 1897," *Notes on Novelists*, p. 442.

58. "The Lesson of Balzac," p. 170; *Two Lectures*, p. 70.

59. Emile Faguet, *Balzac* (Paris: Hachette, 1913), p. 142.

60. "Balzac," *Living Age*, 278 (August 9, 1913), 371–372; Honoré de Balzac, 1913." *Notes on Novelists*, pp. 157, 159.

61. "Honoré de Balzac," p. xxx; "Honoré de Balzac, 1902," p. 131.

62. Edel, *Henry James: The Middle Years*, p. 340.

63. Edel, *Henry James: The Treacherous Years*, p. 274.

64. Pp. 490, 498.

65. "Emile Zola," *Atlantic*, 92 (August 1903), 194; *Notes on Novelists*, p. 27.

66. "The Present Literary Situation in France," pp. 498–499.

67. "Emile Zola," pp. 208–209. 198; *Notes on Novelists*, pp. 60, 36.

68. "The Lesson of Balzac," p. 175; *Two Lectures*, pp. 92–93.

69. "Emile Zola," pp. 202–204, 196; *Notes on Novelists*, pp. 46–49, 32.

70. Ibid., pp. 206–207, 199, 201, 210; *Notes on Novelists*, pp. 55–56, 39, 43, 63, 64.

71. Jan W. Dietrichson, "Henry James and Emile Zola," *Americana Norvegica* (Philadelphia: University of Pennsylvania Press, 1968), II, 128.

72. *The Art of the Novel*, pp. 297–298. Typically, James regrets that he could not have rendered Lionel Croy in more detail.

73. "Emile Zola," p. 208; *Notes on Novelists*, p. 58.

74. "London," *Harper's Weekly*, 41 (July 31, 1897), 754; "London Notes, July 1897," *Notes on Novelists*, p. 439.

75. "Ivan Turgenieff," *Library of the World's Best Literature*, ed. Charles Dudley Warner (New York: International Society, 1897), XXV, 15062.

76. "The Novel in *The Ring and the Book*," *Transactions of the Royal Society of Literature*, 2nd. series: Vol. 31, pt. IV, 1912, 269–298; *Notes on Novelists*, pp. 405–406.

77. "Ivan Turgenieff," p. 15058.

78. "The Younger Generation," *The Times Literary Supplement*, No. 635 (March 19, 1914), 133–134; "The New Novel," *Notes on Novelists*, pp. 319, 321, 322.

79. Wells, "Digression About Novels," in *Henry James and H. G. Wells*, ed. Leon Edel and Gordon Ray (Urbana: University of Illinois Press, 1958), pp. 222, 223.

80. "The Younger Generation," pp. 133–134; "The New Novel," pp. 325, 331, 333.

81. *Henry James and H. G. Wells*, p. 127.

82. "The Younger Generation," *Times Literary Supplement*, No. 637 (April 2, 1914), 157–158; "The New Novel," pp. 339–340, 354–356.

83. Millicent Bell, "Edith Wharton and Henry James: The Literary Relation," *PMLA*, 74 (December 1959), 634–636; Edel, *Henry James: The Master*, p. 254.

84. The second volume, dealing with Michael Fane's career at Oxford, had not yet been published.

85. "The Younger Generation," pp. 157–158; "The New Novel," pp. 359, 358.

86. Ibid., pp. 133–134; "The New Novel," pp. 318, 329.

87. Edel, *Henry James: The Master*, pp. 55–56.

88. "The Younger Generation," pp. 157–158; "The New Novel," pp. 345, 355, 349.

89. I disagree with Ian Watt on this point. See his "Conrad, James, and

Chance," in *Imagined Worlds: Essays on Some English Novels and Novelists in Honor of John Butt* (London: Methuen, 1968), p. 316.

90. *Chance* (Garden City: Doubleday, 1930), pp. 251, 99–100.

91. Watt, p. 314.

92. Loc. cit.

93. "The New Novel," p. 351. This remark appears only in the second version of the essay.

94. *The Art of the Novel,* pp. 9, 269, 319, 16, 309, 201.

Notes to Chapter XIV

1. *The Novels of Henry James,* p. 375.

2. *The Melodramatic Imagination,* p. 2.

3. My phrase is borrowed from Robert Falk, "Henry James's Romantic 'Vision of the Real' in the 1870's," in *Essays Critical and Historical Dedicated to Lily B. Campbell* (Berkeley: University of California Press, 1950).

4. "The Founding of the 'Nation,'" p. 44.

Index

225